A Guide to Anglo-Saxon Sites

In preparation by the same authors
A GUIDE TO NORMAN SITES IN BRITAIN

A Guide to Anglo-Saxon Sites

Nigel and Mary Kerr

GRANADA
London Toronto Sydney New York

Granada Publishing Limited
Frogmore, St Albans, Herts AL2 2NF
and
36 Golden Square, London W1R 4AH
866 United Nations Plaza, New York, NY 10017, USA
117 York Street, Sydney, NSW 2000, Australia
100 Skyway Avenue, Rexdale, Ontario M9W 3A6, Canada
61 Beach Road, Auckland, New Zealand

Published by Granada Publishing 1982

British Library Cataloguing in Publication Data

Kerr, Nigel
A guide to Anglo-Saxon sites
1. Anglo-Saxons 2. England – Antiquities
– Guidebooks 3. England – Description and
travel – Guidebooks
I. Title II. Kerr, Mary
942.01 DA152.2

ISBN 0-246-11775-3 (hardback)
ISBN 0-586-08423-1 (paperback)

Typeset in Palatino by A-Line Services, Saffron Walden

Printed in Great Britain by Fakenham Press Limited,
Fakenham, Norfolk

Contents

Acknowledgements

Many people have helped us during the preparation of this Guide, and we would particularly like to thank the following: David Dawson, Alistair Haldane, Blaise Vyner and Peter Warner, who provided accommodation and photographs; Peter Moore for developing the films and Ron and Wendy Brown for looking after the cats and rabbit during our prolonged absences from home.

For permission to reproduce copyright material we are grateful to:

The Bodley Head for the lines from 'The Battle of Maldon' translated by Henry Treece in *Hounds of the King*

Macmillan, London and Basingstoke, for the lines from *Beowulf* translated by Kevin Crossley-Holland

The National Trust for Places of Historic Interest or Natural Beauty for the second verse of 'Norman and Saxon' from *A History of England* by Rudyard Kipling

Dedicated to the memory of Dame Kitty Anderson, a great Englishwoman

Introduction

This guide is concerned with the physical remains of the long period of England's history between the end of Roman government in Britain early in the 5th century and the Norman Conquest in 1066. Although it deals with a historical period, it is not a 'history book'; it aims to provide basic information and comment about the sites it contains, together with clear directions as to how they can best be reached. It is a guide book, and as such is not intended as a comprehensive reference work for a whole subject, but merely to be a source of information and enlightenment for the traveller.

The illustrations which complement the text are designed to give a foretaste of the delights in store. Most of the photographs are our own work, and many of our drawings were actually made on site. The drawings are deliberately bold, and seek to reproduce the vigour and quality of the original compositions rather than to reflect the evidences of time and damage which have befallen the objects since they were made. By comparing our illustrations with the objects 'in the flesh' the visitor will perceive not only the design as the artist intended it to be seen, but also the traces of wear and tear which add to an appreciation of the antiquity of the material. Like a piece of fine antique furniture, it is both the original design and the patina of age which delight the eye.

The 101 sites in the book are not by any means a complete catalogue of Anglo-Saxon remains in England. If such a compendium were ever assembled, it would run to several thousand entries, since hundreds of churches contain traces of Anglo-Saxon workmanship in their fabrics, and many more house pieces of sculpture; and when barrows, dykes, settlement sites and other field monuments are added, the sheer weight of evidence is staggering.

Most of such sites would be exceedingly unrewarding to visit, however, and are more the province of the dedicated student who wishes to see every example of a particular class of monument. What is presented here is a personal selection of the very many sites which we have visited. The basis of that selection has been either that a site is a good example of a particular type of monument, or that it has strong historical or other associations, or else that it has a fine setting. Many of the sites possess all three attributes. We hope that you will derive as much pleasure from your travels among the ruins of Anglo-Saxondom as we have whilst compiling this guide!

Anglo-Saxon England

Unlike the Battle of Hastings which ended the period, the beginnings of Anglo-Saxon England are obscure. German mercenaries employed by the Romans were an important factor in the early period, and they may have 'spearheaded' the settlements of their kinsmen. It also appears that the *Adventus Saxonum* – the coming of the Saxons – was not quite the cataclysmic affair that was once supposed. Few burnt villas and lacerated corpses have been found in excavations, and it seems that some form of town life as well as agriculture was being carried on by the Romanized Britons well into the 5th century in some areas. Bloodshed there must have been, but not the wholesale pillage and slaughter which has generally been imagined.

By 'Anglo-Saxons' we mean the various tribes, or 'nations' as the Venerable Bede described them, who were living on the northern coasts of Holland and Germany during the period of the Roman Empire. They had a long history of piracy in the North Sea before the Romans withdrew the British garrisons in 410, and when Britain lay largely undefended they changed from pirates into settlers. The earliest settlements, which were located on the fertile flood plains of the great eastern rivers, were apparently well-established by 450, so little time was lost.

The first settlements were doubtless fairly haphazard affairs, and depended upon the degree of resistance encountered from the British inhabitants. The settlers fanned out westwards from their eastern bridgeheads, forcing back or absorbing the Britons as they went. Briton and Saxon must have coexisted in many areas, and we know that the region about modern Leeds was a British enclave for 200 years or so after the Saxons arrived. Some organized British resistance was encountered, as the Battle of Badon in 500 or thereabouts tells us, but the details of the British reaction are so hedged about with Arthurian myths and the later pontification of churchmen, who regarded the Saxon settlement as an expression of the wrath of God on a wicked people, that facts are in short supply.

After the first settlements, the newcomers gradually sorted themselves out into larger groups, and from these groups the first kingdoms emerged. At first there were many of them, and all sorts of warband leaders called themselves 'kings', but a process of natural selection ensured that the more powerful kingdoms

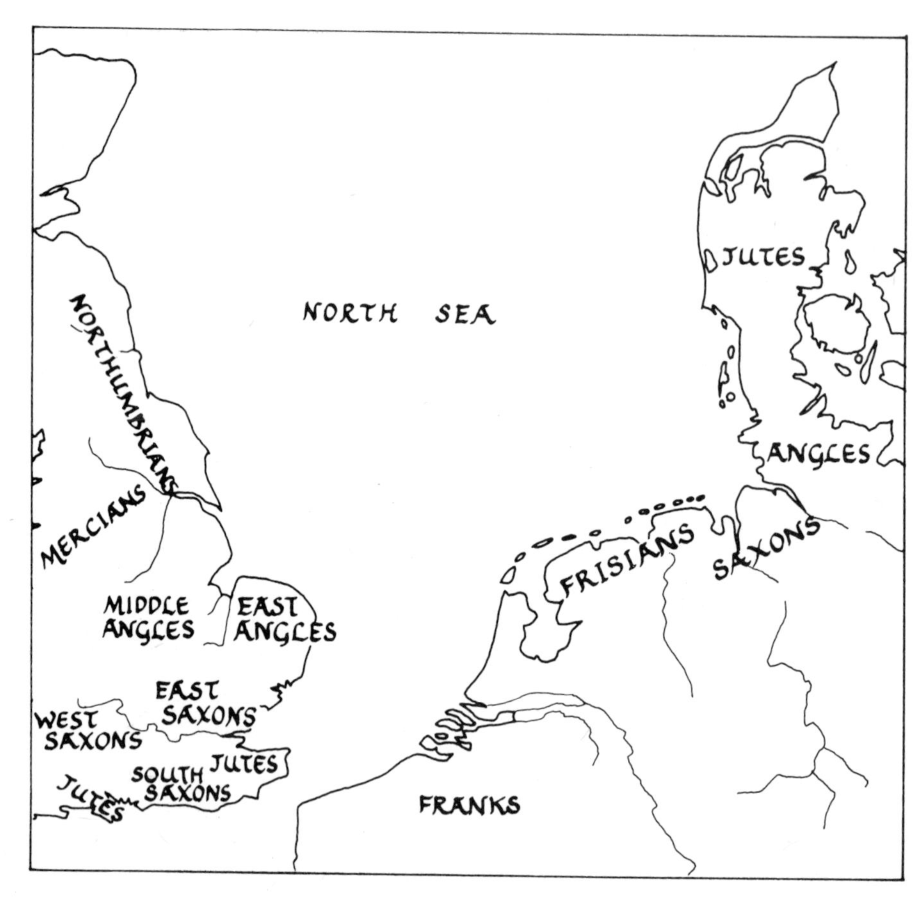

absorbed the smaller ones. Eventually there appeared four major power blocks: Northumbria, East Anglia, Mercia and Wessex, whose fortunes were to shape the history of the land. The story of Anglo-Saxon England, of the rise and fall of the various powers and of the final triumph of the house of Alfred of Wessex which united the country, is best traced through the histories of these major powers and short summaries of each will be found in the relevant sections of the guide.

The history of Anglo-Saxon England is long and complicated. This should occasion no surprise since the period lasted for over 600 years, the time which separates us from Geoffrey Chaucer. The pace of change was slower than today, but change there was, and some of it must have appeared radical indeed.

The coming of Christianity, which was to bring Anglo-Saxon England into closer contact with the Continent, was a major watershed. From the time of St Augustine's mission in 597 onwards, literacy, architecture, the arts and all the other trappings of classical civilization which the early settlers had ousted in England were to return. The Anglo-Saxons were not slow to adopt new ways, and the history of English Christianity, from its tentative beginnings in the different kingdoms to the terrible disruption caused by the Danes, to the flowering of the great revival during the more peaceful times of the 10th century, is an inspiring one. Perhaps no force was so influential in the develop-

SCOTLAND
YORK
LINCOLN
DERBY
NOTTINGHAM
STAMFORD
NORTHAMPTON
WALES
ENGLISH MERCIA
WESSEX
**** The Danelaw was north and east of this line

SCOTLAND
NORTHUMBRIA
MERCIA
EAST
ANGLIA
WALES
WESSEX

ment of Anglo-Saxon society than was Christianity itself.

A second major event was the settlement of the Danes in England. The progress of the Scandinavian settlement was similar in many respects to that of the Anglo-Saxons. They began by raiding and piracy, and ended as settlers and farmers. From the end of the 8th century, they began raiding the coast of England, and in 865 a great army bent upon conquest and settlement landed in eastern England. A large part of the country fell under their sway, and had it not been for the resistance of Alfred of Wessex, the whole country would have fallen. In 886, he was forced to come to terms with the Danish leader Guthrum, and England was effectively cut in half by a 'Berlin Wall', with Englishmen on one side and the Danes on the other.

The 'Danelaw', as the Danish territory was called, did not last long. The rulers of Wessex won back the land during the early 10th century, and united England in the process, but further troubles were not far over the horizon. Later Viking raids culminated in the reign of Canute during the 11th century, who was the first and last Danish ruler of England. After him, Anglo-Saxon England drew rapidly to a close, with the final tragedy being played out at Senlac near Hastings where yet another invading force won England for its own.

What has this formative period of England left to us: what is the legacy of the Anglo-Saxons? The answer to this question is that the legacy is so overwhelming that we who are part of it cannot objectively discern it. The very word 'England', the shire counties, more than half the words we use, many of our villages and parish boundaries, the qualities of fair dealing and respect for justice and fairness, our monarchy and many of our governmental institutions all have their roots in our Anglo-Saxon heritage. England is inseparable from its Anglo-Saxon origins, and however 'Englishness' is defined, it is the identification of the very characteristics which we have inherited from the first Englishmen.

Another aspect of the Anglo-Saxon inheritance is the physical evidence of the period, the churches and crosses, the sculptures and frontier dykes, the barrows, cemeteries and settlement sites; it is with this aspect that this book is concerned. Whereas the ancient feats of Stonehenge, Avebury and Hadrian's Wall are a commonplace, the achievements of our Anglo-Saxon forefathers are but dimly appreciated. We believe that this is largely because no guide has been available directing the visitor to these Anglo-Saxon remains and explaining their interest. With this book we hope to redress the balance, and make the sites of Anglo-Saxon England as familiar to the general reader as those of the preceding ages. In the words of the great Anglo-Saxon poem *Beowulf* there is:

many a fine sight
for those who have eyes to see such things.

How to Use This Book

We have divided England into four parts, roughly along the lines of the four major kingdoms. The boundaries were seldom static during the Anglo-Saxon period, but the areas correspond to the broad divisions. Each kingdom forms the basis of a separate section of the book, and each is prefaced by a brief outline of its history. A key map showing the modern county boundaries will also be found at the beginning of each section, and the numbers on it correspond with the consecutive descriptions in the text. If you wish to look up one particular site, consult the index at the end of the book in order to find its page number.

Each site is located in detail, and a six-figure Ordnance Survey grid reference is provided. An Ordnance Survey 1:50,000 metric map, which has replaced the old one-inch survey, is a valuable tool when visiting sites, but it you don't have the relevant map, the directions can be followed quite easily from a good road atlas. Most of the sites lie in villages, but any which are particularly difficult to find have been located by a small map showing nearest major roads and other features as well as a verbal description. Where appropriate, nearest towns and villages are indicated, together with their distances from the site.

Some of the sites in this book are on private land, and their inclusion does not imply any right of access. Nevertheless owners are generally very cooperative, and are pleased to allow genuinely interested people access to sites on their land. Many of the sites are churches, and it is hoped that visitors will behave in a suitable manner; a contribution to the fabric fund is not only courteous but also helps to ensure the survival of the very sites which the visitor sees. When in the countryside please follow the Country Code, and never, in any circumstances, dig into a site. This is a very complicated business which archaeologists spend a lot of time learning about!

Certain of the sites are in the care of the Department of the Environment, and this is indicated under the relevant entries. Some are open at all reasonable times without charge, others have special opening hours which are indicated in the entries, while most open during standard hours which are:

	Weekdays	*Sundays*
16 October to 14 March	09.30–16.00	14.00–16.00
15 March to 15 October	09.30–18.30	14.00–18.30

A list of important Anglo-Saxon museum collections, books to read and a glossary of unfamiliar terms will be found at the back of the book.

PART I

Northumbria

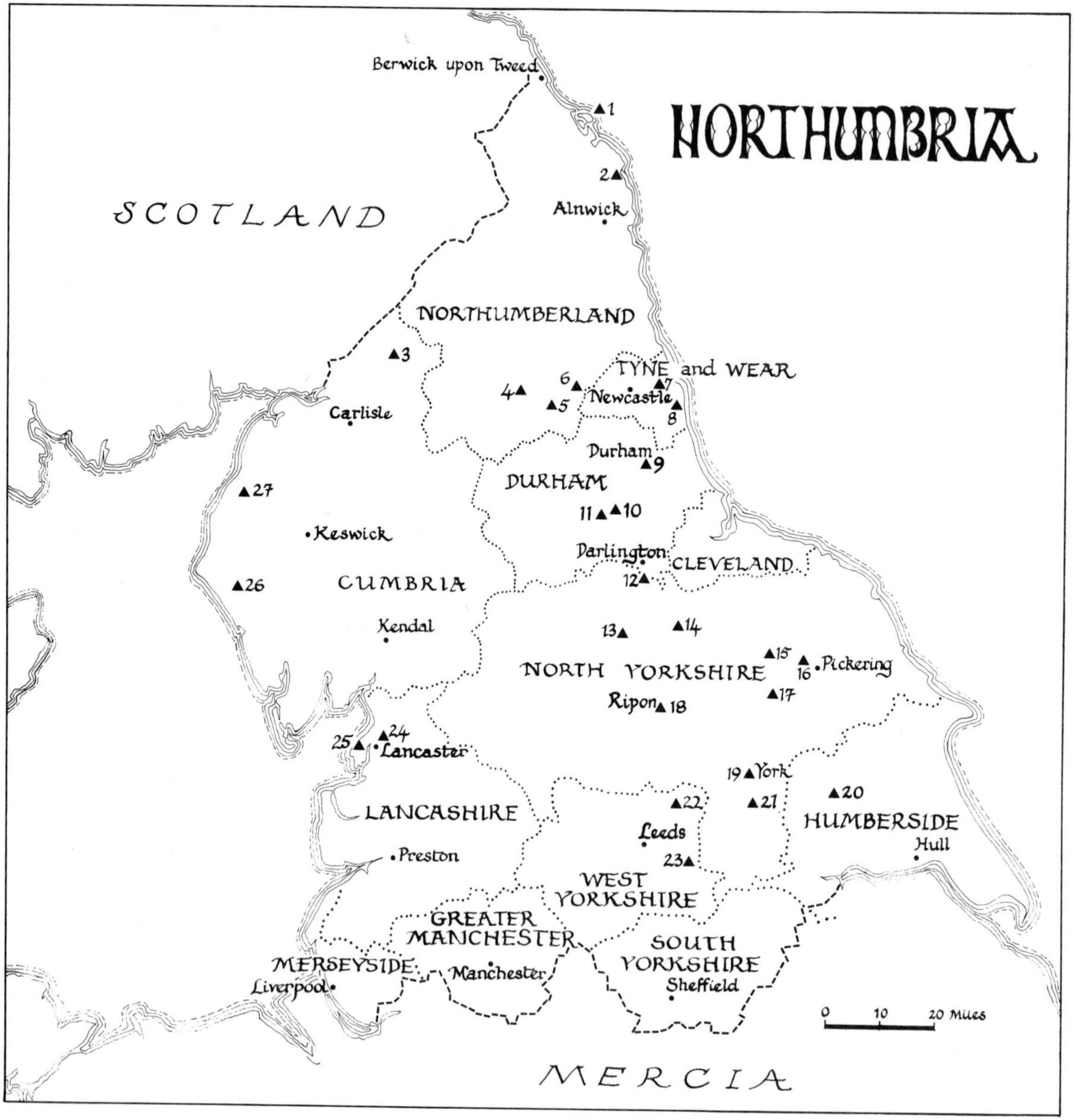

NORTHUMBRIA

SCOTLAND
Berwick upon Tweed
1
2
Alnwick
NORTHUMBERLAND
3
4
5
6
7
8
TYNE and WEAR
Newcastle
Carlisle
Durham
9
DURHAM
27
11
10
Keswick
Darlington
CLEVELAND
26
CUMBRIA
12
Kendal
13
14
15
16
Pickering
NORTH YORKSHIRE
17
Ripon
18
24
25
Lancaster
19
York
20
21
22
LANCASHIRE
HUMBERSIDE
Leeds
Hull
Preston
23
WEST YORKSHIRE
GREATER MANCHESTER
SOUTH YORKSHIRE
MERSEYSIDE
Manchester
Liverpool
Sheffield
0 10 20 Miles
MERCIA

Introduction

The name Northumbria derives from the Old English *Norohymbre*, meaning 'the people living north of the [river] Humber'. It is impossible to draw clear boundaries round the kingdom, because frontiers shifted according to the strength of the rulers and the opposition encountered from British and English neighbours. During the 7th century, at the height of its power, Northumbria extended south of the Humber into north Lincolnshire, and north as far as the Firth of Forth. By the mid-8th century, when its political power had declined, the northern boundary was just north of the river Tweed, whilst the southern frontier lay on the Humber estuary.

Northumbria developed from two originally separate kingdoms: Deira to the south centred on east Yorkshire, and Bernicia to the north in Northumberland. Deira, traditionally founded by King Aelle, had its capital at York, and Bernicia had its citadel at Bamburgh, on the harsh north-eastern coast. It was to these centres that the first Christian missions came: Paulinus from Kent who became Bishop of York in 627, and the later, more successful mission from Iona in Scotland in 634, which was based on the Island of Lindisfarne, just across the sea from Bamburgh.

The Venerable Bede, who lived at Jarrow, provides the source for much that is known of early Northumbrian history. His *History of the English Church and People* charts the vigorous expansion of the northern kingdom during the 7th century when the great Northumbrian kings Edwin, Oswald and Oswiu won great victories against the Scots, Welsh and Mercians, and came close to establishing permanent ascendancy over the rest of England. Upon the firm political foundations built by these men were to rest the cultural attainments of the 'Golden Age' of Northumbria in the late 7th and 8th centuries.

The political dominance of Northumbria did not last long. An expansion far into Scotland ended with defeat and the death of Ecgfrith at the hands of the Picts at Nechtansmere in 685. His earlier defeat by the Mercians on the River Trent in 674, began a period of Mercian supremacy which was to culminate in the reign of Offa, the first Anglo-Saxon king to achieve European renown.

But the quality of Northumbria which set it apart from the rest of Anglo-Saxon England was its artistic and cultural magnificence. During the 7th and 8th centuries, great centres of learning sprang up in the north which produced scholars of international standing such as Bede at Jarrow and Alcuin at York. The arts of manuscript illumination, metalwork, architecture and sculpture have left us a rich legacy of priceless objects. How was it that these comparatively inhospitable northern lands nurtured such richness?

To understand the artistic development of early Northumbria, we must appreciate the importance of Christianity, for it was in this kingdom that two great Christian traditions, the Celtic and the Latin, met together and jointly produced the works of art for which Northumbria is famous. The Irish and Scottish Celtic churches had kept alive the old British traditions of abstract art, which had their roots in the pre-Roman Iron Age. When this rich source was joined with the influence of Mediterranean styles, which concentrated more on naturalism and recognizable representations of subjects, the Lindisfarne Gospels, together with sculpture like the Acca Cross at Hexham, resulted. In the meeting of the two styles, a new strain of creativity was born which was greater than the sum of its parts. The monasteries were the power houses which generated the new styles and designs, and with lavish lay patronage they remained great centres of learning and culture until their destruction in the Viking raids of the 9th century.

It should not be imagined, however, that the fusion of the Celtic and Latin traditions was easily accomplished. During the first half of the 7th century, there was considerable enmity between the two parties. The Celtic church, which espoused a loosely-knit structure of small monasteries and churches, and which advocated a simple and austere way of life, was far removed from the wealth and accomplishment of its Latin counterpart. Apart from such general dissimilarities, there was a fundamental disagreement over the method by which the date of Easter should be calculated. This may sound a trifling matter, but it was a major stumbling block which attempts at reconciliation could not surmount. Easter was the major festival of the Christian year, and the divergence on this issue was symptomatic of the deep rift between the churches.

At the famous Synod held in 664 at Whitby, the Northumbrian royal house was forced to make a clear choice. Was the kingdom to continue to follow the traditions of the Celtic church in Ireland and western Britain, or was it to align itself with Canterbury, Europe and Rome? Bede records the Synod in great detail, and he explains the arguments raised by either side, but in the end St Wilfrid, who presented the Latin case, prevailed. The Celtic monks had either to accept the church of Rome and the primacy of the Pope, or retire to the outlying parts of Britain which remained loyal to their observances. The stage was now set for the 'Golden Age' of Northumbria to begin.

The Latin church brought with it Mediterranean learning and ideas, as well as writing, sculpture and architecture. Within ten years of the Synod, Wilfrid himself had founded two great churches at Ripon and Hexham, and shortly afterwards Benedict Biscop gathered masons and glaziers from France to build his new double monastery at Monkwearmouth and Jarrow. The various centres attracted schools of illustrators, sculptors and metal-workers whose works were prized throughout Europe.

The influence spread from the monasteries into the countryside. Great stone crosses were raised at Bewcastle, Bishop Auckland and Croft, and churches such as those at Escomb, Ledsham and Bywell were built. Moreover, missionaries were sent to northern Europe, and St Willibrord, who was educated at Ripon by St Wilfrid, founded the great abbey of Echternacht near Trier which lies in modern-day Luxembourg. Churchmen travelled frequently to the Continent, and Wilfrid himself made three journeys to Rome. We are fortunate indeed that in Bede's *History* we have not only a unique personal monument, but also a very full account of those halcyon days of Northumbria.

The holocaust of the Viking raids appears even more tragic in the light of what had gone before. Well might Anglo-Saxon churchmen pray: 'From the fury of the Norsemen, good Lord deliver us.' In 793, Lindisfarne was the first place in England to suffer at the hands of the Danes, an event which the Anglo-Saxon Chronicle records was preceded by 'dire portents'. Immense whirlwinds and flashes of lightning afflicted Northumbria, and 'fiery dragons were seen flying in the air'. For the next seventy years, raids were made on the rich and comparatively peaceful land which was totally unprepared for such attacks. By the middle of the 9th century, the sporadic seasonal raids gave way to the landing of great armies. By 875, York, the Deiran capital, was captured. In the same year the Danish king, Halfdan, 'shared out the lands of Northumbria, and the Danes were quietly engaged in ploughing and making their living' (Anglo-Saxon Chronicle).

The Danish settlement of Yorkshire, together with the later influx of Norse settlers into Lancashire and Cumbria, was to have decisive effects on the development of northern art. The new settlers were gradually converted to Christianity, and during the 10th century we see distinctive Anglo-Scandinavian monuments appearing in Yorkshire at such places as Middleton, Nunburnholme, Collingham and Brompton, and in Lancashire and Cumbria at Heysham, Gosforth and Dearham. These sculptures with their mixed iconography of pagan and Christian images are the physical evidence of the conversion process, of the gradual retreat from the paganism of their Scandinavian forebears.

Although the north and east of England had given way to Viking pressure, the south – and particularly Alfred's Wessex – had not. It was from that quarter that help finally came in the person of Athelstan, Alfred's grandson. He recaptured York in 927, and Eric Bloodaxe, last King of York, was finally expelled in 954.

After the restoration of Northumbria to the united English kingdom, the development of the north largely followed national fortunes. Further Danish raids culminated in the reign of Canute, who ruled wisely and well until his death in 1035, when England reverted to her national rulers. The last attempt by the Norwegians to invade the north was crushed by King Harold of Wessex at Stamford Bridge in Humberside on the eve of the Norman Conquest. After Hastings, England came once more under foreign domination, and the old Anglo-Saxon kingdom of Northumbria passed finally into history.

1

Lindisfarne Monastery Museum, Northumberland

Lindisfarne (Holy Island), the very name of which conjures up images of saintly men quietly engaged in their devotions, is an extraordinary place. The only access is afforded by a sandy ridge linking the island with the mainland, which is only exposed for a few hours around low tide. The village itself, with its fishing boats and small cottages, huddles close by the austere remains of the Norman abbey of St Peter, which looks out across the North Sea. It was to this place that St Aidan came from Iona in 634. Aidan had left his similarly desolate island off the west coast of Scotland in response to the call of Oswald, king of Northumbria. Oswald was later to be martyred by the heathen Penda of Mercia who had killed the Christian king Edwin but two years before.

With the death of Edwin, the cause of Christianity in Northumbria had almost come to nothing. Paulinus' mission had retreated southwards, and paganism again held sway. But Aidan's monks stood fast in Lindisfarne and, despite the death of their patron Oswald in 642 at the Battle of Maserfield in Shropshire, they retained their influence in the northern kingdom.

In 685, St Cuthbert became Bishop of Lindisfarne and, although the saint was perhaps the most famous inhabitant of the island, he was bishop for only two years before returning to his life of almost complete solitude and contemplation on the Inner Farne. It is perhaps appropriate that the Farne Islands, once believed to be under Cuthbert's special protection, are now a sanctuary for birds, seals and other wild life under the care of the National Trust.

On 7 June 793, the Holy Island was attacked by Danes who burnt the monastic buildings and slew most of the inhabitants. This attack had the dubious distinction of being the first Danish raid on the coast of England. In the words of the Anglo-Saxon Chronicle: 'the harrying of the heathen miserably destroyed God's church in Lindisfarne by rapine and slaughter.'

Map Reference: NU 126418 (metric map 75. 1-inch map 64)
Nearest Town: Bamburgh
Location: Access to Lindisfarne is by a dramatic causeway reached by turning east off the A1 about 9 miles (14.5 km) south of Berwick-upon-Tweed. The causeway can only be crossed at low tide.

The abbey ruins are well signposted and parking is available. The museum is adjacent to the abbey. Both sites are in the care of the Department of the Environment, and are open standard hours; a small admission charge is payable.

Grave marker bearing a lively carving of warriors on one face, and a scene of a cross with the sun and moon on the other. The warriors may be Viking raiders, but it is possible that the stone represents an evocation of Doomsday, which was a strong theme of Anglo-Saxon Christianity. The warriors would thus portray one of the portents of Doomsday cited in Matthew 24:6: 'And ye shall hear of wars and the rumours of wars', whilst the other face shows the cross, symbol of the Son of God, which will appear in the heavens and outshine both the sun and the moon.

There were doubtless further attacks on the little community, but the monks did not finally abandon the island until 875, when it was so severely attacked that it was impossible to remain. Carrying with them the body of their beloved Cuthbert, the monks wandered about the eastern part of Northumbria for some seven years until they set up a church at Chester-le-Street. They stayed there until they went to the site above the River Wear which later became the City of Durham in 995.

Although none of the fabric of the pre-Conquest abbey has been found, excavations on the site have yielded a considerable collection of carved stones and crosses dating from the 7th to the 9th centuries. These include a remarkable pillow stone, probably from the cemetery of the early abbey, which may illustrate some of the Vikings who attacked the monks.

The later Norman monastery, begun in 1082, may be built on the site of the earlier buildings, which would probably have been of fairly flimsy construction. Bede himself tells us that even the church was made of wood, but there are literary references to a communal refectory, which implies the existence of other major buildings. It is highly improbable that there were any buildings here of the scale or quality of those at Monkwearmouth and Jarrow. Lindisfarne was a creation of Celtic Christianity, and owed little to the Roman traditions to which Benedict Biscop aspired. In these differences lay the seeds of the confrontation between the Celtic and Latin churches which was to culminate in the Synod of Whitby in 664.

What Lindisfarne lacks in buildings, it makes up for in the richness of its Christian associations and, of course, in its Gospels. Whatever the lowly circumstances were in which those beautiful pages were produced, there can be no doubt as to their quality, which still acts as a beacon for art historians of all nations. After making the pilgrimage to Lindisfarne, the visitor must go to the British Museum in order to appreciate what the monks achieved on this remote Northumbrian island before the Danish warbands prevailed.

Before leaving Lindisfarne, the visitor might pause to ponder this story told by Bede of St Cuthbert. He relates that the saint spent a whole night praying in the sea, the water up to his neck: 'At daybreak he came out, kneeled on the sand, and prayed. Then two otters bounded out of the water, stretched themselves out before him, warmed his feet with their breath, and tried to dry him on their fur. They finished, he blessed them, and they returned to the sea whence they came.'

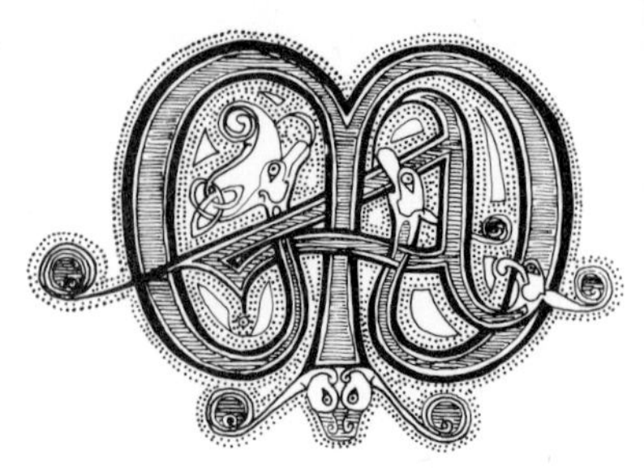

Drawing of the initial letters M A from the Latin Vulgate version of the Four Gospels written at Lindisfarne in about the year 700, now to be seen in the British Museum.

2

Ebb's Nook Hermitage Chapel, Northumberland

The situation of the small ruined chapel at Ebb's Nook is all-important. It stands bleakly beside the North Sea, looking up the forlorn and storm-swept coast of Northumbria, and we may well wonder at the piety and faith which made men choose this of all places to build a chapel. There can be few more powerful examples of the juxtaposition of the spiritual and the elemental than this small outpost of Christianity.

The ruins of the chapel, originally a simple two-roomed structure of nave and chancel which was later extended by a western annexe, were uncovered in 1853. There is no certain date for the building, but the place name recording its association with St Ebba, stepdaughter of Ethelfrith, king of Northumbria, suggests a site of ancient usage.

St Ebba, whose feast day is 25 August, fled from Northumbria to Scotland when Edwin invaded the kingdom in 616. She later became a nun and was famed for her wisdom. She reputedly secured the release of St Wilfrid on

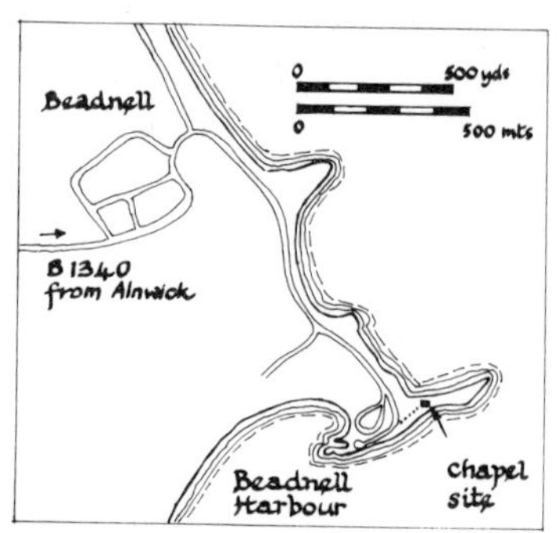

Map Reference: NU 239286 (metric map 75. 1-inch map 71)
Nearest Town: Bamburgh
Location: Beadnell is situated on the east coast beside the B1340, about 5 miles (8 km) south of Bamburgh. At Beadnell, follow the signs to Beadnell harbour (a dead-end road). Look for a telephone box by the yacht club and park nearby; it is likely to be rather crowded in summer. Take the path to the shore by the telephone box. The site is on the promontory and is marked by a green and white official notice. This notice misleadingly describes the site as 13th century.

The ruins of the chapel lie on the higher ground to the left of the picture. Such exposed coastal sites were especially favoured by devout hermits, and it is possible that the remains of a small hut used by such a man lie undiscovered beneath the sand nearby.

one occasion by telling Ecgfrith, the king who had imprisoned him, that his wife's illness was a divine punishment for depriving the saint of his freedom: he was speedily released! Later, however, St Ebba was criticized for the relaxed state of her community of nuns at Ely. Particular attention was drawn to the nuns' weaving of fine clothes with which they sought to attract the attentions of 'strange men'. Despite this temporary lapse from grace, Ebba's reputation for holiness continued after her death, and she was especially venerated during the 12th century in the north of England and south Scotland following the discovery of her relics.

Perhaps, therefore, the little chapel on Ebb's Nook is of the 12th century, and was constructed when her cult underwent a revival. But in lieu of direct evidence to the contrary, we will follow the confident assertion of the 19th-century excavators that this was the site of a chapel dedicated to her during the halcyon days of Northumbria in the 7th century.

3

Bewcastle Cross, Cumbria

The countryside about Bewcastle is splendidly remote and steeped in Border memories. Set in the wild land north of Hadrian's wall, Bewcastle today consists of little more than a farm, a small church and a rectory. The church lies within the circuit of the walls of a Roman fort, and its hexagonal plan can still be traced on several sides. A ruined castle, built during the reign of Edward I, Hammer of the Scots, stands to the north-east. In the churchyard is Bewcastle's famous cross – a superb example of Northumbrian art.

The head of the cross, which was recorded during the 17th century, is now sadly lost. It had an incomplete runic inscription upon it which read 'of the powerful Lord' or 'of the Lord's power'. The shaft, which is cut from a single stone, is richly decorated with panels and vegetation. On the main west face are

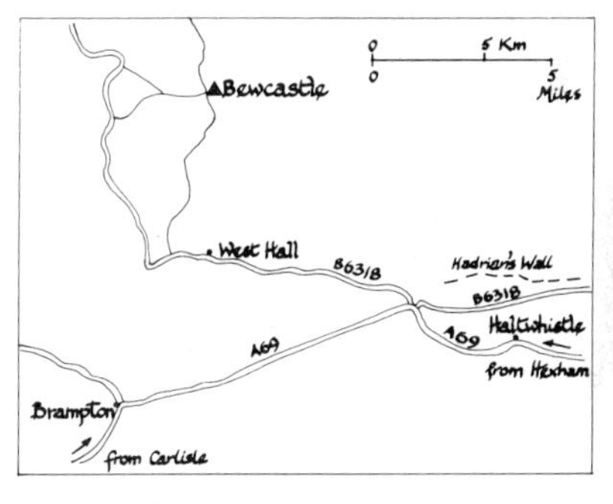

Map Reference: NY 565746 (metric map 86. 1-inch map 76)
Nearest Town: Carlisle
Location: North of Hadrian's Wall, in an area more associated with Roman remains, the cross stands in the churchyard at Bewcastle. This is reached by travelling 4 miles (6.5 km) up an unclassified road, a northward turning off the B6318 one mile (1.6 km) west of West Hall.

three figure panels representing St John the Baptist holding the Agnus Dei, Christ in Majesty, and a figure with an eagle or hawk on its wrist which is generally identified as St John the Evangelist. The eagle was John the Evangelist's symbol, but as the bird more closely resembles a hawk, it has been suggested that the figure represents a portrait of the secular donor of the cross attired for the hunt. An inhabited vinescroll fills the eastern face, whilst the northern and southern faces each have fine panels of interlace, vegetable scrolls and chequers, one of which contains a sundial.

Apart from the quality of the figure carving on the cross, it is of exceptional interest because of the runic inscriptions which it bears. Unhappily, most of the inscriptions are illegible, and many fanciful 'translations' have been offered. The inscriptions are set between the decorative panels, with the main inscription, nine lines in length, below the Christ panel. It has been suggested that this inscription was altered in the 19th century, with the result that most of its letters cannot now be read with certainty.

It seems likely that it was some sort of memorial inscription, since the phrase 'this victory monument' has been traced within it. Such a purpose for the cross might explain its presence in this remote place and the high quality of its carving. Other decipherable words are *gessus Kristtus* (Jesus Christ) above the Christ panel, what was probably a further *gessus* on the head of the north side, and the female name *kyniburga* which occurs on the same face. Since Kyniburga was the wife of King Aldfrith, the clear identification of her

Right: *The west face of the cross with the figures of St John the Baptist at the top, Christ in Majesty in the centre, and the man with the hawk below. The worn lines of the main inscription are visible between the two lower panels.*

name on the monument has encouraged acceptance of the supposed recognition of her husband's name in the long inscription on the west face of the cross.

Aldfrith reigned in Northumbria from 685 to *c.* 704, and was a noted patron of the arts, as well as a scholar of some renown. Stylistically the cross may well date from the period of his reign, since it belongs to the years about 700. We do not know where Aldfrith died, but it is possible that it was here at Bewcastle and that this splendid monument was a commemoration of one of Northumbria's most able and learned kings. Whatever the purpose for which this great sandstone column was erected, it stands as a lasting tribute to the 'Golden Age' of Northumbria, when the influence of Latin Christianity waxed in the northern kingdom.

4

Hexham: St Andrew's Crypt and Sculpture, Northumberland

It is sad indeed that so little now remains of St Wilfrid's great church at Hexham, which inspired his chronicler Eddius to write: '. . . nor have we heard of any other house on this side of the Alps built on such a scale.'

Eddius may have been somewhat biased in his account of Wilfrid's activities, since he naturally wished to impress the accomplishments of the saint upon his readers, but even in the 12th century William of Malmesbury could still write that 'those who have visited Italy allege that at Hexham they see the glories of Rome.' What now remains of this beauteous place which Eddius 'was quite at a loss for words to describe'?

The most notable survival is the crypt; its plan and construction are so similar to that at Wilfrid's other church at Ripon that there can be no doubt as to their common origin. Eddius tells us that Hexham was built between the years 672 and 678, during Wilfrid's period of office as Archbishop of York. The crypt is just west of the crossing of the present church, and it is entered by a steep flight of stairs which are mostly original. The stairs terminate in a small anteroom from which the main chamber, which would have contained venerable relics, opened to the east. This eastern chamber would probably have been closed off from pilgrims by an iron grille: they would have prayed at the entrance to the sanctuary and then departed by way of the exit passage on the north side of the antechamber. A small bowl scooped out of the wall on the south side would have contained oil or tallow with a floating wick to provide light; a ventilation hole in the roof was for escaping smoke. Within the eastern chamber are three more lights which would have made it brighter than the antechamber, thereby increasing the wonder of the pilgrims. The nature of the Hexham relics is uncertain, but we may guess that Wilfrid would have done his best to obtain some exceedingly precious objects for this wonderful church on his visits to Rome.

The walls of the crypt would probably have been plastered, and the rich 'picture gallery' of Roman inscriptions which is now visible on the inside walls would have been obscured. As well as being one of the finest Saxon crypts in England, Hexham also provides a dramatic illustration of the re-use of Roman stonework by Saxon builders. Here is an altar to the God Apollo, and stones bearing such famous names as Marcus Aurelius, Geta and other Emperors whose fame echoed through the Empire. Yet here at Hexham their glory is diminished, the stones having been plundered from the nearby Wall fort of Corstopitum for use in Wilfrid's glorious enterprise.

Other than the crypt, few traces of Wilfrid's church survive. Beneath a trapdoor in the choir the sturdy foundations of an apse may be seen, which probably represents the extreme

Map Reference: NY 935641 (metric map 87. 1-inch map 77)
Nearest Town: Hexham
Location: The town stands on the south bank of the River Tyne. It can be reached from the A69 trunk road between Newcastle and Carlisle. The abbey church is at the west side of the market place.

Part of the vinescroll ornament on the Acca Cross. This superb piece of sculpture dates from c.740, a tribute to the 'Golden Age' of Northumbria.

eastward extension of the Anglo-Saxon church. The original west wall probably followed the line of the present one, whilst the south wall also follows the earlier line. On the north, however, it appears that the Saxon church was nearly ten feet (3 metres) wider than the present nave, so we must imagine a substantially broader nave than at present, though of the same length. The church would therefore have had a basilican plan, rather like the early Kentish churches at Canterbury and Reculver. The inner nave walls would have been pierced by arches, like those at Brixworth in Northamptonshire, but unlike Brixworth there appear to have been columns behind the main arches which divided the side aisles into two long corridors. Whether or not these side aisles were divided up to form small chapels called porticus is uncertain.

Within the church there is a vast array of Saxon sculpture, some of the highest quality. Particularly notable is the great cross-shaft in the south transept called 'Acca's Cross'. Acca, who was a disciple of Wilfrid and became bishop after him, is said to have 'ennobled' his master's church yet further during his period of office. The superb vinescroll decoration on the cross with its scintillating rhythm is a fitting tribute to a man who was celebrated for his chanting of the holy offices. In support of the identification, the name ACCA was apparently visible on the cross in the last century.

Two further objects must be mentioned in the midst of so many which claim our attention. In the choir is the stone 'frith stool' which is reputed to have been used by men seeking sanctuary in the church from lay authority. Tradition links it with Wilfrid himself but the style of the decoration suggests a 9th century date: the chair has been claimed as the coronation seat of the kings of Northumbria. This rare survival of a piece of Anglo-Saxon church furniture serves to remind us that there must have been many such objects in both stone and wood of which but a handful survives.

Finally the small copper-gilt chalice on display in the church must be seen. This almost certainly came from a priest's grave, and is one of only five Anglo-Saxon chalices which are known. It may have been made as a token object for burial, or else it could have been a small portable cup carried by a priest from the mother church at Hexham to outlying parts of the kingdom where he would have preached God's word and administered the sacraments. In either case, it is a rare survival from the early days of Northumbrian Christianity.

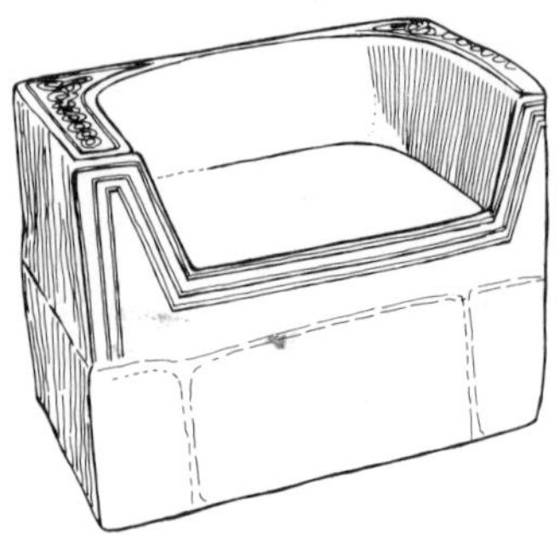

The frith stool. This has been variously claimed as St Wilfrid's episcopal seat, the coronation chair of the kings of Northumbria, or as a sanctuary seat for those seeking protection from the civil authorities. Since the word 'frith' meant 'peace' in Old English, it might be that the sanctuary theory is most probable. In the 10th-century laws of Alfred it is declared that 'if a man exposed to a vendetta reaches [the church] running or riding, no one is to drag him out for seven days . . .'

This small copper gilt chalice, which stands less than three inches (7.6 cm) high, was probably used with a small portable altar like the one found in St Cuthbert's coffin at Durham.

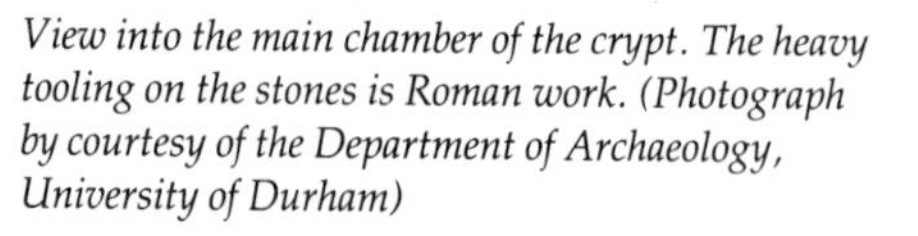

View into the main chamber of the crypt. The heavy tooling on the stones is Roman work. (Photograph by courtesy of the Department of Archaeology, University of Durham)

5
Bywell: St Andrew's and St Peter's, Northumberland

The two churches of St Peter and St Andrew are both of Anglo-Saxon origin, and present a most unusual spectacle in a settlement which today is scarcely more than a hamlet. They were presumably built to serve two Anglo-Saxon estates, both of which were based in the village. Standing beside the Tyne, Bywell may well have been a bridge point across the river in Roman times, which would have contributed to its early importance. The chronicler Simeon of Durham recorded that Egbert was consecrated twelfth Bishop of Lindisfarne in Bywell in 802 by Eanbald, Archbishop of York. The church used may have been a monastic one, and the size and early evidence from St Peter's suggests that it was the place. We can only speculate about Egbert's feelings upon his new appointment: it was a great honour, but Lindisfarne had been sacked by the Vikings only nine years before and the community probably lived in constant fear of further marauding.

Not much is left of the Anglo-Saxon church of St Peter, but indications suggest that it was a major building. The height and thinness of the nave walls provide the first clue to their age. The nave was slightly over 60 feet (19 metres) long and probably had a small western annexe, now obscured by the later tower. The north and east nave quoins are still visible, externally in the first instance and in the organ chamber in the second. The most striking indication is provided by the four windows in the north wall. One of these has been altered, but the others retain their monolithic heads and thin strip-like jambs. In the north chancel wall is a blocked flat-headed doorway of early character which may have led to an attached porticus, as at Escomb in Durham. The presence of such a doorway, which is probably of

The tower of St Andrew's church. The heavy quoin-stones bonding the angles can be seen, and note the simple but well-proportioned lights in the top belfry stage with the delicate stripwork arch above.

Map Reference: NZ 049614 (metric map 87. 1-inch map 77)
Nearest Town: Corbridge
Location: Bywell lies on the north bank of the River Tyne, about 4 miles (6.5 km) east of Corbridge and 12 miles (19 km) west of Newcastle. From Newcastle take the A695, after Stocksfield cross the Tyne to Bywell, which is now only a small hamlet. St Andrew's church stands by the entrance to Bywell Hall. Close by, on the bank of the Tyne, is St Peter's church.

8th-century date, together with the porticus and the grand scale of the plan, suggests that we are looking at the remnants of the church in which Egbert was consecrated nearly 1,200 years ago. When we add to this the great height of the chancel walls, which equals those of the nave, it is clear that St Peter's was a substantial foundation, and a fitting location for such an important event as the enthronement of a bishop of Lindisfarne, itself the nerve centre of Northumbrian Christianity.

St Andrew's splendidly displays its Anglo-Saxon origins by virtue of its tower. This is a well-proportioned structure with prominent side alternate quoins and fine windows. The lower part of the tower appears to pre-date the upper stages; a change in the colour and texture of the stonework is visible above the bottom south tower window. In the photograph, this can be seen as a junction between the coarser and generally smaller rubblework above the window as against the larger, smoother stones below. The upper stages are likely to be immediately pre-Conquest, owing to the relatively advanced design of the belfry lights, whilst the lower section, which may have formed an early towerless entrance porch, as in the early phase at Monkwearmouth, is probably 10th century. Part of the west wall of the nave is also of Anglo-Saxon date. The early nave roof was somewhat higher than the present one, since the Anglo-Saxon quoins rise several feet above the eaves of the existing roof. Inside, there is a rather undistinguished fragment of a stone cross-shaft.

Unhappily, St Andrew's church is now redundant, scarcely surprising in view of the fact that the modern community is barely enough to fill one church, never mind two. But St Peter's is brightly kept, and the little hamlet is a wonderful place in summer.

6

Ovingham: St Mary's Tower and Sculpture, Northumberland

Map Reference: NZ 085637 (metric map 88. 1-inch map 78)
Nearest Town: Prudhoe
Location: On the north side of the River Tyne about 10 miles (17 km) west of Newcastle. It can be reached from the A69 trunk road, turning south onto a minor road to Ovingham and Prudhoe. The church is in the centre of the village.

St Mary's church, which stands in a secluded churchyard, has one of the finest of the simple Northumbrian Anglo-Saxon towers. There are five stages, and it is only in the uppermost that any sizeable windows appear. These are simple double belfry openings, outlined in stripwork, with arched lintels and mid-wall balusters which have crudely cut capitals and bases. Above the belfry lights are simple circular openings cut through single blocks of stone which are rather similar to those at St Andrew's, Bywell. The absence of a west door lends the tower a somewhat stark appearance, and we are reminded of the later Northumbrian peel towers which acted as places of refuge in troubled times. The fabric of the tower consists of squared blocks of greyish stone, some of which are re-used Roman work. The angles are tied in with large side alternate quoins.

The west wall of the nave is probably also Saxon, since it is bonded into the east tower wall. As there is no discernible break with the other walls of the nave, it is possible that their upper parts above the tall Early English arcades are also Saxon. On the first floor there is a round-headed doorway leading from the tower into what must have been the roof-space above the nave. Two fragments of Anglo-Saxon sculpture are preserved in the church: part of a cross-shaft in the south porch and a cross-head beside the pulpit.

The openings visible in the tower are all of Anglo-Saxon date. The austerity of the structure suggests that it may have served as an early 'peel tower' to protect the thane and his folk from hostile attack.

7

Jarrow: Bede's Home Monastery, Tyne and Wear

It was at Jarrow that the Venerable Bede spent all save his earliest years, and it is with his name, together with his great reputation as a scholar, that St Paul's church will be forever associated. Standing beside the steep bank of the Tyne, now set amongst cranes and factories, it is hard at first to imagine the place as it must have once been: a group of buildings set in open country with the church towering above. Yet in this place were created magnificent manuscripts and a new philosophy of history which has lasted to the present day. Bede was the first historian to date events before and after the birth of Christ (BC and AD), and his thoroughness in checking sources for his great *History of the English Church and People* is still a model approach to the writing of history.

Jarrow was founded some ten or eleven years after its sister house at Monkwearmouth; precision is possible because the dedication stone is preserved in the nave, recording that the church was dedicated on 23 April 684 or 685. The two houses together formed a single monastic family, as Bede called it: 'the monastery of St Peter and St Paul which is at Wearmouth and Jarrow.' But Bede was by no means the only monk at Jarrow and Wearmouth; at the time of the death of Abbot Ceolfrith in 716 there were over 600 monks in the community and this great monastery must have been one of the largest in the land.

As with Monkwearmouth, Jarrow was founded by that enterprising Northumbrian nobleman Benedict Biscop, who obtained a grant of land for the purpose from King Ecgfrith. The chancel of the present church is the only standing element of the original building. It seems somewhat small to be the nave of the monastic church, and it is generally assumed that the present chancel was a small chapel lying to the east of the main church, which probably had a basilican plan similar to that at Hexham. The chancel has an original north doorway, now blocked, and three round-headed single-splayed windows in the south wall. The tower, which joins the chancel to the modern nave, is also Anglo-Saxon, though of a later date than the work in the chancel. It may have been a porch entrance, and it was certainly raised in the later Anglo-Saxon period, as can be seen outside.

Externally, the side alternate quoins of the east wall of the chancel demonstrate the Anglo-Saxon origins, together with the windows in the south wall. It is possible that there was an eastward extension of the chapel, since there are two upright stones in the east wall which suggest a doorway. The tower, which may have been built after the site was sacked

the chancel. The window head is carved from a single block of stone, as are the other members.

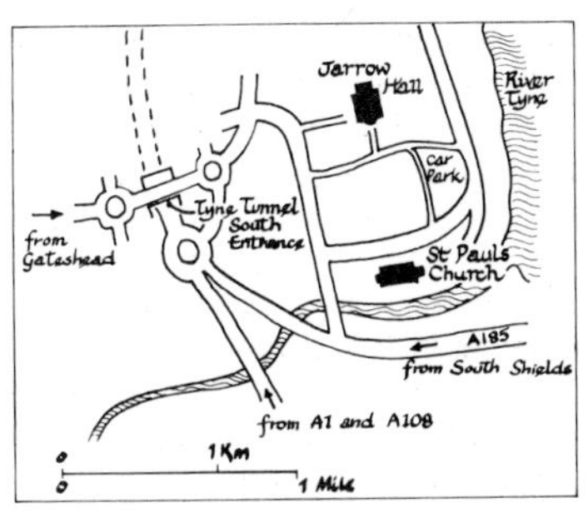

Map Reference: NZ 339652 (metric map 88. 1-inch map 78)
Nearest Town: South Shields
Location: The church and nearby museum in Jarrow Hall are best approached by following signs to the Tyne Tunnel. At the southern entrance roundabout, take the A185 to South Shields and then follow the signs to St Paul's church, Jarrow. There is ample car parking space at the site.

The monastery is in the care of the Department of the Environment, and is open free of charge.

St Paul's church and Jarrow Hall are open as follows:

Apr–Oct	Mon–Sat	10.00–5.30
	Sun	2.30–5.30
Nov–Mar	Mon–Sat	11.00–4.30
	Sun	2.30–5.30

Jarrow Hall is closed every Monday except Bank Holidays. There is a small admission charge.

by the Danes in 794, is rectangular in plan at the base, and square, or nearly so, at the belfry stage. The scar of an earlier taller chancel roof is visible on the east side of the tower. The rest of the church, including a broad nave, side chapels and a western tower, was demolished during the 18th century, but fortunately a drawing in the British Museum records the original structure.

The monastic buildings were located to the south of the church, and nothing now remains above ground. It is doubly unfortunate that the area is also obscured by the standing walls of the later medieval monastery; even the very Anglo-Saxon-looking triangular-headed doorway is of Norman date. Recently, excavation has elucidated the Anglo-Saxon layout, and the Department of the Environment has marked out the lines of the early walls; these can readily be followed by reference to the coloured plan to the south of the nave.

There were two main structures called prosaically 'A' and 'B'. Both were on an east-west axis approximately 13 yards (12 metres) south of the church; the space between was used as the monks' cemetery. Building A, the more westerly, was apparently used as a refectory or dining hall. The building was substantial, with plastered stone walls, a stone slated roof, a mortar floor strengthened with chips of tile and windows glazed with coloured glass. The solid construction of the walls, together with

Right: *The church from the south, looking up from the steep bank of the Tyne. One of the small Saxon round-headed windows is visible to the left of the down pipe, on the right-hand side of the picture. The masonry in the foreground is part of the later medieval monastic buildings; the Anglo-Saxon ones lie under the grass beyond.*

Two of the many fine sculptural fragments in St Paul's church.

the occurrence of buttresses, led the excavator, Professor Cramp, to suggest that it was a two-storey building.

Building B was divided into three rooms, one of which was very large, whilst the other two were subdivided from it by a wall, and from each other by a wooden screen. It is suggested that the two small rooms were used by the Abbot as a 'cell', which consisted of a living-room and separate oratory (chapel) with a small altar set against the east wall. The other, larger room was probably a place of assembly for the community, and may also have been a 'scriptorium' or writing room in which books were written and illustrated. This building was also plastered and glazed with plain glass.

Below these main buildings on the slope down to the river, several small wattle huts were found which may have been used for such crafts as glass-working, judging from the finds made in them. This reminds us that these early monasteries were probably important trading centres as well as religious communities. But it should not be imagined that these early monks were other than frugal in their ways; no costly personal objects or other tokens of luxury have been recovered from the site, and fish appears to have been the staple diet, as became holy men. We should also remember that the Venerable Bede himself possessed only pepper, incense and napkins when he died.

North of the church lies Jarrow Hall, which is now a museum containing material excavated from the site. Many finds are preserved there, and there are exhibitions on the structure and decoration of the monastery. It is much to be recommended, and even affords the rare facility of a pleasant coffee room!

8

Monkwearmouth: St Peter's Tower and Sculpture, Tyne and Wear

Bede's account of the founding of Wearmouth, of the grant of royal land for the purpose to Benedict Biscop, and of that young nobleman's desire to create a church along the lines of a Latin Christian community is filled with fascinating detail. Bede tells how Biscop sent his friends to France in order to secure the services of skilled masons, and how later in the building programme they returned to France to find glaziers to beautify the new church. Major masonry buildings and glazed windows had probably not been seen in Northumbria for 250 years before Biscop began his work at Wearmouth, and it is a tribute to his zeal that he almost single-handedly reintroduced the techniques of Roman building construction. Wearmouth, founded in 674, just ten years after the Synod of Whitby, was a symbol of the victory of the Latin Church over the Celtic. It introduced monasticism on a scale and of a quality which the north of England had never seen before.

The west tower and some fragments of sculpture are all that is left of the monastery, and little is known of its history. For a century and more, Wearmouth must have been a dynamic centre of Northumbrian Christianity until the Danish raids took place. Later, in 1070, the abbey was burnt by Malcolm, King of Scots, but about the period between its foundation and that tragedy the record is remarkably quiet. Apart from the monastic church, there appear to have been two lesser churches, as well as oratories and a dormitory, but we know little about them. We must be content to look at the fragments which remain.

The west tower of the present church consists of five storeys, all of which seem to be later in date than the west wall of the nave. This suggests that they are later than the foundation date of 674, but before 686 because in that year Eosterwine, joint abbot of St Peter's, died of the plague and was, according to Bede, buried in the west porch. It is possible of course that all traces of that early porch have disappeared, but it is generally accepted that the lower stages of the existing building belong to the porch which Bede described.

The porch, which originally consisted of the lowest storey, together with a room above, opened into the church by way of a partially blocked doorway. The head of this may be seen in the west wall of the nave, slightly askew to the later west doorway. The north and south doorways in the porch presumably opened into side chapels or chambers. The scar of the gabled roof of the early porch can be clearly seen in the west wall of the tower, just above the second string-course. A patch of large stones above the window in the first floor was probably the reverse side of a large sculpture of the Crucifixion, as at Romsey in Hampshire and Langford in Oxfordshire. The upper parts of the tower, including the double belfry lights, are probably of the 10th century, and mark the end of the architectural development.

The porch must have been a magnificent composition, as the turned baluster shafts and carvings of twined birds on each side of the entrance indicate. The western opening appears to have had no door, so the porch would have been open as we see it today. Unhappily, the animal carvings on the lowest string-course of the tower are now almost obliterated by weathering, but they must have added to the richness of the impression which the porch created.

Excavations to the south of the church have exposed a number of Anglo-Saxon structures, but nothing now remains above ground level. The buildings were plastered, as at Jarrow, and finds of window glass attest the work of Biscop's French glaziers. The use of lead in the buildings, together with their architectural

Map Reference: NZ 402577 (metric map 88. 1-inch map 78)
Nearest Town: Sunderland
Location: St Peter's church, Monkwearmouth, stands on the north bank of the River Wear close to the bridge to Sunderland on the south bank. A lonely site, set in the midst of industrial and housing development, it can be reached from the north by the A184 from Newcastle. Continue towards the centre of Sunderland, but take the left turning, called Dame Dorothy Street, immediately before the bridge.

St Paul's church has a museum and is also a tourist information centre. It is open daily from 10 to 5 and can open outside these hours by prior arrangement.

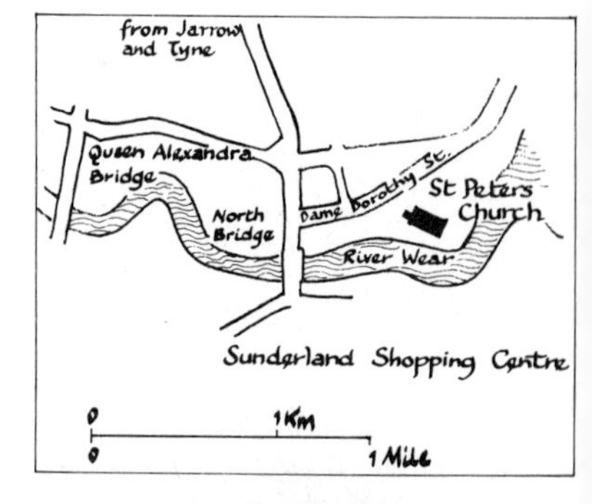

Two of the interlocking heron heads on the porch. The bodies are elongated to form narrow intertwined strips which terminate in broad fish-like tails.

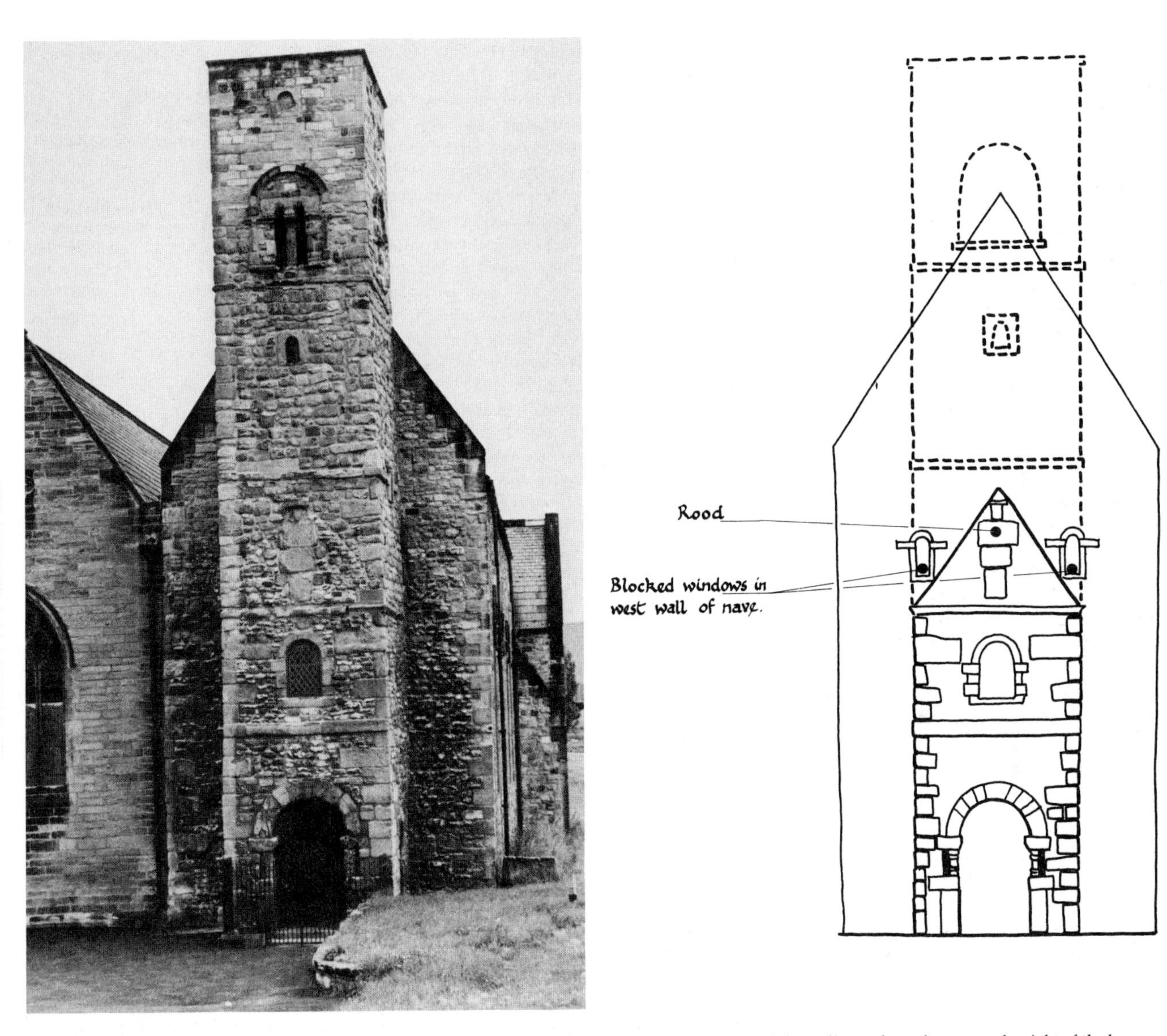

The Anglo-Saxon tower. Originally it consisted of a lower porch two storeys high; the diagonal scar of the earlier roof may be seen to the right of the large stones set above the first floor window. The porch is thought to have been built between 674 and 686, and was the burial place of at least one Anglo-Saxon abbot of the monastery of Wearmouth and Jarrow.

sophistication, strongly supports the accuracy of Bede's account of the building of the monastery.

We are told that Ceolfrith, who was Abbot of the monastery of Wearmouth and Jarrow between 688 and 716, greatly enriched the churches here and enlarged the monastic library. One great project which he ordered was the making of three copies of a Latin Bible which he had brought back from Italy. This work took place here at Wearmouth, and it would be fascinating to know more of it. One of the copies has survived because Ceolfrid took it to Rome in 716 as a gift for the Pope.

This book, called the *Codex Amiatinus* is claimed to have originated at St Peter's, and is now a prized treasure of the Laurentian Library in Florence. It is the oldest complete Latin Bible in existence, and it has been estimated that the skins of 500 calves would have been required to make its vellum pages. The work is beautifully illustrated, and it is reckoned that seven separate hands can be recognized in it.

It is perhaps ironical that this most precious relic of Anglo-Saxon Christendom should lie far away in Italy, but when we consider Ceolfrith's pains in taking it there – it weighed 75½ pounds (34 kg) without any packing – it is perhaps fitting that it should remain there undisturbed.

9

Durham: St Cuthbert's Relics, Bede's Tomb and Sculpture, Durham

Although nothing now remains of the Anglo-Saxon church or churches at Durham, it commands our attention not only because it is the last resting place of two of Northumbria's greatest saints, Cuthbert and Bede, but also because of its unrivalled collection of sculpture. All these treasures are housed in the great cathedral which stands high above the river, the noblest English example of Norman ecclesiastical architecture.

Cuthbert's body was brought here by the devoted monks of Lindisfarne. He was consecrated Bishop of Lindisfarne, but held office for only two years before returning to his life of contemplation shortly before his death in 687. His reputation for great holiness was enhanced when his body was exhumed ten years after his death and was found to be undecayed. A shrine was erected, and Lindisfarne became a major centre for pilgrimage.

The Danish raids 200 years later shattered the peace of the Holy Island, and the monks, following Cuthbert's wish that his bones should be carried from the island if ever the monks departed, took his body with them. They eventually came to the high fastness above the River Wear – the future site of Durham – and built a 'white church', perhaps so-called because of its plastered walls. The bones of Cuthbert have never left Durham since, and he lies now in a place of honour east of the high altar.

The tale of Cuthbert does not end there; his shrine was destroyed at the time of the Reformation though his body was reburied in the same spot. It lay undisturbed until 1827, when his tomb was excavated and a remarkable collection of objects was found.

These included the original wooden coffin made for the saint's body, which was decorated with carvings of the Twelve Apostles, the Virgin and Child, and the Seven Archangels. Inside the coffin were his gold and garnet pectoral cross – a splendid object that owes much to the jewellery styles at Sutton Hoo – his portable altar and an ivory comb. Additionally, there were substantial parts of embroidered vestments comprising a stole, maniple and girdle, which may have been presented to the saint's shrine when it rested in Chester-le-Street. If these pieces of textile were indeed presented on that occasion, then they were royal gifts bestowed by King

Map Reference: NZ 273420 (metric map 88. 1-inch map 85)
Location: The Monks' Dormitory is in the cloisters of the cathedral; this houses a rich collection of sculpture of our period culled from all over Northumbria and beyond.

The Cathedral Treasury, which contains the Cuthbert relics, is also near the cloister.

Cuthbert's gold pectoral cross set with garnets. The technique by which the garnet 'cells' are formed is similar to that used in the jewellery from the Sutton Hoo ship burial. The cross would have hung round the saint's neck; the suspension loop for the cord is visible at the top.

One of the Apostles carved on the side of Cuthbert's wooden coffin.

Athelstan on his recorded pilgrimage to the tomb in 934. This would be consonant with their quality, which is of the very finest, and provides ample testimony of the skills of Anglo-Saxon needleworkers. All these delights are now displayed under modern conditions in the Cathedral Treasury exhibition. For those of us who recall the frightful circumstances of their erstwhile public exposure in the Monks' Dormitory, the new display is a blessing.

The Venerable Bede lies in the very westernmost projection of the cathedral, beneath a simple stone slab in the Galilee Chapel. Originally buried at his home monastery at Jarrow where he died in 735 'still praising God', Bede's body was removed to Durham in 1022. The precise circumstances of the translation of the body are unclear. A monk called Alfred Westlow was apparently responsible, and it has been suggested that the remains were stolen in order to swell Durham's comprehensive collection of northern saints' relics. If those venerable bones were indeed the subject of some sordid adventure, it cannot detract from the life of a man who has been an inspiration to many generations of scholars. His bones were finally laid with due reverence in their present position in 1370, and we must trust that they will not be disturbed again.

Finally, a visit should be made to the Monks' Dormitory on the west side of the cloister south of the cathedral. In this long gallery lie over seventy pieces of sculpture of our period culled from a wide area of the north. Most are original, though casts augment this comprehensive collection. A rudimentary catalogue is available. Particularly notable are the casts of the Ruthwell and Bewcastle crosses. The former lies in Scotland, alas beyond the scope of this work, whilst the other is on the high moors of Cumbria. If the visitor cannot reach such a remote place where buses seldom run, he must content himself with this replica, but the sight of the cross with the hills behind is well worth the journey.

10
Bishop Auckland Cross, Durham

The great cross of St Andrew, Auckland, stands at the west end of the nave, under the tower arch. It is unusual in that it has retained its massive base stone, which is carved with figures probably representing disciples. The shaft itself is rectangular in section, and tapers markedly towards the top. The Auckland carver was much more at home with the birds and beasts contained in the vinescroll panels which run up the sides than with the human figures in the main panels. The creatures have vitality and naturalistic poses, whilst the figures are rather wooden, with features crudely cut into the flat surfaces.

Cable ornament decorates the angles and also separates the panels. On one side, the creatures contained in the vinescroll roundels are menaced by an archer who is portrayed in the action of shooting his bow upwards towards them. The figure panels on the front and back contain nimbed figures, two of whom are identified by abbreviated versions of their names; PA[VLV]S 'Paul' and AND[REAS] 'Andrew' executed in capitals contained within rectangular tablets. Although unnamed, it is likely that the other male figures are also disciples, whilst a further panel depicting two female figures may represent the Annunciation.

Although the Auckland cross, which dates from the later 8th century, is less competently executed than, say, the nearly contemporary Acca's Cross at Hexham, it is nevertheless a forceful product of its time. Sir Thomas Kendrick's famous comment that it reflected 'the hard and violent barbarism of the age' is certainly justified by such ungainly details as

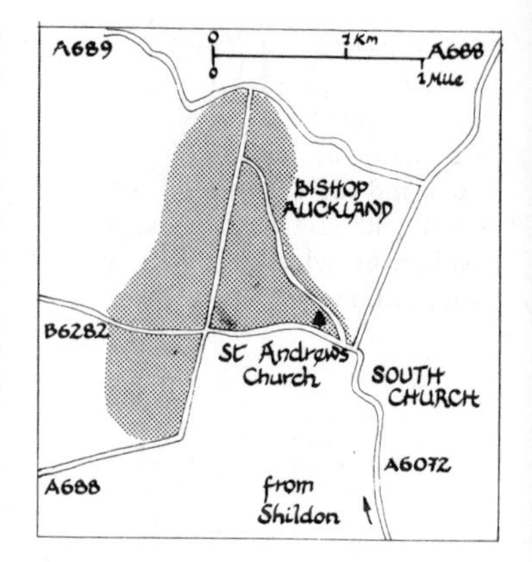

Map Reference: NZ 218285 (metric map 93. 1-inch map 85)

Location: St Andrew's church lies on the outskirts of Bishop Auckland in a settlement known as South Church on the south-east side of the town. It lies on the road between Bishop Auckland and Shildon on the left-hand side from Bishop Auckland, on a hill.

It is best to plan a visit to coincide with pub opening hours(!) as the key must be obtained from the Red Alligator nearby.

The crude expressions and over-large hands of these figures on the base-stone of the cross are typical of the human representations, but the birds and animals on the sides are much more sympathetically carved.

the over-large hands and the flat expressions. But when we look at the birds and beasts on the sides of the cross, we see that the carver was more at home with his subjects. The Auckland carver executed the inhabited vine-scroll with detail and care which belie the 'barbarism' which Kendrick attributed to the composition.

11

Escomb: The Celebrated Church of St John, Durham

The little church of St John is an excellent example of early Anglo-Saxon work. Standing tall and austere in an almost circular churchyard, its majestic antiquity is unmarred by the tasteless modern houses which surround it. This is one of the best-preserved Anglo-Saxon churches in England and, apart from a short break during the last century, worship has probably continued here for 1,300 years.

Nothing is known of the foundation of the church, and the dedication is unhelpful. The main fabric is of 7th-century date, and some have claimed that its simplicity shows con-

Map Reference: NZ 189301 (metric map 92. 1-inch map 85)
Nearest Town: Bishop Auckland
Location: From Bishop Auckland take the B6282 to the west; after 2 miles (3 km) Escomb is signposted to the right; the church lies at the end of this minor road.

The key may be obtained at reasonable hours from a house near the church; the address is on the church door.

Escomb church from the south-west. Apart from the later porch and the absence of a west door which was probably originally present, the church is virtually untouched after 1,300 years.

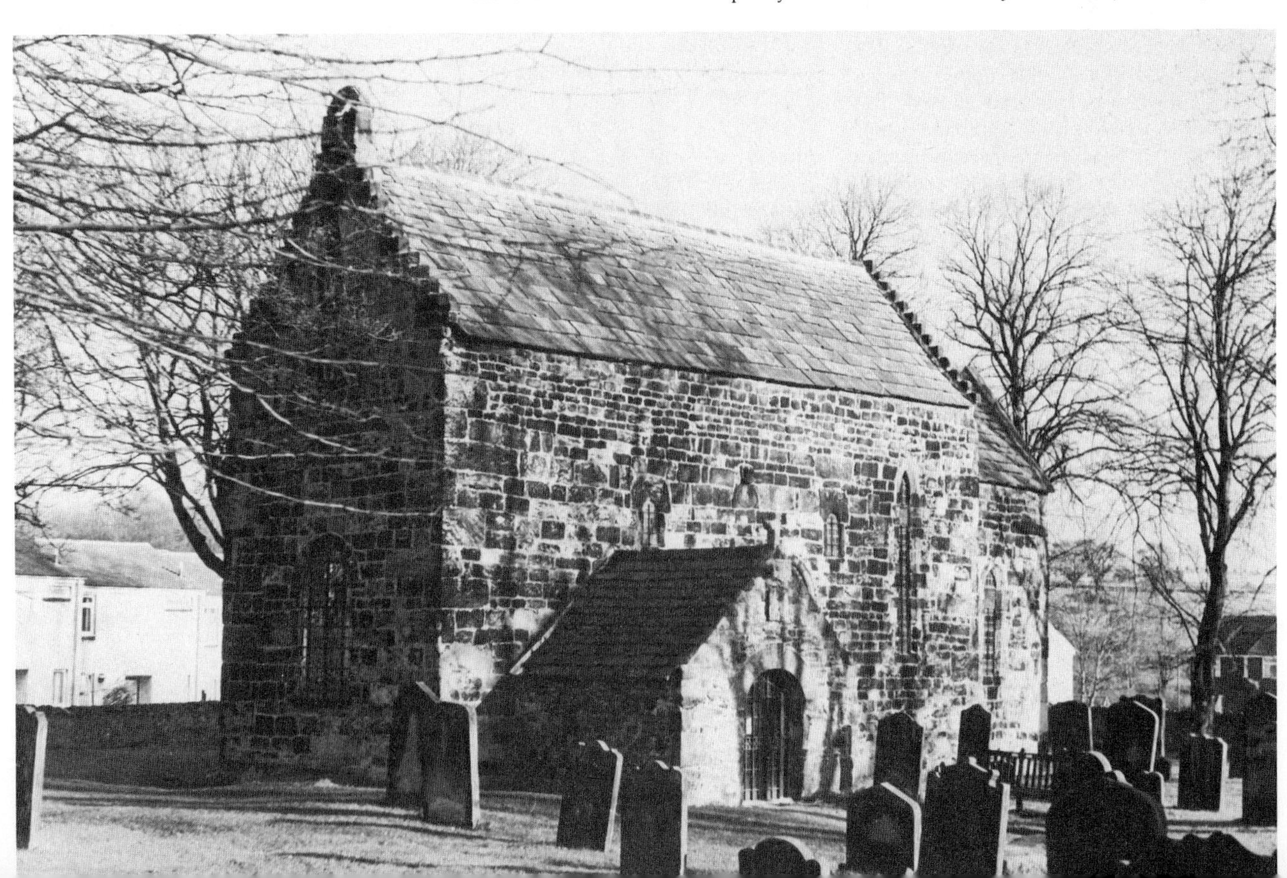

tinuity from Celtic timber buildings. The Venerable Bede makes no mention of the church in his *History of the English Church and People* which was finished in 731. This has led some to question the early dating, but Bede only mentioned churches germane to his narrative, so the omission is not critical.

The gables of the nave have been restored; the 'crow step' pattern may therefore be later. The walls are over two feet (61 cm) thick and 23 feet (7 metres) high. Huge quoin-stones, some nearly two feet (61 cm) high and three or four feet (1 metre) long, are set on edge and extend along each wall alternately; hence the name 'side alternate' quoins. Many of the stones show characteristic Roman diamond tooling and were doubtless taken from the nearby fort at Binchester. A steeply pitched roof line, perhaps of a porch, can be seen on the west wall. The blocked doorway in the north wall of the chancel led into a small chapel, called a porticus, which was excavated in 1968. The present south porch is later. Just to the east of it, high up in the wall, an original sundial may be seen, decorated with a carving of a serpent.

Internally, the lofty nave is complemented by a tall chancel arch, a further example of re-used Roman work. The small chancel has a simple Saxon carving behind the altar. The four Saxon nave windows, round-headed on the south side and square on the north, are strongly splayed internally to admit more light. They are now glazed, but vertical grooves for wooden shutters show the original arrangement; some window glass was found during the excavation of the north porticus, however. A small section of early cobbled flooring is preserved at the west end of the nave.

As Escomb is older than St Lawrence's at Bradford-on-Avon and Odda's Chapel at Deerhurst, it is the earliest largely complete Anglo-Saxon church in England, and well worth a visit.

12

Croft Cross Fragments, North Yorkshire

Map Reference: NZ 289099 (metric map 93. 1-inch map 85)
Nearest Town: Darlington
Location: Croft, right beside the Tees, is on the Yorkshire side of the river, about 4 miles (6.5 km) south of the centre of Darlington on the A167 to Northallerton. The church stands close to the bridge. Unfortunately, it is kept locked owing to vandalism, and access other than on Sundays must be made by prior arrangement.

Since it is very difficult to gain access to the church at Croft, the replica of the Croft cross in the library of the Dean and Chapter at Durham is vital for students of Anglo-Saxon art. The cross at Croft is justly famous since it is one of the finest pieces of Northumbrian sculpture. It dates from the late 8th or early 9th centuries.

The piece itself is quite small, a mere fragment of a cross-shaft less than two feet (61 cm) high, but the scroll decoration on it is remarkable for its innovation and quality. On one face, roundels contain fabulous beasts and birds which are vigorously carved in attitudes of frozen movement. The roundels are not

A vertical tree scroll with paired volutes containing griffins and other creatures.

mechanical, but subtly alter shape according to the attitude of the creatures which they contain. Springing from a simple centre shaft, the elements fill the available space and form one of the most perfect artistic compositions to survive from Northumbria.

The other face is also spectacular, but the upper panel which contains two opposed birds is unfortunately broken off below the top. The balance and life which are such notable features of the roundel panels are also present here; two birds and dog-like creatures stand like coiled springs amongst the foliage. It is fortunate that, although mutilated, the shaft is remarkably unworn. It now stands on the north windowsill of the Milbanke Chapel while a further cross fragment stands by the north door.

13

Hornby: St Mary's Tower, North Yorkshire

The western tower of Hornby church is a good example of very late Anglo-Saxon building. Indeed, it has even been thought to be of post-Conquest date, but the presence of added Norman buttresses on the western angles suggests that the tower is probably late Saxon.

There were three storeys originally, the present fourth-floor belfry stage having been added in the 15th century. Apart from the fine third-storey double belfry openings, only one other window, in the south wall of the middle stage, is original. There are two doorways in the east and west sides; the west door has a flat lintel surmounted by a rather misshapen relieving arch. The door into the nave is a massive affair with a heavy voussoired head.

Although outside the scope of this guide, the medieval painted screen dividing off the south chapel from the south aisle of the church should not be missed.

The west tower from the south-east. The Norman buttresses added to the bottom stage are clearly distinguishable by their larger square stones. Each section of the tower is of similar height, and each is slightly stepped inwards, which not only lends added structural strength, but also makes the tower appear more slender.

Map Reference: SE 222937 (metric map 99. 1-inch map 91)
Nearest Town: Richmond
Location: Hornby is 2 miles (3 km) west of the A1, and can be reached by a minor road signed to Hackforth and Hornby 3 miles (4.5 km) north of the major turning to Leeming Bar. The fine parkland of Hornby Park is traversed before the village is reached; the church stands in the centre.

14

Brompton: Anglo-Danish Hog-back Tombstones, North Yorkshire

The Brompton hog-backs. The general form of the stones is derived from architectural prototypes, but the symbolism of the bears is unclear.

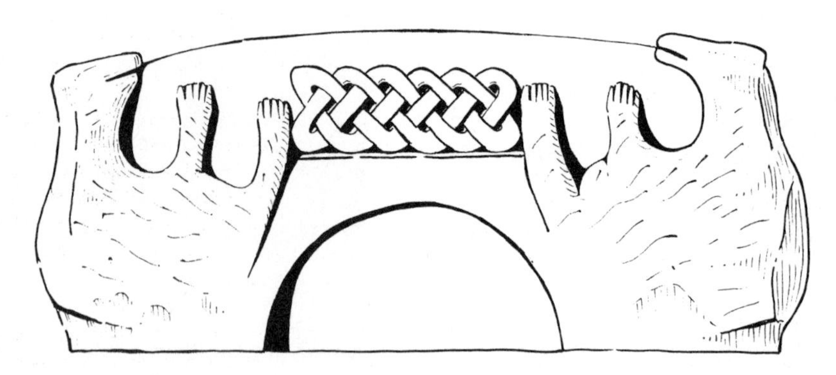

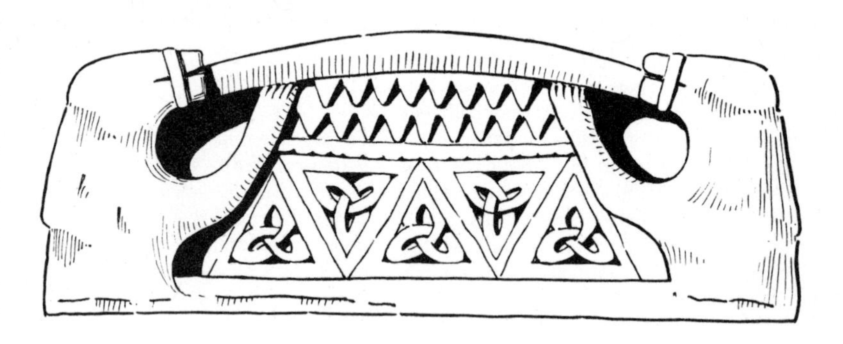

The village of Brompton is the fortunate possessor of two large greens, beside one of which stands the church of St Thomas. The church is all of post-Saxon date, but inside are some of the finest hog-back tombstones in the country. The stones lie just west of the chancel arch, where they present a strange and slightly disturbing spectacle.

Hog-backs, so-called because of their shape, being higher at the middle than at the ends, were intended to portray houses. The idea of such house-tombs has a long history, and has resulted in such diverse monuments as the pyramids of Egypt and prehistoric burial mounds in Britain. In this instance the idea seems to have come from a fusion of Scandinavian architectural styles with British stone-working techniques.

The Brompton examples clearly exhibit their architectural origins; the upper parts imitate roofs with heavy down-curving ridges and triangular wooden 'shingles' (roof tiles). The walls below are reduced to decorative panels, though the middle stone appears to show walls constructed of plaited wattles represented by interlace patterns. The stone nearest the chancel also shows a round-headed arch, which may be intended as a doorway. The evidence provided by hog-backs has been used in attempts to reconstruct the appearance of Scandinavian halls in both Britain and the northern homelands.

The ends of the Brompton stones are carved in the form of opposed muzzled bears which clasp the gable ends of the houses. The meaning of this symbolism is unknown, though it may relate to some idea of guarding the tomb. The bears are not particularly fierce, and two appear to be smiling broadly and rolling on their backs. An attempt has been made to represent their fur by light picking of the stone surface. The worn condition of the upper parts of the stones suggests that they were originally outside in the churchyard; they were found during the 19th century built into the foundations of the later church.

Elsewhere in the church are fragments of several crosses. One by the font has panels containing birds which have been identified as cocks but look more like ducklings. All the surviving cross-heads are wheel-shaped, the arms being linked together by segments of a circle. Brompton has been claimed as the source of this pattern.

The Brompton monuments are a reminder of the early days of Scandinavian Yorkshire, when the Danish settlers were accepting the new ways of Christianity. These stones, with their essentially pagan symbolism yet Christian context, are a material expression of this age of transition. Although the finest of the Brompton sculpture is retained in the church, the visitor may wish to see the other fragments preserved in the great collection housed in the Monks' Dormitory at Durham cathedral.

Map Reference: SE 373963 (metric map 99. 1-inch map 91)
Nearest Town: Northallerton
Location: About one mile (1.6 km) north of Northallerton, a left turning off the A684. The church stands by the green on the south side of the village.

15

Kirkdale: St Gregory's Minster and Sundial, North Yorkshire

The small church at Kirkdale is filled with interest for the Anglo-Saxon student. Set on a restricted flat site beside the wide moors which form the northern boundary of the Vale of Pickering, it is an idyllic place in summer.

Before entering the church, it is worth walking round the outside in order to see the good quoins at the west end of the nave, and the re-used Saxon cross-shafts incorporated in the later walls; they may be seen in the south wall of the nave, and in its west wall north of the tower. The nave is basically Anglo-Saxon, and its date can be fixed with unusual precision since above the south doorway is the famous sundial which bears an original inscription translated as follows: 'Orm, the son of Gamal, bought St Gregory's church when it was broken and fallen, and had it made anew from the ground in honour of Christ and St Gregory, in the days of Edward the King and Tosti the Earl.'

The king to whom the inscription refers is Edward the Confessor, and Tostig, who was brother to the ill-fated Harold, was Earl of Northumberland, 1055-65. St Gregory's church, or minster as it is generally called, is therefore one of the most closely dated of our Anglo-Saxon churches.

The earlier church to which the inscription refers all but disappeared during the 11th-century rebuilding, but the fragments of cross-shafts and other stones re-used in the fabric probably came from it. It has also been suggested that the large quoin-stones at the foot of the south-west angle of the nave may pre-date the later building. Local tradition associates the earlier church with St Cedd, who was bishop of the East Saxons in the mid-7th century, but the reference by Bede to his having founded a church at 'Leastingaeu' is normally associated with the nearby village of Lastingham, whose impressive Norman church contains several pieces of Anglo-Saxon sculpture.

Inside St Gregory's church are several important pieces of sculpture, the most notable being the two decorated coffin lids in the north aisle. The earlier of these, the so-called 'Ethelwald Stone', is probably of 8th-century date. The 'Cedd Stone' with its fine interlace decoration is of the 10th century. The latter is interesting because, apart from the excellence of its carving, it has a side decoration of V-shaped tassels with little ball ends. This may be a representation of a pall, which was a cloth draped over a coffin. If it was, then the work was doubtless very fine, providing another

Map Reference: SE 677857 (metric map 100. 1-inch map 92)
Nearest Town: Helmsley
Location: St Gregory's Minster is signposted off the A170, and lies between Helmsley and Pickering on the north side of the road. The first sign from the Helmsley direction is on the far side of Beadlam.

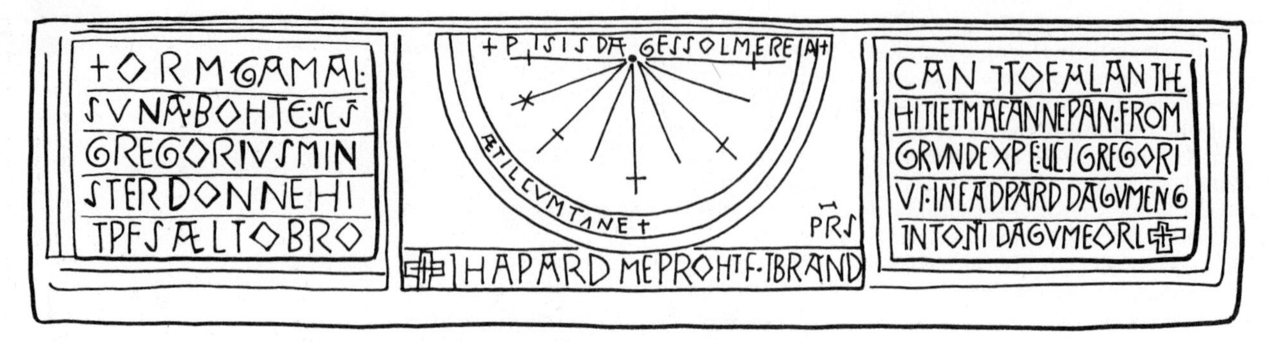

The two outer panels of the sundial record the facts that Orm rebuilt the church in the reign of Edward the Confessor, and the central inscription reads, in translation: 'This is the day's sun-marking at every hour. And Hawaro made me, and Brand, priest[?].'

The lines with cross bars correspond with 6 a.m., 9 a.m., noon, 3 p.m., and 6 p.m, the uncrossed lines divide each tide into one-and-a-half-hour periods. The line with a cross on it on the left hand side of the dial denotes 7.30 a.m., which marked the beginning of 'day time'.

outlet for the needleworking skills of Anglo-Saxon ladies.

Apart from the coffin lids there are several cross fragments in the north aisle of which the central one – a cross-head – clearly shows how the design was made by a series of 'pock marks' rather than being cut in a continuous line.

16

Middleton: The 'Warrior' Cross and Others, North Yorkshire

The fabric of St Mary's church is of considerable interest. It has a late Saxon west tower, the doorway of which, despite horrendous later mutilation, is a fine composition. Above the doorway is a weathered equal-armed cross cut on a square stone; its simple ornament is just visible if the light is kind. It seems that the nave, which is late Saxon in its present form, was preceded by an earlier and narrower structure. The evidence for this is provided by the survival of the quoins of the earlier building, now partially obscured by the later tower. Perhaps at some time after the tower was built, the nave was enlarged by some three feet (90 cm) on either side to its present width.

It is the sculpture inside Middleton church which commands our greatest interest. In the north aisle there are three Anglo-Danish wheel-head crosses which bear unusual decoration. These crosses belong to a sculptural tradition located in North Yorkshire and the Tees Valley in which the depiction of armed men is a notable feature. More generally, the secular character of the carving reflects a common preoccupation of sculptors in areas subject to Scandinavian influence.

The most celebrated of the carvings is the westernmost one, which bears the 'Middleton warrior'. It was long supposed that this simple carving of a man clad in a conical helmet and cuffed tunic, and bearing a complicated sword sheath, was of a pagan warrior newly converted to Christianity. The scene of the man

Map Reference: SE 782855 (metric map 100. 1-inch map 86)
Nearest Town: Pickering
Location: The village is one mile (1.6 km) west of Pickering on the A170 to Helmsley. The church is on the north side of the village.

surrounded by his battle-axe, sword, shield and spear was interpreted as a representation of a pagan burial in which the dead man was placed in the grave with his weapons laid about him in the time-honoured pagan manner.

That such a pagan burial rite should be commemorated on a cross-shaft which seemingly had Christian significance was explained by the assertion that, like King Raedwald at Sutton Hoo, the warrior was a new convert to the faith who also clung to the old ways. This attractive hypothesis therefore placed such warrior stones at the threshold of the conversion of the Scandinavian inhabitants of Yorkshire, and marked a 'transitional phase' in that process.

But it has been recently suggested that the Middleton 'warrior' may in fact be a chieftain, and he is shown surrounded not by personal weapons of combat, but by symbols of his office. Thus the portrait is a secular one, but not necessarily of pagan inspiration. Additionally it has been argued that the dragon on the reverse of the cross, derived from the Scandinavian 'Jellinge' style, should really belong to the 10th century rather than to the 9th, which would place the stone later than the period of the conversion of this part of Yorkshire. So, although nothing is finally decided about the sculpture, debate now rages fiercely as to whether it belongs to the 9th or the later 10th century. It is symptomatic of the difficulties in dating this Anglo-Danish work that a range of a hundred years or so separates expert assessments!

The other stones are also of great interest: one bears a hunting scene with a dog, and a dragon on the reverse; another has interlace ornament, and three other fragments lie on the east windowsill of the aisle. Together they provide a compelling indication of the influence of the Vikings during the period of their dominance of Yorkshire in the 9th and 10th centuries.

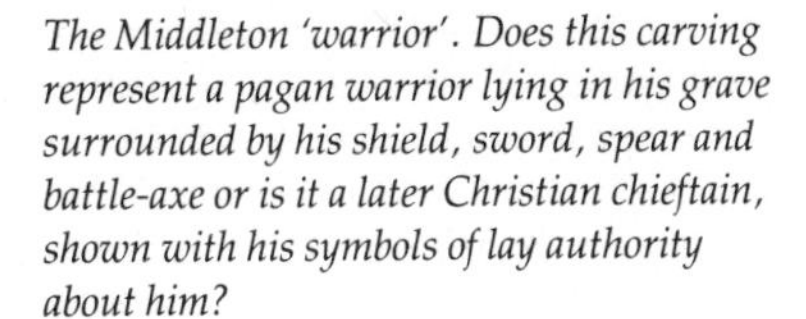

The Middleton 'warrior'. Does this carving represent a pagan warrior lying in his grave surrounded by his shield, sword, spear and battle-axe or is it a later Christian chieftain, shown with his symbols of lay authority about him?

The dragon on the reverse of the 'warrior' shaft. This rather sad beast perhaps represents a late and despairing attempt to imitate the vigour of the early Scandinavian style from which it derived.

17

Hovingham: All Saints Tower and Sculpture, North Yorkshire

The church of All Saints in the attractive village of Hovingham stands by the gates of the Hall. The west tower is the most striking feature of the structure, and is of late Saxon date. Three storeys are neatly demarcated by plain square section string-courses, the whole being surmounted by a rather uncompromising 19th-century coping which rests on small rolled corbels.

The tower has good rectangular side alternate quoins for the most part, and contains a fair collection of re-used stonework, including a crude cross-shaft above the north belfry window. These fragments presumably derive from an earlier church on the site, as at Kirkdale. An equal-armed cross, similar to that at Middleton, may be seen above the west doorway and is probably of 9th-century date – hence also re-used in its present position.

In the uppermost storey of the tower there are four tall double belfry openings, each head being cut from a single block of stone. The western doorway is a handsome affair with a round head accentuated by four orders of moulding; the use of circular angle shafts in the recessed jamb of this door marks this composition out as a very advanced design. It is only the absence of bases and the very rudimentary capitals which indicate a late Saxon rather than a Norman date.

Inside the church is a rare treasure which was itself originally built into the upper parts of the tower as a common building stone. Sadly the weathering of many centuries has taken a heavy toll of what must once have been a superb piece of friezework. The stone now forms the reredos behind the altar in the south aisle.

Though redolent of the splendid Mercian friezes at Breedon-on-the-Hill and the Hedda Stone in Peterborough cathedral, it is finer than both. The work has been variously claimed as being of 8th- or 9th-century date, with the balance of evidence favouring the later dating.

The composition comprises eight arched panels containing nimbed figures which stand above a 'pediment' of continuous vinescroll frieze inhabited by birds and beasts. The stone, which is over five feet (1·6 metres) long, may have been the altar frontal in the earlier church on the site. We may guess from the superior quality of the carving that Anglo-Saxon Hovingham enjoyed the patronage of some powerful lay or ecclesiastical personage who was doubtless attracted to the fair Vale by its rich agricultural land.

Map Reference: SE 666757 (metric map 100. 1-inch map 92)
Nearest Town: Helmsley
Location: Lying in the Vale of Pickering, Hovingham is on the B1257 between Helmsley and Malton, about 7 miles (11 km) north-west of Malton itself. The church is in the centre of the village, close to the Hall.

The tower from the south-west. The ornate west door is visible on the left, and the re-used cross-shaft may be seen above the centre of the double belfry opening on the south side of the tower.

18

Ripon: St Wilfrid's Crypt, North Yorkshire

Eddius, the chronicler of the life of St Wilfrid, tells us that at Ripon he 'built and completed from foundation to roofbeam a church built of dressed stone, supported with columns and side aisles.' Eddius later recounts the pomp and circumstance attendant upon the consecration of the new church on St Peter's Day (29 June) 672. Two kings, Ecgfrith and Aelwine, together with sub-kings, abbots, sheriffs and all kinds of dignitaries were present. The altar was dedicated and covered in purple woven with gold. Wilfrid stood before it and read out the list of lands which had been bequeathed to the abbey by monarchs past and present. This was a glittering occasion, and marked one of the greatest peaks of a remarkable career. Here at Ripon and slightly later at Wilfrid's other great church at Hexham, Latin Christendom was beginning to reap the fruits of royal patronage.

The dynamic character of Wilfrid, who warred constantly with other clerics, as well as with kings and other important people, was to make a vital impression on the affairs of Northumbria. The pernicious rivalry between the Celtic and Roman churches – the foundation of which was a dispute over the calculation of the date of Easter – was a running sore in the side of 7th-century Christianity. Finally, at Whitby in 664, the two parties met and argued their claims; Wilfrid supported the Latin case so well that the Celtic church was routed and retreated back into the north and west, never thereafter able to compete with the authority of the Pope. It is perhaps ironical that the land which Wilfrid received for his church at Ripon had originally been granted to a group of Scottish (Celtic) monks, who had left the place rather than accept the traditions of Rome.

The major survival of Wilfrid's church is the crypt, which now houses the cathedral treasury. It is fitting that fine artifacts of gold and silver should again fill this place, reminding us that it would have presented a very different appearance from the bare stonework that now confronts us. The crypt closely resembles that in Wilfrid's other church at Hexham, but is somewhat simpler in plan. The stonework of the crypt walls is indeed fine, as Eddius's description suggests, and some of the plasterwork may be original. Five small recesses in the walls of the chamber held oil lamps; they would have been simple wicks floating in oil. A large recess in the east wall of the main chamber contained the relics themselves. These were perhaps brought from Rome by Wilfrid himself on one of his three trips there, the last of which was accomplished on foot when he was almost seventy years of age!

Although Ripon is primarily associated with Wilfrid, a recent discovery on the site reminds us of its later Christian associations. In 1974, a fragment of a stone cross-head was found in the foundations of the north transept. It bears a picture of the Scandinavian hero Sigurd sucking his thumb after burning it whilst roasting the heart of a dragon. Other scenes from Sigurd's tale occur widely on the Anglo-Scandinavian monuments in the North, notably at Halton (site No 24, in which entry the legendary feats of Sigurd the Volslung are discussed in more detail). The discovery of the cross-head emphasizes the impact of the Danes in Yorkshire during the 9th and 10th centuries, long after Wilfrid and his zealous Romanism had passed away.

Map Reference: SE 313711 (metric map 99. 1-inch map 91)
Location: Ripon is 4 miles (6.5 km) west of the A1 and is signposted north of Boroughbridge. The A61 passes through the town and the cathedral is close to the market square.

There is a token admission charge to the crypt.

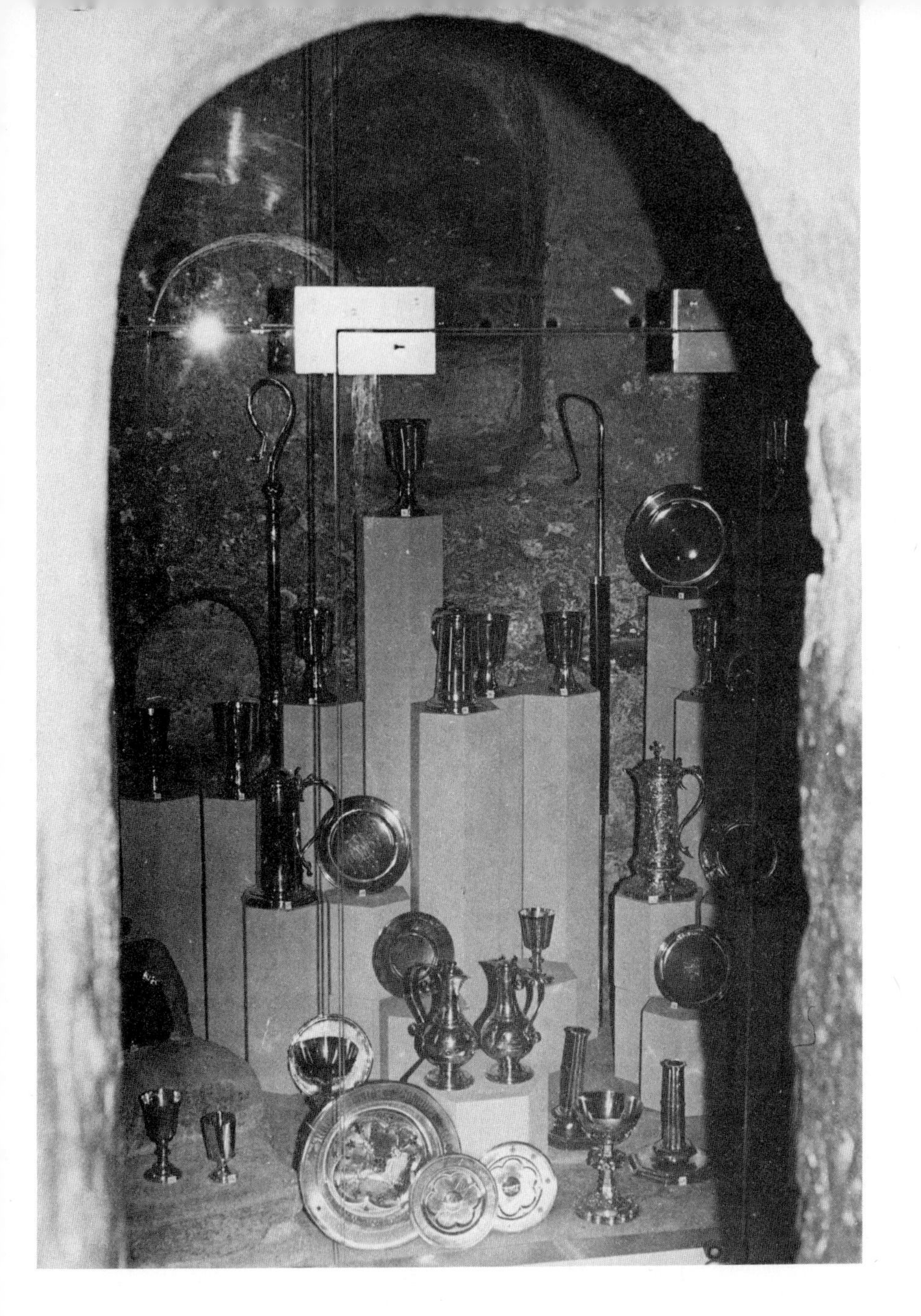

Viewed through the doorway into the eastern chamber of the crypt, the modern visitor must gain an impression not dissimilar from that experienced by the Anglo-Saxon pilgrim. An array of brightly lit rich objects contrasts with the gloom of the entrance passage.

19

York: The Anglian Tower and St Mary Bishophill Junior, North Yorkshire

Despite Bede's detailed description in his *History of the English Church and People* of the introduction of Christianity to York under King Edwin, little survives from the 7th century within the city. Most of the evidence comes from excavations, and a few objects are all that can be seen. The little wooden church built by Edwin for his baptism in 627 has not been traced. No trace has been found even of its larger, later form when it was rebuilt in stone and provided with glazed windows. It was presumed that the early church lay under the site of the Minster, but extensive excavations on the site have yielded no definite structural evidence, though a concentration of Anglian tombstones in the area strongly suggests that the Anglo-Saxon church of St Peter cannot be far away.

King Edwin chose 'Eoforwic', as the place was then known, for the site of his baptism because it was the capital of his kingdom of Northumbria. It was at some time during this period that the 'Anglian Tower' was built against the back of the old Roman fortress walls. This tower is a unique English fortification. It owes much to its Roman precursors, and it would be interesting to know just how old it is.

The existence of the tower suggests that the Roman defences of the city were being kept in a state of reasonable repair. Doubtless the king and his court had their headquarters in the city, perhaps in some of the surviving Roman buildings. York may have supported a larger population than the royal entourage, but little is known of the way in which the people lived. We know that traders from Frisia, across the North Sea, were calling at the city from the 7th to the 9th centuries, but this might reflect no more than regal purchasing power. Churches were being founded elsewhere in the city at this period, however, as a fragment of early sculpture from St Mary Bishophill Junior indicates.

In 865, the Great Army of the Vikings seized York and defeated the Angles. York, or 'Jorvik' as it was then known, was to be in Scandinavian hands until it was recaptured in 927 by Alfred's grandson Athelstan. Even then it was to be a further fifteen years before Eric Bloodaxe, the last Scandinavian king, was finally expelled. There is nothing to be seen of Viking Jorvik unless you are fortunate enough to visit one of the York Archaeological Trust's excavations. Finds from the recent Coppergate excavations may be seen in the Yorkshire Museum, however, and these range from am-

Map Reference: **The Anglian Tower** SE 599521 (metric map 105. 1-inch map 97)

St Mary Bishophill Junior SE 600514

Location: The Anglian Tower is on the Roman Wall in the grounds of the Yorkshire Museum. The tower is found on the long stretch of wall which runs from the multiangular tower at the west angle of the fortress behind the city library.

St Mary Bishophill Junior is within the walled city, and is best approached from Micklegate. From the Micklegate Bar, proceed towards the city centre, turn right into Priory Street and then left into Bishophill. Bishophill Senior, also a Saxon church, was demolished during the 1960s.

Left: *A 10th-century lead alloy brooch from the Coppergate excavations, decorated with a cross motif formed from bound tendrils.*

Right: *One of the double openings into the belfry stage of the 11th-century tower of St Mary Bishophill Junior.*

The tower of St Mary Bishophill Junior. Note the herringbone work carried out in the lighter coloured stone above the nave roof.

The Anglian Tower is set against the back of the Roman fortress wall. Earth ramparts had been piled over the top of the Roman wall nearby in order to heighten it. The tower was probably two storeys high with a lookout platform at the top. The simple form of the doorways without the use of dressed stone provides few clues to the date of the structure which presumably falls between the 7th and 9th centuries when the city was the political centre of Northumbria.

The south door, showing the ironwork on the wooden door panels set in the Norman door arch. Apart from the ship, there are great curving hinge pieces which terminate in gaping mouths, as well as smaller 'knots' made from twisted bars of iron. All the metalwork probably pre-dates the Norman Conquest.

Anglo-Saxon England at all. The church of St Helen appears to be entirely of post-Saxon date, but the south door has some remarkable iron fittings which might just be of pre-Conquest manufacture.

Before looking at the doorway, the dedication of the church is of interest. St Helen, whose feast day is 16 October, was mother of the Roman Emperor Constantine who was acclaimed emperor by the army in York after his father, Constantius, died there in 306. Under Constantine's rule the Edict of Milan in 313 extended freedom of worship to Christians, and he was revered thereafter. His mother's cult was strong in Britain and dedications to her are relatively common in the north-east, presumably because of Constantine's connection with York.

To return to Stillingfleet church, its particular interest belongs to the late Saxon period, probably to the 11th century. The south doorway is a handsome Norman creation, with five orders of carving about its head. But on the wooden panels of the door, which appear to be very old, are several pieces of wrought-ironwork, one of which is in the form of a ship. Only the stern of the ship survives intact, but the curling dragon-head finial denotes a clear Viking tradition. The form of the stern, with its great steering oar and dragon head, is straight out of the Viking sagas where time and again they tell of dragon heads on large ships. King Hakon's long ship is described as a 'dreki' (dragon ship) with gold ornamented figure-heads, and this was by no means exceptional. Indeed, even as late as the Norman Conquest, William the Conqueror's ship is depicted on the Bayeux Tapestry as having a hornblower aft as its decoration and emblem.

Whatever the date of the Stillingfleet ironwork, the sleek lines of the craft remind us of the great fleets of Scandinavian ships which plied the North Sea, such as those in the Danish King Sven's invasion of England in 1013, when the chronicler tells us: '. . . the signal was suddenly given, they set out gladly, and, as they had been ordered, placed themselves round about the royal vessel with level prows, some in front and some behind. The blue water, smitten by many oars, might be seen foaming far and wide, and the sunlight, cast back in the gleam of metal, spread a double radiance in the air . . .'

22
Collingham: St Oswald's Church and Crosses, West Yorkshire

Map Reference: SE 390460 (metric map 104. 1-inch map 96)
Nearest Town: Wetherby
Location: Collingham lies about 2 miles (3 km) south-west of Wetherby on the A58 Wetherby to Leeds road at the junction with the A659 to Harewood. It is only one mile (1.6 km) west of the A1, and can be reached directly from that road by following the signs for the A58. The church stands alone on the north-east side of the village.

The church of St Oswald, martyred king of Northumbria, is very pleasantly situated near the main road from Wetherby to Leeds. Despite the close proximity of such a busy road, the churchyard has retained a distinctly rural aspect, and it is a quiet place to visit as a break from a journey along the A1.

Little of the Anglo-Saxon fabric of the church now remains; the chancel was rebuilt in 1840, and in 1870 extensive restoration must have taken a heavy toll of the early evidence. However, as with so many restorations, something escaped to indicate the Anglo-Saxon origins of the building – in this case the tall, thin nave walls together with their southern quoins. The restoration also led to the discovery of two crosses of our period which were embedded in the south wall of the nave. They now stand by the chancel arch, and well repay examination.

The earlier of the crosses, which probably dates to the early 9th century, is the 'Apostles Cross'. Although rather worn, the images of Christ and eleven of his apostles may be discerned, set in arched panels flanked by cable decoration. These figures are somewhat similar to those on the St Andrew, Auckland, cross, which means that although rather primitively executed, they do show variety and some attempt at characterization. The surviving part of the shaft probably belonged to the central section of the whole. It has been suggested that the original form was somewhat similar to the Gosforth cross in Cumbria, with a round lower shaft giving way to a square upper part. The Gosforth cross has a wheel-shaped head, but fragments of similar monuments from elsewhere in West Yorkshire, notably at Masham and Dewsbury, suggest that the Collingham cross-head may have been of simpler form.

The second cross, called the 'Aerswith Cross', has given rise to much speculation since its discovery. Decorated with opposed beasts, a dragon and interlace, the piece has been identified as a late 9th-century attempt to reproduce Viking Jellinge style ornament. If this is so, then the Collingham shaft belongs to the early years of the Viking settlement of Yorkshire around 875. In the generation or so separating these two crosses, cataclysmic changes had occurred in Yorkshire which these stones reflect in their divergent styles of decoration.

But the major difficulties surrounding the Aerswith Cross concern the worn runes which now occur on two sides of the lower part of the shaft. In 1857, D. H. Haigh, who was a noted antiquary and amateur runologist, claimed to be able to trace runes on all four sides of the lower part of the shaft, and he reconstructed an inscription which purportedly read: 'OEdilblaed this set up after her nephew Auswini the king pray for his soul.'

Later, in 1870, Haigh varied his reading somewhat and this tends to detract from both his attempts to 'read' the stone. Sadly, the reading claimed by Haigh must be treated with grave suspicion, and little significance can be attached to the mention of 'Auswini', presumably meant for 'Oswin', king of Deira, who died in 651 when Oswiu, king of Bernicia, tried to re-unite the two halves of Northumbria in the face of Mercian aggression.

The cross itself certainly dates from well after the time of Oswin's death and whilst the inscription could be a record of the original foundation purpose of the church, the absence of further evidence must preclude certainty. Modern runologists have puzzled over the stone, but no clear evidence of the additional runes which Haigh claimed to have seen has been found. It is possible that the runic inscription is an afterthought, since the characters are rather oddly positioned on the stone. As mod-

These fine beasts on the 'Aerswith Cross' are derived from Viking 'Jellinge' style work. The runes occur just below the lower panel.

ern readings suggest that 'in memory of . . . swith' can be traced, the cross may simply have been re-used as a grave marker by a local Anglo-Scandinavian chieftain whose name was misread by the optimistic Haigh. There are four other cross fragments on the western windowsill of the nave.

23

Ledsham: The Forest Church of All Saints, West Yorkshire

Ledsham is not far from the busy A1, yet the setting of the church in the centre of the village, together with the great interest of its fabric, marks it out as a pleasant spot for repeated visits.

A small sandstone church was built here in the 7th or 8th century, at a time when Ledsham lay in the great Forest of Elmet. The original structure was a simple nave and chancel but, if the claim that Ledsham was the 'monastery that lies in Elmet Wood' as mentioned by the Venerable Bede is correct, it may have been more significant in the past. Bede tells us that an altar stone was brought to the Elmet monastery after the church which contained it was destroyed by pagans. The destroyed church had been built near the royal residence of 'Campodunum', which may have been at Doncaster, and the altar may have been brought to the remote site at Ledsham for safe-keeping. We may imagine that the 'most reverend priest and abbot Thrydwulf' would have taken great care of this relic from the royal church. No trace of the altar stone now survives if it ever was at Ledsham, but the church is a fascinating building in its own right.

The walls of the early nave survive, but the chancel was replaced in the 13th century. The original simplicity of the structure did not last long, however. A two-storeyed gabled porch was added to the west end and a small chapel, a porticus, was built against the centre of the south wall; there was probably a balancing one to the north of the nave. A door was cut through the nave wall into the new porticus, and traces of it survive above the medieval south door. The new door was a magnificent feature, taking the Anglo-Saxon love of tall narrow openings to a whizzing extreme; the door was fully 14 feet (4·3 metres) high, but only two feet (61 cm) wide! It has been suggested that this extraordinary door was designed to allow a processional cross to pass through it, but as with so many aspects of these early churches, we cannot be certain.

Map Reference: SE 456297 (metric map 105. 1-inch map 97)
Nearest Town: Castleford
Location: The peaceful village of Ledsham is only a short distance from the A1. Only 4 miles (6.5 km) north of Ferrybridge with its massive cooling towers, Ledsham can be found on a minor road to the west, opposite the A63 turning to Selby. The church is in the centre of the village, near a convivial hostelry.

The south tower doorway. The carving probably dates to the restoration of 1871, but it might follow the original scheme.

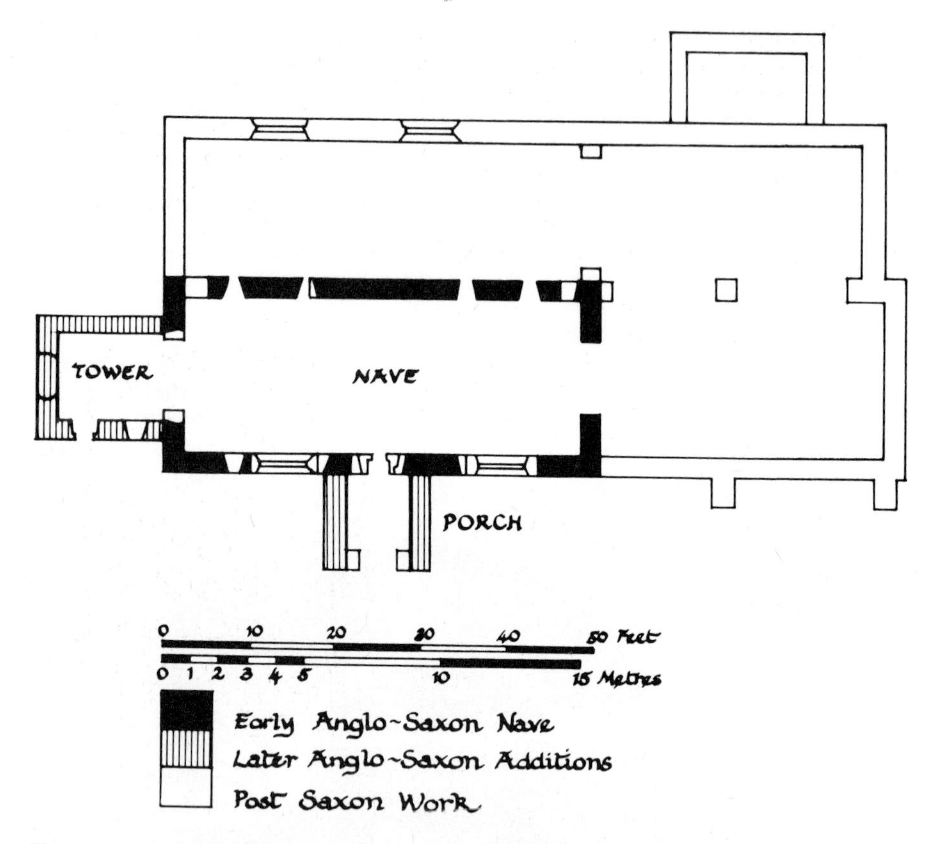

The porticus was later converted into a porch by which the church is now entered.

The tower, which today consists of three storeys, is a combination of a Saxon tower porch two storeys high – a similar structure to that at the west end of St Paul's, Monkwearmouth – with an added Norman belfry stage. Two windows in the south side of the tower mark the Anglo-Saxon floor levels within, and the line of the original gabled roof is visible in the east wall of the clock chamber.

The main interest of the tower is centred on the south doorway, since this bears some most unusual carving. The photograph shows this, the imposts enriched with interlace ornament, and the stripwork surround with a vinescroll motif. Unfortunately it may be that much of this work dates from a major restoration of the church in 1871, but it might reflect the former arrangements. Such elaboration is unusual in Saxon doorways, but a traveller to Ledsham in 1862 before the restoration recorded some 'rude sculptures' on the jambs of this door. If the doorway was indeed richly decorated, it would attest the importance of Ledsham as a Christian centre in the midst of Elmet Forest over 1,000 years ago.

24
Halton: The Sigurd Cross, Lancashire

Although the church at Halton is of comparatively recent date, it has an interesting collection of sculpture of both Anglian and Anglo-Scandinavian character. Inside the church, at the west end, fragments of 10th-century Anglian crosses have been reconstructed. These bear images of saints in arched panels, scrollwork and smaller panels illustrating an archer shooting at a bird caught in a vine-scroll – rather like the archer at St Andrew, Auckland – and a flock of sheep. The sheep are presumably intended to represent the faithful upon earth whom the saints above inspire. The crosses probably date to the period immediately before the Scandinavian settlement of the area, and it is to this period of settlement that the other monument at Halton, the so-called 'Sigurd Cross' belongs.

The Sigurd Cross stands in the churchyard and, although somewhat worn, bears lively scenes from the life of the hero. The saga of Sigurd was plainly an important one, since representations of it occur widely in the north of England, the Isle of Man and Sweden; carvings of the saga can be seen at Ripon and Nunburnholme and are described earlier in this book. The following is a brief outline of the Sigurd tale, which, amongst other great works, inspired Richard Wagner to compose his epic *Ring of the Nibelungen*.

Sigurd was approached by a certain Regin, who asked him to kill a dragon who was guarding a treasure hoard. Regin, who was disguised as a smith, merely wanted to use Sigurd as a pawn in order to obtain the treasure for himself. Unbeknown to Sigurd, Regin, with his brother Fafnir, had already murdered their father to obtain the gold, and the dragon was none other than Fafnir, who had transformed himself into that shape to guard the treasure and so prevent Regin from sharing it.

Regin offered to re-forge the mighty sword belonging to Sigmund, Sigurd's father, which had been given to him by the god Odin. The bottom scene on the Halton shaft shows Regin busy in his forge, working the blade with a hammer. He is shown surrounded by the tools and products of the smith's trade – pincers, bellows, what is probably a coat of mail, and a helmet. Regin prepared the sword, and Sigurd duly slew the dragon. Regin then asked Sigurd to roast the dragon's heart, meaning to eat it himself. Sigurd accidentally burnt his thumb whilst roasting the heart – hence the scene depicted on the centre panel where Sigurd stands beside the fire sucking his injured thumb. This scene also occurs at Ripon.

But there was a spot of dragon blood on his thumb when Sigurd put it into his mouth. When the blood touched the hero's tongue, he was suddenly able to understand the speech of birds. In the tree above his head two nut-hatches warned him of Regin's evil intentions towards him; the birds are shown on the top panel, perching on curved interlacing branches. Sigurd reacted immediately by cutting off Regin's head. Sigurd then loaded the treasure onto his horse Grani and rode away. All was not well, however, since the treasure included a gold ring which had belonged to a dwarf called Andvari, and which was accursed. Sigurd enjoyed but a short life thereafter, which was full of misfortune.

So here in the peaceful churchyard at Halton, we are reminded of that rich spring of Scandinavian mythology which inspired so many craftsmen of the time. But on the reverse side of the shaft is a cross with two figures standing beside it, which asserts the Christian inspiration of the monument. The Sigurd Cross is an important survival from the twilight years when Christianity and paganism battled in the minds of men.

Map Reference: SD 503650 (metric map 97. 1-inch map 89)
Nearest Town: Lancaster
Location: Halton lies beside the M6, and can be reached from Junction 34. From there, take the A683 to the east and turn left to Halton across the River Lune. Alternatively Halton can be reached by turning east off the A6 5 miles (8 km) south of Carnforth at Slyne.

The false Regin reforging Sigurd's sword.

25

Heysham: St Patrick's Chapel and Parish Church, Lancashire

Heysham is fortunate indeed to possess both the surviving Anglo-Saxon churches in Lancashire. Sadly, little of the former seclusion of the place remains to us and much imagination is required to conjure its original solitude out of the present throng of sweet shops and cafés around the lower edge of the churchyard. But at St Patrick's chapel, which stands alone above the great sweep of Morecambe Bay, some appreciation of the site can be obtained.

The ruins of the small rectangular chapel, which is associated with the great Irish saint St Patrick, may be of the 9th century. The angles of the building, where they survive, have side alternate quoins which attest its antiquity. The head of the south doorway is curiously decorated with three concentric raised ribs separated by hollow mouldings. Dr H. M. Taylor compares this feature with the north doorway at Somerford Keynes in Gloucestershire, which is safely of Anglo-Saxon date. A further remarkable feature of the site is the presence of a number of rock-cut graves about the chapel; these have been variously dated to the 10th and 13th centuries. Whilst the general form of the graves, some of which have separate holes for the head, is redolent of medieval stone coffins, the existence of small square sockets at the head end might suggest that each was marked by a stone or wooden cross, which is a well-known pre-Conquest tradition.

The parish church of St Peter, which lies immediately below the headland upon which St Patrick's chapel stands, also contains early elements. The west wall of the Anglo-Saxon nave is largely intact, and portions of the south wall and the east wall above the chancel arch are original. The blocked west doorway is the most notable feature, which is similar to the opening in St Patrick's chapel. In the south-west corner of the churchyard, an early doorway discovered behind a buttress in the north wall of the nave during building operations in 1860 is preserved. It was the discovery of this doorway, and the recognition of its similarities to that in the nearby chapel, which led to the realization that St Peter's was also of pre-Conquest date.

In the south aisle of the church is a fine hog-back tombstone, which has a bewildering frieze of animals and men upon its side panels. The 'roof ridge' is emphasized by a zigzag line below which is a simple moulding. The ends of

Map Reference: SD 409616 (metric map 97. 1-inch map 94)
Nearest Town: Morecambe
Location: Drive through the resort of Morecambe and follow the A589 coast road to Heysham village. Parking is restricted near the site, but a car park is provided close by the bus station in the village centre. Follow the signs to St Peter's church and the shore. St Patrick's chapel stands on a promontory above St Peter's churchyard.

Base of a 9th-century cross-shaft in the churchyard. This may depict the visit of the Three Marys to the sepulchre.

This strange hog-back tombstone, decorated with pictures of a stag hunt, may refer to the legend of Sigurd, which was well-known among the Anglo-Scandinavian settlers of the north-west.

The little chapel of St Patrick, probably of 9th-century date, which stands high above Morecambe Bay.

the stone are clasped by two creatures whose nature might best be described as midway between bears and dachshunds. It has been suggested that the occurrence of a stag in the hunting scene on this monument might indicate some connection with the Sigurd myth (see the entry on Halton, No. 24). When Fafnir the dragon asked Sigurd who he was, the hero answered that he was *gofugt dyr*, which means 'splendid deer' or 'noble stag'. The stag certainly occupies a prominent position in one of the panels, and it is quite likely that elements of the great legend were in the mind of the Anglo-Scandinavian sculptor who created the monument.

In the churchyard there is a short section of a cross-shaft beside the path near the church. This stone bears a strange representation of a 'house' with three faces in the upper windows and a clothed or shrouded figure in the doorway below. This scene has been variously interpreted as the raising of Lazarus (he being the shrouded figure), or alternatively it is claimed as a picture of the visit by the Three Marys to the sepulchre, since the tomb is sometimes represented as a small Byzantine church in early Christian art. On the west side of the Heysham shaft is a round-headed panel similar to those on the Halton Cross, enclosing a nimbed figure of a saint holding a book. The foliage scrolls below this figure and up the sides of the shaft are of 9th-century character.

So here at Heysham we have an interesting group of monuments; perhaps beginning with the little chapel on the headland, which is more akin to Celtic traditions than the Anglo-Saxon, and together with the parish church below, we see a rare survival of an early west coast Christian site. The 'sepulchre shaft' is probably contemporary with these two buildings, and the rock-cut graves may have been used slightly later. In the 10th century, Viking influences make themselves felt, resulting in the hog-back tombstone with its complicated iconography. Few sites provide more complete evidence for the development of Christianity during our period on the remote coastland of the Irish Sea than does Heysham.

26
Gosforth Cross and Sculpture, Cumbria

The great cross in the churchyard at Gosforth is a deservedly famous monument; it is probably the finest product of 10th-century Anglo-Scandinavian art in the north of England. Perhaps the most striking quality of the cross is its graceful shape – the tapering rounded lower section fits neatly into the discreet stepped base, whilst the transformation from the circular to the square upper panels is made into a pleasing feature. It is miraculous that the red sandstone of which it is made has survived a thousand years of weathering so well.

As at Dearham, the ring-chain pattern of surface ornament is much in evidence, and this links it closely with a long series of Norse crosses on the Isle of Man. The upper panels are filled with jumbled scenes comprising men and dragons, wolves and twined beasts. Attempts have been made to fit the various elements into contemporary Norse mythology, and the general interpretation that it portrays the triumph of Christ over the Old Gods seems likely enough. The only Christian element on the cross, apart from its head, is a carving of Christ Crucified on the east face. If the reading is correct, this scene occupies the most significant position amongst the jumbled images, since it occurs at the end of the series shortly after the symbolic destruction of the gods. The cross, which is probably of 10th-century date, exemplifies the religious turmoil of its time, which continued in these remote north-

The Norse god Thor fishes for the Great Serpent, using an ox head for bait. The interlace at the top of the panel might be intended to represent the Serpent.

The cross from the south-west. The ring-chain decoration on the lower part is clearly visible, as are the figures of beasts, men and interlace serpents in the upper panel. Note the original stepped base.

Map Reference: NY 072036 (metric map 89. 1-inch map 88)
Nearest Town: Whitehaven
Location: Gosforth is situated on the A595, 12 miles (19 km) south of Whitehaven. The cross stands in the churchyard which is beyond the village centre and up a left turn on the east side, towards Wellington. The turning is opposite a chapel on the right-hand side.

Right: *Part of the upper panel on the west side. The lower figures may represent the God Loki, who was condemned to lie bound beneath a serpent which dripped poison onto his face. The knotted snake appears just below the head of the inverted horseman, who may be the Norse god Odin, and Loki lies across the base of the panel. The worn figure between the snake and Loki may be Sigyn, who caught the snake's venom in a cup to prevent her husband's death.*

western areas right up to the Norman Conquest, and in some cases even later.

Inside the church, there is an interesting group of stones which were mostly discovered in the Norman foundations during the last century. There are two good hog-back tombstones (see Brompton, No. 14), one of which depicts two armies confronting one another – each man carries a great circular shield, with a banner at the head of one host. The other stone has a crucifix at one end, and biting serpents on the side. There are also further cross fragments, one of which depicts the Norse god Thor fishing for the Great Serpent which was believed to lie curled about the centre of the earth; Thor is using an ox head for bait, as described in Norse mythology.

It is tantilizing to imagine the nature of the church at Gosforth; it was plainly a place of considerable importance to the Anglo-Scandinavian farmers in the vicinity. The quality of the carving on the cross might well suggest that some royal, or at any rate chiefly, patronage was extended to the site, but excavation alone will provide the answers, if there are any to be had.

27
Dearham Cross and Sculpture, Cumbria

Map Reference: NY 073364 (metric map 89. 1-inch map 82)
Nearest Town: Maryport
Location: Dearham lies south of the A596, about 2 miles (3 km) east of Maryport. The church is in the old part of the village, near the post office, and is signposted off the main street. The village can also be approached on the A594 Maryport to Cockermouth road.

The dedication of the church to St Mungo is of interest. This was the pet-name of St Kentigern, monk, bishop and evangelist of Strathclyde and Cumbria. Kentigern lived during the 7th century, and was probably an Irish monk of the Celtic church. He was consecrated bishop of the kingdom of Strathclyde in central Scotland, but was exiled to Cumbria. The nine English dedications to the saint, mostly in Cumbria, attest his local importance. Many legends were current about him during the 11th and 12th centuries, including his reputed discovery of a queen's missing ring in the stomach of a salmon.

The church is of Norman and later date, but it contains three earlier carved stones. A piece of cross-shaft in the west window of the tower is called the 'Kenneth Cross', and is held to be ornamented with scenes from the life of St Kentigern. One panel shows a bishop (Kentigern) being rescued from drowning by an eagle. The wheel-shaped head of this cross is built into the north wall of the vestry.

The finest sculpture is the complete 10th-century wheel-head cross which stands in the nave. This has characteristic Scandinavian ring-chain decoration on the front, with crude interlace on the sides and back. Low down on the front panel, two birds can be seen on either side of a whale-like fish. The fish might be intended as an additional Christian symbol, but the significance of the birds is more difficult to understand. It has been plausibly suggested that they might be intended for the Norse god Odin's ravens, who scanned the world of men and brought back news to their master. Such Scandinavian influence would be natural enough in this part of the country, and perhaps parallels stones with both pagan and Christian symbolism noted elsewhere.

The third Dearham stone, called the 'Adam' stone, is on a windowsill on the north side of the nave. It is elaborately carved with figures, rosettes, a quatrefoil, a cross and a bearded head. Some of these elements, including the deeply-cut name 'ADAM', are probably later additions. One feature which appears to be original is a runic inscription at the opposite end from the name. The beginning of the inscription is broken, and the rest makes no sense in either Scandinavian or English; the stone was probably a grave marker.

This handsome 10th-century cross is decorated with designs the Norse settlers brought with them from Ireland and the Isle of Man.

Part II
Mercia

NORTHUMBRIA
MERCIA
Sheffield
▲32
▲31
Chesterfield
CHESHIRE
▲30
Chester
▲28
NOTTINGHAMSHIRE
▲29
Matlock
Crewe
DERBYSHIRE
▲33
WALES
Stoke on Trent
35
Derby
Nottingham
STAFFORDSHIRE
▲36
34▲
▲37
EAST
Shrewsbury
Stamford
Leicester
▲38
SHROPSHIRE
▲39
40
Peterborough
WEST MIDLANDS
LEICESTERSHIRE
41
46
Birmingham
▲43
CAMBRIDGESHIRE
▲47
NORTHAMPTONSHIRE
▲44
HEREFORD & WORCESTER
Warwick
Northampton
▲45
▲42
WARWICKSHIRE
Worcester
Hereford
ANGLIA
▲48
▲49
▲50
GLOUCESTERSHIRE
Gloucester
0 10 20 Miles
▲51
▲52
WESSEX

Introduction

The origins of Mercia – the kingdom of the people of the 'Mierce' or boundary, presumably the boundary with the Welsh – are very obscure. Traditionally the settlement of the Midlands began with a westward exodus from East Anglia under the leadership of Crida, who became the first king in 585. The earliest Anglo-Saxon settlements in the area were in the middle Trent, where good arable land was to be had. Later concentrations of cemeteries in north-west Derbyshire and Staffordshire show the expansion of the initial land-taking. In 650-70, the Mercian advance had reached westwards to the border of Wales, while the River Wye marked the limit of advance to the south.

The heartland of Mercia lay in what are now the modern counties of Derbyshire, Staffordshire and the West Midlands. The capital was at Tamworth for most of the period, with important ecclesiastical centres at Lichfield and Repton. From an early date the Mercian rulers controlled the region called 'Outer Mercia', which included the area west to the Welsh March, south to the Severn Basin and east to the Wash south of the kingdom of Lindsey, which was itself subject to Mercia during the 7th century.

Mercia did not become a major political force until the reign of the pagan Penda during the first half of the 7th century. He warred with the Welsh and with Northumbria, and although Mercia passed briefly into the control of Northumbria after his son Paeda's death in 656, his second son Wulfhere restored Mercian fortunes. Wulfhere, who was a Christian, resisted the Northumbrian advances and gradually came to dominate the whole of the south of England. By 665 he had annexed the kingdom of Essex, and London itself fell soon afterwards. The power of Northumbria was finally shattered at a battle on the River Trent in 678, which was won by Wulfhere's successor Aethelred. From this time on Mercia was effective overlord of all England south of the Humber.

The 8th century was to see the true dominance of Mercia. From the accession of Aethelbald in 716 to the final defeat at the hands of Egbert of Wessex in 825, the Mercian hegemony was to be absolute. Although a Christian, Aethelbald was the last of the barbarians; he was a ruthless man whose immorality was castigated by churchmen, and whose followers were notorious for their violence and extortion. Under his leadership Mercia emerged as a strong political entity which, although embracing many small units rather than being a centralized power, was nevertheless very effectively organized. Aethelbald was responsible for Wat's Dyke, the first major artificial demarcation of the boundary with the Welsh, and in this, as in much else, he was setting the scene for the reign of his cousin Offa, whom some have called 'Great', who succeeded him in 757.

Offa described himself in one of his charters as *rex totius Anglorum patriae*, 'King of the whole of England'. This was no exaggeration: he was master of the whole of England south of the Humber, and Northumbria was held by his pliant son-in-law. Where Aethelbald had been a barbarian, Offa was civilized, and while Aethelbald had been insular, Offa was the first English king to perceive the benefits of trade and contacts with Europe. So successful was Offa's foreign policy that he was the only European ruler whom the Emperor Charlemagne treated as an equal. They exchanged letters and gifts, the courteous communications of two powerful and civilized men. Offa stimulated national and international trade, and the towns of his kingdom flourished. He was the first to introduce on a wide scale the silver penny, the basis of the monetary economy until the 14th century. He was a patron of monasteries, and actually established an archbishopric at Lichfield in opposition to Canterbury. Offa has been hailed as the first Anglo-Saxon monarch of European standing and the mighty dyke which bears his name is his imperishable memorial.

When Offa died in 796, it must have appeared that Mercia's fortunes were firmly fixed, but his son and successor Ecgfrith survived him by only a few months and the kingdom passed into the hands of a distant kinsman.

The power of Mercia lasted for a further quarter of a century, but in 825 Egbert of Wessex defeated the Mercians at the Battle of Ellendun in the 'debateable lands' between the kingdoms south of Swindon.

There was a recovery of Mercian fortunes under Wiglaf in 830 or thereabouts, but there seems little doubt that Wessex held the whip hand until the Danish invasion of 865, after which the kingdom effectively disappeared. The Danelaw boundary divided Mercia roughly into two halves, with Danish Mercia to the north and east and the rump of the old kingdom to the south. Nottingham and Derby, which had been two of its principal towns, together with Stamford and Northampton in 'Outer Mercia', became part of the Danish territory of the Five Boroughs, and the overlordship of Offa became no more than a memory.

Mercia has left an interesting legacy of monuments of which Offa's Dyke and the lesser known Wat's Dyke are the most imposing. Shorter earthworks existed along many parts of the

Mercian frontiers, built either by the Mercians themselves or by the adjacent kingdoms which they threatened.

During the 7th century, the influence of Christianity began to be felt in the Midlands, and a series of important monasteries at Breedon-on-the Hill, Repton, Peterborough and Deerhurst was founded. These sites bear witness to the artistic and architectural accomplishments of Mercia, which was for long thought to have been a state geared to war rather than to peace. The incomparable sculptures at Breedon, the Angel at Deerhurst and the great church at Brixworth all indicate that this was far from the case. Although not as celebrated as the achievements of Northumbria or those of the 'Winchester School' in Wessex, these monuments attest a lively and flourishing culture. The crypt at Repton and the tower at Earls Barton are two of the finest gems of Anglo-Saxon architecture.

Perhaps the most remarkable attribute of Mercia was the tremendous production of stone crosses in the region. This was doubtless due in part to the plentiful local supplies of stone suitable for carving, but it also seems possible that churches were not established in Mercia as quickly as elsewhere, and that preaching crosses were therefore in greater demand. The crosses, which date from the 9th to the 11th centuries, are particularly common in the northern parts of the kingdom, and there was evidently a production centre at Bakewell in Derbyshire. Fine examples may be seen at Leek, Eyam, Bakewell and Sandbach, whilst at Newent in Gloucestershire may be seen not only an interesting cross-shaft bearing a Mercian beast, but also a curious carved tablet which may have been a portable altar. From the very end of our period come the lively tympanum at Southwell and the stylish church at Great Paxton, which was probably built by Edward the Confessor.

28
Sandbach Crosses, Cheshire

Map Reference: SJ 759609 (metric map 118. 1-inch map 110)
Location: Sandbach is on the west side of the M6 and can be reached directly from Junction 17. The crosses stand in the market place at the centre of the town.

The great crosses of Sandbach have stood in the market place since at least the 16th century, and probably long before. They were disturbed during the 17th century, however, when religious zealots demolished them and were not finally reinstated until 1816. Both appear to retain their original monolithic bases, but the platform upon which they stand dates from the 19th century. Their survival in such a busy spot is remarkable, and the citizens of the town must be congratulated on their good taste. Both crosses are now in the care of the Department of the Environment.

Neither of the crosses is complete, but the taller northern cross has retained the whole of its shaft and the lower part of the head. All faces of the cross are richly decorated, the decoration terminating near the base in triangles which clasp the angles of the shaft. The east face is the most notable, and working up from the base there are angels in the basal triangles, and a circle holding three figures, one of which is Christ. Above again is a scene of the Transfiguration with a dove in the top right-hand corner. This is followed by a Nativity scene with an ox and ass stooping over the crib whilst Mary looks on. Above again is a fine Crucifixion with Our Lord set rigidly upon a flaring-armed cross, surrounded by the signs of the four Evangelists. The various figures above are of uncertain significance. On the west and north faces are small figure panels, with a scene of Christ before Pilate in the middle of the west face, and a dragon at the top of the north face. The south face has rather languid vinescroll decoration which on the lower part is inhabited by a man and wolves which may represent a hunt. Above is a good panel of tight interlace.

The southern cross is similarly carved, but differs in detail. The basal triangles reappear, but the main west and east faces have curious plaited borders adorned with human masks. The west side has lozenge-shaped panels, each containing figures of uncertain meaning; the middle figure on the west side might represent the Resurrection of Christ. The south and north sides are divided into small double figure panels.

These crosses, which date from the 9th century, are doubtless from the same workshop and, whilst some of their details are known elsewhere, are nevertheless very unusual. Single figures and vinescrolls are known from Northumbria, and it seems likely that the Sandbach work represents some Mercian memory of the 'Golden Age' of its rival, Northumbria.

The great crosses have stood in the market place since at least the 16th century; they perhaps represent some dim recollection of Northumbria's 'Golden Age' in Middle England after the source of the inspiration had been cut off by the Danish raids.

29

Leek Sculpture, Staffordshire

The little town of Leek in north-east Staffordshire was probably an important centre during Anglo-Saxon times. It commands a substantial territory on the Pennine fringe, and it is still often called the 'Capital of the Moors'. The parish church of St Edward the Confessor, dedicated to one of England's most pious rulers, has an interesting collection of sculptures, including the large cross in the churchyard. There is a curious legend associated with the cross to the effect that it sinks imperceptibly lower into the ground each year. As local doggerel puts it:

When the churchyard cross shall disappear,
Leek town will not last another year.

The cross itself is circular for just over half its length, changing to a slighter square profile above, the junction being marked with a raised band of interlace. Below the band are triangular and circular panels, one of which contains an equal-armed cross. Above the band the panels contain either tight interlace decoration or a larger chain-link design. The head of the cross, which was probably wheel-shaped, has unfortunately broken off. The original appearance of the whole would have been similar to the cross at Stapleford in Nottinghamshire but it is not as highly decorated. The general crudeness of the design suggests a very late date, perhaps some time in the 11th century.

A further cross-shaft, this time of rectangular section, may be seen beside the path to the south of the church. This is quite crudely cut, but does have some elegant knotwork on one side. The stone is sadly battered, but on the north side near the base a short runic inscription may be seen. The runes run vertically in two lines up the side of the stone, and the inscription may well have been much longer

Map Reference: SJ 983567 (metric map 118. 1-inch map 111)
Location: On the edge of the Peak District, Leek is an old weaving centre. The town is about 9 miles (14.5 km) north-east of Stoke-on-Trent on the A523 between Macclesfield and Ashbourne. The crosses stand in the churchyard close to the town centre.

Left: *11th-century churchyard cross.*

Above: *An early 9th-century example of the 'Staffordshire Knot'.*

originally. As with so many such fragmentary inscriptions, this one fails to make much sense. Perhaps a further piece of the stone may one day come to light. This cross is probably one of the oldest of the Leek sculptures, and may date from the early 9th century.

Other fragments may be seen built into the west wall of the porch close to the ground, and inside the church under the pulpit and elsewhere. These include parts of a wheel-head cross, and a stone with a depiction of Calvary, all of which date to the late 9th or early 10th centuries. Finally, in the south aisle, there is a substantial hog-back tombstone of Anglo-Danish character.

30

Bakewell: All Saints Church and Sculpture, Derbyshire

The cross in All Saints churchyard is probably the finest of the early 9th-century Mercian group. Standing in the angle of the chancel and south transept, it retains its original socket stone, and is surrounded by a pleasing hand-made wrought-iron fence. Although broken, the head of the cross is sufficiently well-preserved to show a horseman on one side trampling a snake or dragon, with a Crucifixion scene on the other. The horseman might be intended for a representation of Our Lord trampling the powers of darkness whilst riding on his way to victory over death. Below the horseman is a curious cat-like creature which appears to be picking berries in the topmost of the superb curling spiral scrolls. These scrolls are full of movement and flow sinuously into one another. Each has a small cluster of berries, perhaps meant for grapes, at its centre, and a single leaf drops from each volute. The spirals are contained within a sunken panel, and the quality of the carving is very high. On the other side of the shaft there are vinescrolls

The deep curving scrollwork and fine composition proclaim the Bakewell cross as a masterpiece of the sculptural school which existed here during the early 9th century.

Map Reference: SK 216685 (metric map 119. 1-inch map 111)
Location: Bakewell is in the Peak National Park on the A6 halfway between Matlock and Buxton. The church of All Saints is in the centre of the town. Parking in the area is restricted but may be available in King Street adjacent to the churchyard. The cross is in the churchyard in the angle between the chancel and the south transept.

and small animals, the whole making a lively scene. Tight scrollwork decorates the sides of the shaft and is continued round the head.

In the south porch and north aisle of the church is a rich and diverse collection of sculpture. There is so much material at Bakewell, including not merely further fragments of crosses, but figure sculpture and parts of sarcophagi, that it is reasonable to suppose that a school of sculpture was based here. Many local crosses and other sculptures have been shown to be similar in style to material in the Bakewell collection, so it appears that its products were either widely exported, or that its sculptors travelled the surrounding area.

31

Eyam Crosses, Derbyshire

This small village on the eastern edge of the Pennines is famous for the selfless actions of the 17th-century villagers and their devout vicar, Mompesson. They cut themselves off from the outside world in order to contain an outbreak of plague within the village. In our period, Eyam was close to the frontier between Mercia and Northumbria, and the Grey Ditch to the south of the village may have been built by the Northumbrians in an attempt to check the 7th-century Mercian advance.

In the churchyard of the parish church of St Lawrence is a large and impressive cross with a tapering rectangular shaft and a massive, slightly squat head. The top of the shaft is broken, and the head is set too far down, but enough remains to show the quality of the original composition.

The lower part of the western face and the sides of the cross are decorated with circular patterns of interlace, which give way on the western face to an arched panel containing a human figure which seems to hold a horn. Above is a fine cross-head which in form and

Eyam was situated in the frontier zone between the kingdoms of Mercia and Northumbria; the decoration of its splendid cross reflects influences from both north and south.

Map Reference: SK 218765 (metric map 119. 1-inch map 111)
Nearest Town: Bakewell
Location: Eyam, in the Peak National Park, is about 6 miles (9.5 km) north of Bakewell just to the north of the A623 between Chapel-en-le-Frith and Baslow. About 6 miles (9.5 km) from Baslow, turn right up the B6521, Eyam is the first village reached. The church of St Lawrence is in the centre of the village, a west turning off the B road.

layout owes much to Northumbrian models. The use of the central roundel, together with the figures in the arms, attest this northern influence, whilst the use of many angels in the spaces between the main scenes suggests links with the Breedon-style friezes further south in Mercia itself. On the reverse side are spiral trumpet scrolls which are similar to the decoration on the Bakewell cross.

The intermingling of Northumbrian and Mercian styles on this cross perhaps reflects Eyam's location in the 'debateable land' between the two kingdoms. The scrollwork on the eastern face suggests that it was produced in the Bakewell workshop, but its distinctive decoration probably reflects local preference which looked beyond Mercia for inspiration.

32

Carlton-in-Lindrick: St John's Church, Nottinghamshire

Apart from an interesting Anglo-Saxon tower, Carlton also boasts a 'Devil Stone', which was found as recently as 1937. If the agile visitor runs round the stone seven times, he may either enjoy good luck or see the Devil. The art lies in deciding which way to run round the stone. Normally clockwise should ensure good fortune, whilst 'widdershins', i.e. anti-clockwise, will probably have unfortunate consequences!

To return to the western tower: there are two external Anglo-Saxon stages surmounted by a 15th-century belfry. The Anglo-Saxon belfry was on the floor below, and is marked by double openings in the east and west walls with tall mid-wall shafts and curved lintels. There is some good herringbone work below the western belfry window, which may either be patching, or perhaps represents the original fabric which has since been renewed above. The original west door was replaced by a re-used Norman arch in 1831. The great stepped buttresses are, of course, medieval, and date from the time the upper belfry was erected.

Inside, the tower arch is very fine on its eastern face, but severe on the western, perhaps because of later recutting. The arch is of very late Saxon character, and hovers on the brink of Norman influence. The tower appears to post-date the west wall of the nave, which is therefore also of Anglo-Saxon date; the north and south walls may also be original. The chancel arch is Norman, but some crude strapwork of Anglo-Saxon character may be seen on the southern impost.

Map Reference: SK 588839 (metric map 111. 1-inch map 103)
Nearest Town: Worksop
Location: Carlton lies 3 miles (5 km) due north of Worksop on the A60 Doncaster road. The church of St John is in the older part of the village by woods belonging to Carlton Hall. An RAC sign on the main road directs the visitor to St John's church on the west side of the A60.

The original western window of the Anglo-Saxon belfry. Note the fine herringbone work below the opening.

A further curiosity retained in the church is the 'Sun Stone' which is set above the vestry door in the south aisle. It is almost certainly re-used in its present position, as it is somewhat askew at the top, suggesting that it was originally larger. The design, which is contained within a semi-circular moulding, supposedly shows the sun and moon with two stars. Outside the moulding in the spandrels are sprays which might be wings or foliage. A cross has been deeply and crudely incised into the head of the piece, perhaps in order to 'sanctify' it when it was re-used. Whether this piece is Anglo-Saxon, or even Romano-British, is a difficult question to resolve. Either way it is an unusual piece of work, and repays close examination.

33
Southwell Tympanum, Nottinghamshire

The present Minster at Southwell is of Norman and later date, but it stands on the site of an important late Saxon church. Between 955 and 980, England enjoyed a period of peace from Danish raids which enabled the Anglo-Saxon church to reorganize itself. In 956, Eadwig, King of England, called the 'all-fair' because of his beauty, granted an estate centred on Southwell to Osketel, Archbishop of York. It was one of a series of grants made to religious houses at this period, and Southwell thus belonged to the great period of the 10th-century ecclesiastical revival. Southwell acted as a mother church for the surrounding area, as it still does today, and we can imagine that the Saxon church was an impressive structure.

The most important evidence for this late Saxon church is the tympanum built into the head of a later door in the west wall of the early 12th-century north transept. Argument has inevitably arisen about the date of this carving, but it is unlikely that it is later than the middle of the 11th century, as one must allow time for its re-use in its present position.

At the centre of the composition is a nimbed figure of St Michael shown with his archangelic wings; he holds a sword and shield and fights a dragon to the right. This beast shows unmistakeable signs of Scandinavian influence in its sinuous twined body with foliate scrolls. Although greatly developed, it is perhaps

Map Reference: SK 701538 (metric map 120. 1-inch map 112)
Location: Southwell is 7 miles (11 km) west of Newark-on-Trent, and is on the A612 road to Nottingham. The Minster is in a commanding position at the centre of the town.

In this lively composition St Michael fights a fierce dragon, whilst to the left Daniel holds a lion's head.

closest to 'Ringerike' originals. To the left of the panel, which is sadly broken, a kneeling figure holds the lower jaw of a wolf or lion. This is generally interpreted as a representation of Daniel wrestling with the lion. This beast is very similar to the wolf on the font at Melbury Bubb in Dorset.

Along the under edge of the panel is interesting decoration consisting of short runs of interlace, scrollwork and twisted rod, some of which have curious curling terminals. This amalgam of different motifs well illustrates the diverse influences discernible in the main panel. The overall composition may derive from foreign Romanesque designs. The beasts are Scandinavian, whilst the posing of the figures is clearly Anglo-Saxon. The Southwell tympanum thus provides a fascinating glimpse of the artistic material upon which the late Saxon ecclesiastical revivalists could draw for the beautification of their churches.

34

Sproxton Cross, Leicestershire

Sproxton is a delightful ironstone village set in the rolling farmland of east Leicestershire. St Bartholomew's Church lies to the north of the village and commands fine views of the country round about. The pattern of medieval ridge and furrow in the surrounding fields attests a long history of husbandry which doubtless began long before Sproxton Cross was raised during the 10th century.

The cross, which is the most complete example in Leicestershire, stands in the churchyard

Map Reference: **Sproxton** SK 857249 (metric map 130. 1-inch map 122)
King Lud's Intrenchments SK 858280–SK 866280
Nearest Town: Grantham
Location: This site is best approached from the Grantham to Melton Mowbray A607 road. At Croxton Kerrial, some 6 miles (9.5 km) south-west of Grantham, take the first turning south.

Sproxton is reached some 3 miles (5 km) down this road. The church stands on a hill to the north of the village.

Right: *This simple 10th-century cross in Sproxton churchyard was probably a preaching cross around which services were held before the church was built.*

by the south porch of the church. It is possible that this was a preaching cross around which the farmers of the area gathered to hear the holy gospel preached to them by a visiting priest, perhaps from the mother church at Buckminster nearby. Certainly there is no Anglo-Saxon fabric in the church, but evidence of a Norman phase is provided by Romanesque voussoirs built into the west wall of the south porch. The location of the church is curious since it lies so far from the village which it serves. There is no evidence of a deserted settlement around it which might suggest that the village had migrated away from its original site. It might be that the church was sited here because the place had some pre-Christian religious significance.

As befits its rural setting, the cross is a simple rustic piece with a somewhat misshapen wheelhead. The shaft is rectangular, and has a raised band or collar midway along its length. It is now set in a squared stone base, but this is probably much later since an 18th-century print of the cross does not show it, and the use of lead to fix the shaft into the stone suggests a 19th-century date for its erection. The east side of the cross is heavily worn; it is said to have served as a footbridge over a local stream before it was returned to the churchyard.

Time has dealt severely with the decorative scheme, and the details are now very obscure. On the main west face are two creatures carved in low relief. The upper, above the medial band, might be an eagle facing right, perhaps intended as the symbol of St John the Evangelist. Below the band is a standing beast with a wolf-like head and raised forepaws. The body is indistinct, but terminates in a broad tail which curls back behind the body and emerges as a panel of competent three-strand interlace below. The sides and top of the cross are enriched with rather lazy sinuous stems carved in rounded relief. Simple leaf shapes fill the spaces between the curves. On the north side, the lower part has a zone of interlocking circles carved in shallower relief.

35

Stapleford Cross, Nottinghamshire

Map Reference: SK 489374 (metric map 129. 1-inch map 112)
Nearest Town: Nottingham
Location: Stapleford is on the west side of Nottingham close to the M1, and can be reached from Junction 25; it is then signposted off the A52, to the north. The cross stands in the churchyard which is in the centre of the town.

The cross commands the road past St Helen's churchyard, and is pleasantly set about with trees. It is likely that a substantial portion of the top of the cross is missing, since the shaft, although diminishing towards the top, is still quite thick below the 19th-century capping stone.

Unlike the other round-based crosses in the area, such as the Leek shaft, the lower part of the Stapleford cross is profusely if crudely decorated with small squarish panels of interlace. The junction between the round base and the upper squared shaft is handled in the familiar fashion, with three horizontal rings around the shaft and upward curving mouldings above. Three of the upper panels contain interlace work, some of which is quite fine. On the south side is a strange flat figure which appears to be a representation of an angel. Wings are visible behind the emaciated body, and the figure is clad in a skimped tunic or robe, but the whole effect is one of barbarous caricature. This cross belongs to the same 11th-century group as the Leek shaft.

The elaborate shaft is decorated with various types of interlace ornament, and a crude representation of an angel occupies the upper panel on the south side.

36

Repton: St Wystan's Church, Derbyshire

Map Reference: SK 303272 (metric map 128. 1-inch map 121)
Nearest Town: Derby
Location: Repton is about 7 miles (11 km) south of Derby and is signposted off the A38 dual carriageway to Burton-on-Trent and Lichfield. The church of St Wystan is virtually in the grounds of Repton School, which grew up on the site of the later abbey.

Repton, called *Hrypadun* in Anglo-Saxon times, has been an important Christian centre since at least the 7th century. It is recorded that St Guthlac, who later founded a monastery at Crowland in Lincolnshire, took his monastic vows here at some time before 700. The abbey, for such it presumably was, became an important Mercian ecclesiastical centre, and benefited from royal patronage. The Anglo-Saxon Chronicle records that Aethelbald, king of Mercia, was buried here in 757 after his murder at Seckington, some twelve miles (19 km) distant, as were King Wiglaf and his grandson Wystan in their turn. Further mention of Repton is made in the Chronicle in 874-5, when a Danish army wintered here. The Danes apparently did their best to demolish the monastic buildings before they left, and since there is no later reference to a monastery at Repton, it appears that it was never refounded after the Danish occupation.

St Wystan, to whom the church is dedicated, was chosen as king on his grandfather Wiglaf's death in 840. According to legend, he asked his mother Elfleda to rule in his stead. Berhtric, Wystan's cousin, thereupon proposed to marry Elfleda in order that he might seize power himself. Wystan opposed the marriage which he held to be incestuous, and Berhtric murdered him at a place called Wistanstowe, which is probably the modern Wistow in Leicestershire. Wystan was buried at Repton, and the church became a place of pilgrimage before the Danish invasion. Tales are told of miraculous happenings at the site of Wystan's murder. During the 12th century an ecclesiastical commission set up by Archbishop Baldwin of Canterbury investigated the reported appearance of hair growing on the murder site upon the saint's feast day, 1 June. The commission duly reported that this story was true, and this must have added to the saint's already considerable popularity. Wystan's body apparently remained at Repton during the Danish occupation, but it was later removed to Evesham at the instigation of King Canute.

Only the eastern parts of the Anglo-Saxon church survive. The chancel and crypt are largely intact, whilst some parts of the early crossing and transepts escaped later remodelling. Externally, the chancel is nearly all Anglo-Saxon work, but there are three separate phases of construction. The lowest part, which comprises the crypt walls, is visible in the trench below ground and probably belongs to the 8th century. Above is a later Saxon chancel wall with massive square quoins at the angles. Above again is the latest Saxon phase which has a string-course below it, and narrow vertical pilaster strips on the three walls of the chancel; this is probably of 9th-century date. Parts of the early transepts are incorporated into the eastern walls of the aisles on either side of the chancel. The continuation of the string-course suggests that they belong to the 9th-century phase.

Inside, the sculpture in the south porch is of interest, and there is a particularly fine cross-shaft decorated with human figures and foliage. At the east end of the 14th-century nave, stairs lead down to the early crypt. The stairs are worn, doubtless by the passage of pilgrims, and the descent into the crypt, which is one of the finest Anglo-Saxon rooms in England, is a remarkable experience. Although small in area, the crypt chamber gives an impression of space and considerable size.

Four free-standing pillars carry the eight ceiling arches which spring from square pilasters set against the walls. The pillars have roughly squared capitals, incised spirals on the shafts and simple sweeping circular bases; they must have appeared exceedingly fine when they were newly cut. The narrow vaults of the roof provide the strangely contemporary impression of a 'coffered' ceiling. The square

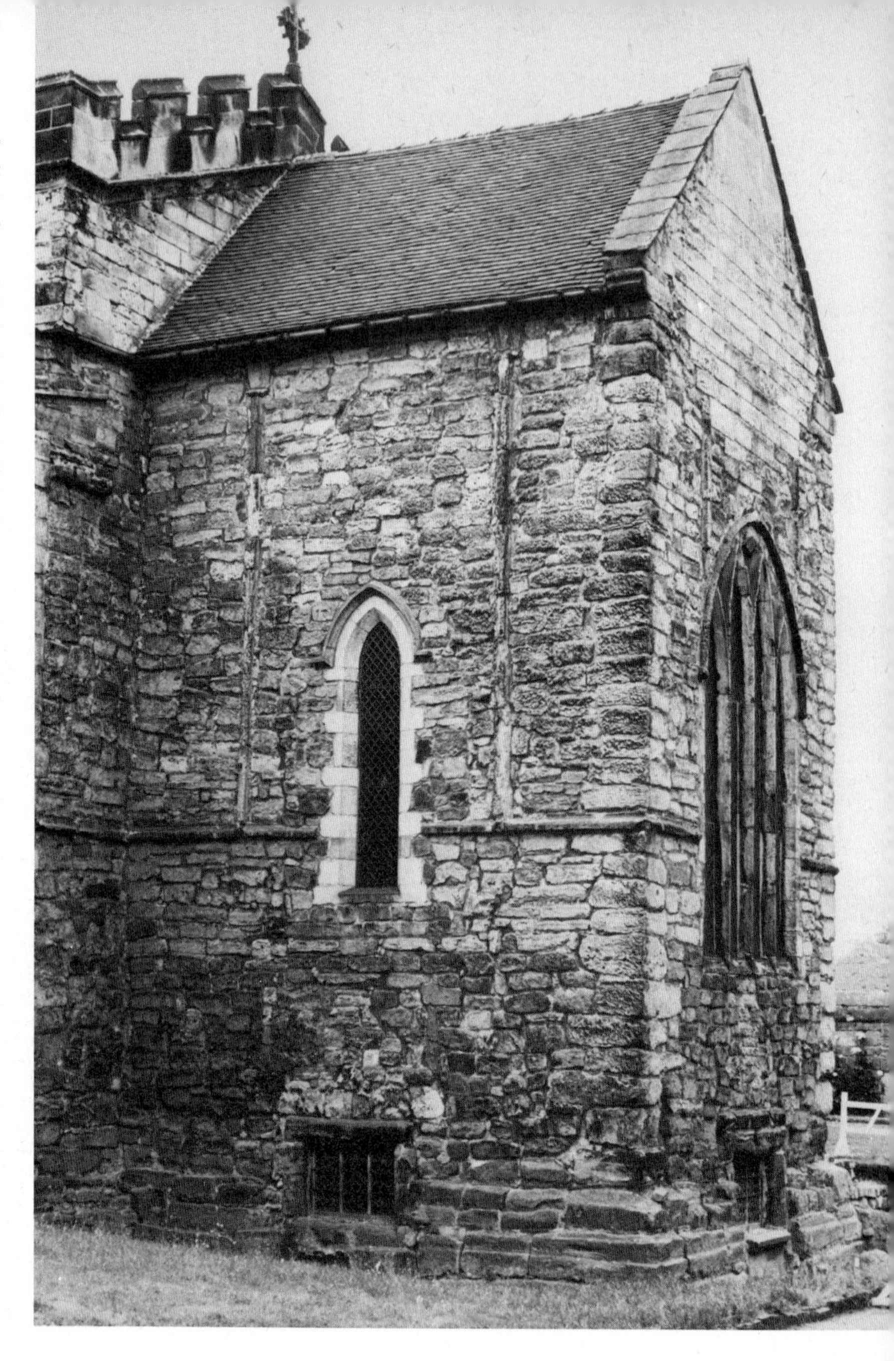

shape of the crypt is extended in the middle of each side by rectangular recesses which were doubtless the last resting-places of the kings of Mercia, with St Wystan among them. The western recess seems to be in its original condition; the triangular opening at the back probably accomodated a lamp.

The crypt was originally entered through a door in the north side, and this suggests that it was intended simply as a royal mausoleum, with no access being afforded for large numbers of pilgrims. Later, after the death of Wystan, this place became an important cult centre and the western double flights of stairs were doubtless added to enable pilgrims to enter the chamber more easily. The provision of this new access is an eloquent testimony to the popularity of the cult of Prince Wystan before the Danes occupied the site during the later 9th century.

A programme of excavation and architectural analysis is in progress at Repton, and it is to be hoped that much more information about this important site will be made available in the future. One of the major discoveries is a large ditch near the church which might have been dug as a defence by the Danes during their wintering here in 874-5.

37

Breedon-on-the-Hill: St Mary and St Hardulph, Leicestershire

The church of St Mary and St Hardulph stands on a great hill above the village, defying the modern quarry below. A Christian church has stood on this site for at least 1,300 years, and the Hardulph to whom the church is dedicated was traditionally a hermit who lived on the site before the church was founded. The church stands within the ramparts of an Iron Age hill-fort. Excavations on the site have revealed traces of the early Christian cemetery to the

Left: *The Saxon chancel from the south-east. The upper parts of the crypt may be seen below the small square-headed window. Above is later Saxon work including the narrow pilaster strips of the 9th-century phase.*

Below: *Beneath the chancel is the remarkable crypt in which at least two kings of Mercia as well as St Wystan were buried.*

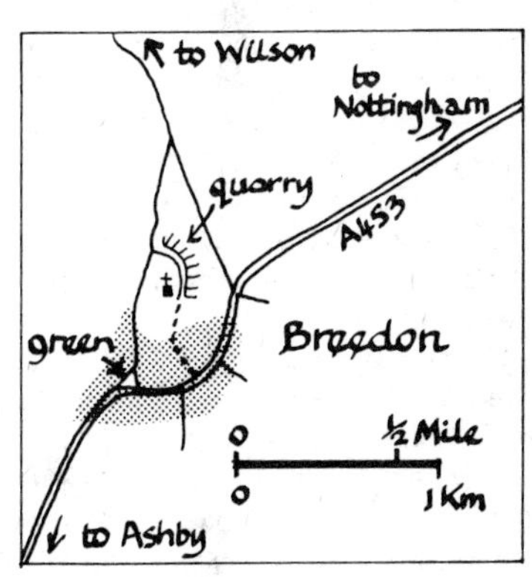

Map Reference: SK 406233 (metric map 129. 1-inch map 121)
Nearest Town: Ashby de la Zouche
Location: Breedon is about 5½ miles (9 km) north-east of Ashby on the A453 to Nottingham. Approaching the village from Ashby, look out for the triangular village green on the left and take the turning that runs beside the green. Carry on up Melbourne Lane out of the village and after about a quarter of a mile (0.4 km), take the unmarked right fork which leads straight up the hill to the church. There is ample parking near the church.

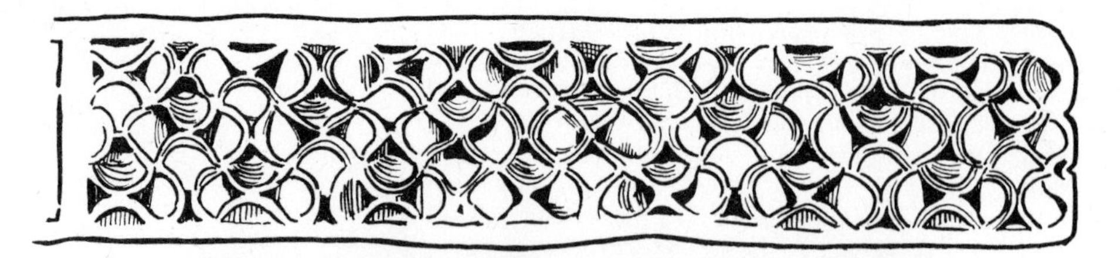

Pelta and inhabited vinescroll ornament on the 8th-century friezes which decorated the monastic church.

east of the church. Breedon Hill is a commanding site, and it is possible that a pagan shrine stood here before the conversion of Mercia since local field-names such as Thunderbush meadow suggest worship of the pagan god Thor.

A monastery was founded here in around 675 by King Aethelbert, son of the pagan Penda. The new community must have been instrumental in the conversion of the eastern part of Mercia, but little is known of its later history. The Anglo-Saxon buildings have largely disappeared, though it is possible that the nave walls are original. However, a rich legacy of architectural sculpture attests the lavish nature of this royal foundation.

Inside the church are exquisitely carved figures and friezes which adorned the monastery. The richness and variety of the carvings are quite remarkable, and it is a rare treat to spy them out where they have been incorporated into the later structure. It seems that some sections of the friezework on the side walls of the nave may be in their original positions. This suggests that the nave walls are therefore of 8th-century date and formed part of the early plan. Most of the sculpture is in the tower, nave and south aisle, but one vinescroll frieze inhabited by long-legged birds is set high up in the east wall of the north aisle.

Some illustrations of the 8th-century friezework are included here, but it is impossible to do justice to its diversity. The panels contain birds, animals and men, and two abstract sections bear pelta and 'Greek key' designs which remind us of the Mediterranean origins of the designs. The friezes were made in eighteen-foot (5.5 metre) sections, and probably ran round both the interior and exterior of the church at the height of the remaining fragments in the nave. It is probable that the friezes were originally brightly painted so they would have formed a rich decorative scheme.

Apart from the friezes, there are several important figure panels including an arched female bust in the south aisle which is probably a representation of the Virgin Mary. The panels with smaller figures of saints standing in arcades probably come from stone coffins. It is worth visiting the first-floor ringing chamber in the tower, for built into its south wall is the famous 'Breedon Angel'. This is a full-length portrait, and the delicate folds of the dress, together with the Byzantine-style blessing which the angel administers, clearly indicate the eastern inspiration of the work. This carving has been compared with the drawings in the Book of Cerne, which was probably written at Lichfield during the 9th century; the carving and the book together illustrate the artistic accomplishments of Mercia on the eve of the Danish invasion.

There are three cross-shafts in the north aisle, one of which bears an Adam and Eve scene which is similar to that at Newent in Gloucestershire. A smaller fragment bears Scandinavian 'Jellinge' style beasts which mark the change in art styles which occurred after the Danish conquest of Mercia in the late 9th century. Breedon thus displays a remarkable range of sculpture, from the magnificent friezes produced during the 8th century when Mercia was at the height of her power, to the much cruder cross-shaft produced under the influence of the Danish incomers.

38

Barnack: St John the Baptist, Cambridgeshire

Barnack was an important place in later Anglo-Saxon times by virtue of its quarries which produced fine building stone. The stone was transported over considerable distances by river, and has been found in Anglo-Saxon churches as far away as Essex and Hertfordshire. The site of the quarries, aptly named the 'Hills and Holes', can be seen to the west of the village.

Little is known of the early history of the village, but in 664 Wulfhere, king of Mercia, granted the estate to the monastery of Medehamstede (modern Peterborough). Wulfhere was an important Mercian king, who successfully resisted the Welsh in the west, and pushed the boundaries of Mercia south to include London. Barnack with its quarries must have been an attractive gift to the monastery, which was then still in the course of construction. A monastic estate such as Barnack would almost certainly have had a church, and it is likely that St John's was founded then, although no such early work survives in its fabric.

The Anglo-Saxon work in the church, which is all of 10th-century or later date, comprises the lower two stages of the tower, a fragment of nave arcade, and a piece of late Saxon sculpture. The tower is of exceptional interest and has a number of unusual features. The main entrance is still visible on the south side, decorated with elaborate stripwork. The surface of the tower is divided into rectangular panels by vertical pilaster strips and horizontal string-courses. Although there are only two stages externally, there are four Anglo-Saxon stages within; the upper parts may have pro-

Map Reference: TF 079050 (metric map 142. 1-inch map 123)
Nearest Town: Stamford
Location: Barnack is 2½ miles (4 km) east of Stamford and can be reached directly from the town by the B1443. Alternatively, it is signposted off the A1 south of Stamford. The church is in the centre of the village. The 'Hills and Holes', which are now a nature reserve, can be reached by turning off the Stamford road in the direction of Ufford. They are on the south-west edge of the village, opposite a modern housing estate.

The 'Hills and Holes' to the west of the village was the site of important stone quarries during the Anglo-Saxon and medieval periods.

Barnack tower: The topmost stage is a medieval addition, the Saxon belfry was on the floor below, lit by the triangular-headed lights below the upper string-course.

The southern tower doorway. A remarkable composition in which large pieces of stone are used to emphasize the opening.

vided accommodation for church officials.

The walls of the tower are further elaborated by three carved panels set above the lower string-course. The panels contain patterns of foliage, cut in low relief, which spring from central stems. The branches appear to be 'bound' to the sides of the panels in two instances, a feature which has been interpreted as imitating an original design in metal. Each panel is surmounted by a bird; the southern one is a cock, symbol of watchfulness. It is possible that these panels are re-used sections of rectangular cross-shafts.

There are four remarkable pierced openings in the upper tower in addition to the more familiar triangular and round-headed windows below. These have been the subject of much debate, and are based on Italian pro-

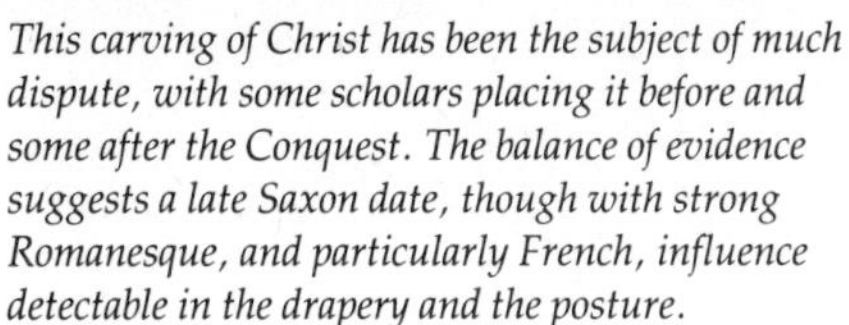

This carving of Christ has been the subject of much dispute, with some scholars placing it before and some after the Conquest. The balance of evidence suggests a late Saxon date, though with strong Romanesque, and particularly French, influence detectable in the drapery and the posture.

One of the pierced screens which lights the Anglo-Saxon belfry stage of the tower.

Perhaps the most distinctive feature of the tower is the incorporation of the fine carved slabs of which this is an example. Each is surmounted by a bird, in this case a dove, and they may be re-used cross-shafts.

totypes, perhaps the result of some early visit to Rome. They are of two types, having simple vertical openings to the east and west, and curvilinear openwork to the north and south. The latter, together with the projecting animal head on the west wall of the tower, suggests strong Danish influence on the building, as would be natural within the area of the Danelaw. There is an original sundial in the south wall which bears a simple foliate design; the hole for the gnomon at the centre is still visible.

Inside, the dominating feature is the huge tower arch. The imposts of the arch look like sandwiches made from thin strips of stone. They are actually cut from three stones and represent a remarkable feat of sculpture. Inside the tower is a unique triangular-headed seat set in the west wall. Further traces of wooden seating were found round the other walls during excavations in the 19th century. The significance of these seats is uncertain, but it has been suggested that civil courts could have met here with the judge occupying the western seat, or perhaps they were used for ecclesiastical meetings presided over by important clergymen.

Other Anglo-Saxon features of note are the fragment of a round-headed arch, presumably from the early nave arcade, behind the pulpit in the north aisle, and the fine sculpture of Christ in Majesty also in the north aisle; this is probably an 11th-century work, but shows strong Romanesque influence.

39

Wittering: All Saints Church, Cambridgeshire

The small church of All Saints, which has close links with the nearby RAF base, has substantial remains of a late Saxon two-cell church within its fabric. As the church is approached from the south side, the antiquity of the nave and chancel is evidenced by fine long and short quoins which clasp the angles of the rubblework walls. Before entering the church, it is worth inspecting the quoins in detail because they have been rebated to take a plaster wall facing. The effect would have been to make the structure look very neat and trim, with plaster covering the rubble walling, which would then have lapped up against carefully cut 'frames' of limestone at the angles. It is also worth noting that the angles of the nave in particular, as at Odda's Chapel

Map Reference: TF 056020 (metric map 141. 1-inch map 123)
Nearest Town: Stamford
Location: The site of an RAF base, Wittering is south of Stamford, some 4 miles (6.5 km) down the A1 on the west side. Turn off the A1 into the village and take the third turn left by the garage into Trent Road. The church of All Saints stands at the end of the village surrounded by modern houses.

Left: *Detail of the fine long and short quoin at the south-eastern angle of the nave.*

Below: *The original two-cell church comprising nave and chancel is largely unaltered; the rebate for plasterwork is clearly visible on the south-eastern quoin of the nave and on the chancel quoin beyond.*

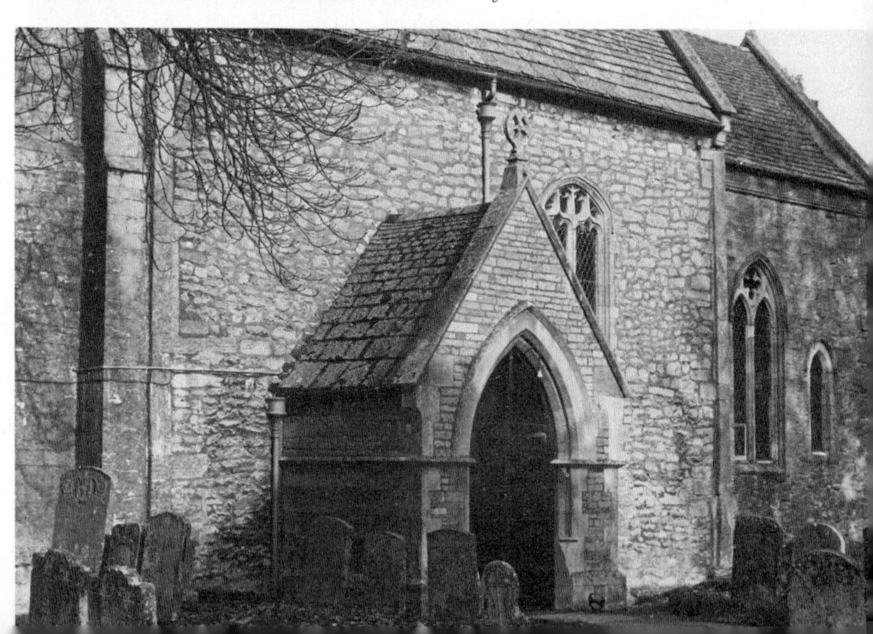

in Gloucestershire, are not truly vertical but actually bow slightly outwards towards the base and sweep gradually inwards towards the eaves. This use of 'entasis', which serves to correct the optical illusion of concavity which would result if the angles were straight, well illustrates the skill of the late Saxon builders.

Upon entering the church through the south porch, the form of the Anglo-Saxon nave is quite clear. The fine chancel arch occupies almost the full width of the east end of the nave, whilst at the west end a later arch gives access to the Early English tower. Although extended by the Norman north aisle and later north chapel, which somewhat upsets the balance of the Anglo-Saxon plan, it is still possible to visualize the original simple structure. The chancel arch is a particularly fine piece of work, with heavily rolled mouldings about its head and fine pilaster strips emphasizing the jambs. The massive chamfered imposts unite in a very pleasing fashion the upper and lower parts of the arch, which though perhaps a little large for the church, is of a very competent design.

40

Peterborough: Remnants of Medeshamstede, Cambridgeshire

Map Reference: TL 194986 (metric map 142. 1-inch map 134)
Location: The cathedral church of St Peter, St Paul and St Andrew is in the centre of the city and stands in its own fine gated close.

The only part of the celebrated Anglo-Saxon abbey church of Medeshamstede which survives lies underground in the area of the crossing of the Norman cathedral. A disastrous fire in 1116 put an end to the building which Hereward the Wake, 'Last of the Saxons', had pillaged in 1070. Eager visitors may gain access to the foundations of the chancel of

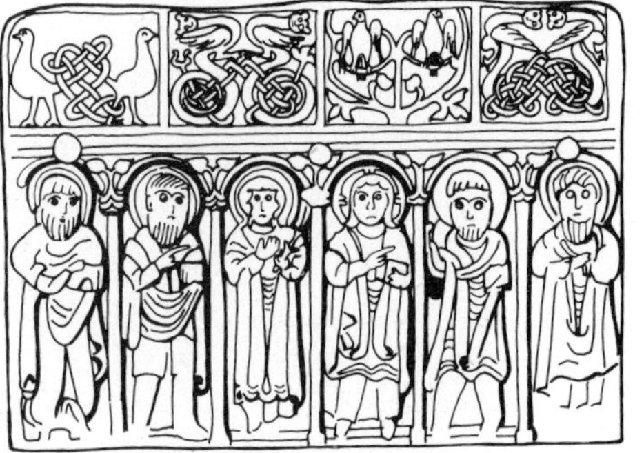

The massive Hedda stone was perhaps a shrine cover, its rich interlace decoration and naturalistic figures connect it with the 8th-century work at Breedon-on-the-Hill in Leicestershire.

This fine grave slab with its languid interlace decoration marked the grave of some 10th-century Peterborough worthy.

the Saxon abbey upon payment of a few pence; the entrance may be found in the south-west angle of the south transept.

Apart from the structure, there are a few pieces of sculpture which recapture some of the Anglo-Saxon flavour of the place. Pride of place must go to the Hedda stone which now stands east of the high altar in the sanctuary. It was traditionally supposed to commemorate the abbot Hedda and his monks who were slaughtered in a Danish raid on the abbey in 870, but it probably belongs to the 8th century since its decoration is similar in style to the Fletton friezes outside the city. The sides of the stone are enriched with arcades containing nimbed figures, most of which are now unidentifiable. Although there are twelve figures, they do not seem to represent the Twelve Apostles since at least one of the figures on the north side is female. As she bears what might be a lily spray it is perhaps a representation of the Virgin Mary. The ends of the stone are plain, and this has led to suggestions that it formed part of a larger screen or similar adjunct to a shrine. In view of its size, it would seem more probable that the stone was not part of some larger arrangement, but formed the top of a shrine containing relics.

Other sculpture in the cathedral includes the handsome gravestone illustrated here, as well as a charming pair of figures standing in arcades which are now set in the west wall of the south transept. All this is little enough to show for over 400 years of Anglo-Saxon monastic life in one of the richest monasteries in Mercia.

41

Fletton Sculpture, Cambridgeshire

The church at Fletton, which stands in something of a wilderness, possesses several fragments of friezework which are similar in character to those at Breedon-on-the-Hill in Leicestershire. Sadly, many of the Fletton pieces are built into the north-east angle of the church, and are therefore exposed to the elements.

The uppermost panel contains a human figure wrestling with, or at least holding, the

Map Reference: TL 198971 (metric map 142. 1-inch map 134)
Nearest Town: Peterborough
Location: Fletton is just south of Peterborough and can be reached by the A605 to Whittlesey. The church is in Old Fletton, a turning west off the main road.

Though sadly weathered, these fragments of friezework built into the later church at Fletton repay close examination.

complex interlaced tails of two cat-like creatures. Below are two panels containing birds (they actually look like obese hens) merging into interlace on the right, and what may be nimbed heads to the left. At the bottom are three nimbed busts framed in architectural arcades in the spandrels of which are debased pelta shapes which have been likened to bats' wings. Inside the church is a further full-length slab, and various other fragments occur within the fabric.

Although similar to the Breedon sculptures, they have been distinguished on the grounds that the human figures are reduced to mere busts, and also that the carvings are flatter, the animal forms less distinct, and tending to be rather mixed up with the background ornament. These differences suggest that the Fletton friezes are a step further away from the Continental models, and are therefore somewhat later in date. How these carvings came to Fletton is a matter for conjecture; perhaps they came from the great monastery of Medeshamstede itself after its destruction, or alternatively Fletton might have derived some benefit from the monastic workshops nearby. Finally, at the west end of the church is a fragment of cross-shaft with a crude horseman carved upon it. The whole is mounted on a 19th-century base.

42
Great Paxton: Minster Church, Cambridgeshire

The substantial late Saxon church of Holy Trinity is probably but the latest of a series of churches on the site. At the time the Domesday Book was compiled, in the years before 1086, it appears that there was only one priest attending the church, but later references record the existence of a small community consisting of a prior and canons, which suggests that the church was a minster. The Domesday Book is a notoriously unreliable record in many respects, and it seems likely that the minster status of the church originated in pre-Conquest times.

Whether or not Paxton was a minster, it is a notable example of a large and sophisticated late Saxon church. It occasions no surprise when we discover that the manor was held by Edward the Confessor, for royal patronage is precisely the milieu from which we would expect such a large and advanced building to have come. Later additions and encroach-

Map Reference: TL 210642 (metric map 153. 1-inch map 134)
Nearest Town: St Neots
Location: Great Paxton is on the B1043 which follows the line of the River Ouse between St Neots and Godmanchester. It is about 3 miles (5 km) north of St Neots. The church can be seen from the main road on the west side, and is reached via Church Lane.

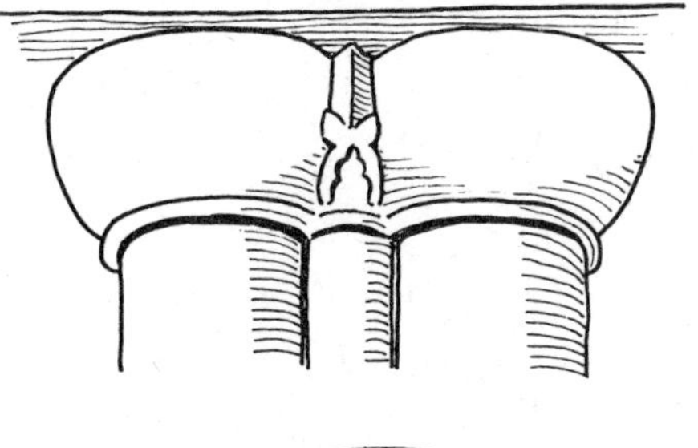

Left: *Detail of a capital in the north nave arcade. The bulbous form of the capitals together with the foliate sprigs is curiously medieval in character.*

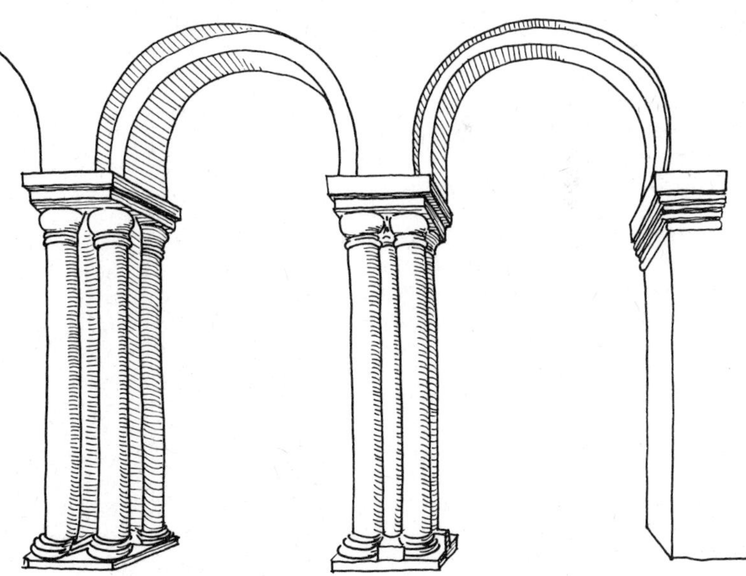

Below: *The mighty arches of the nave arcades would dwarf many a chancel arch elsewhere and attest the grand scale of the original conception.*

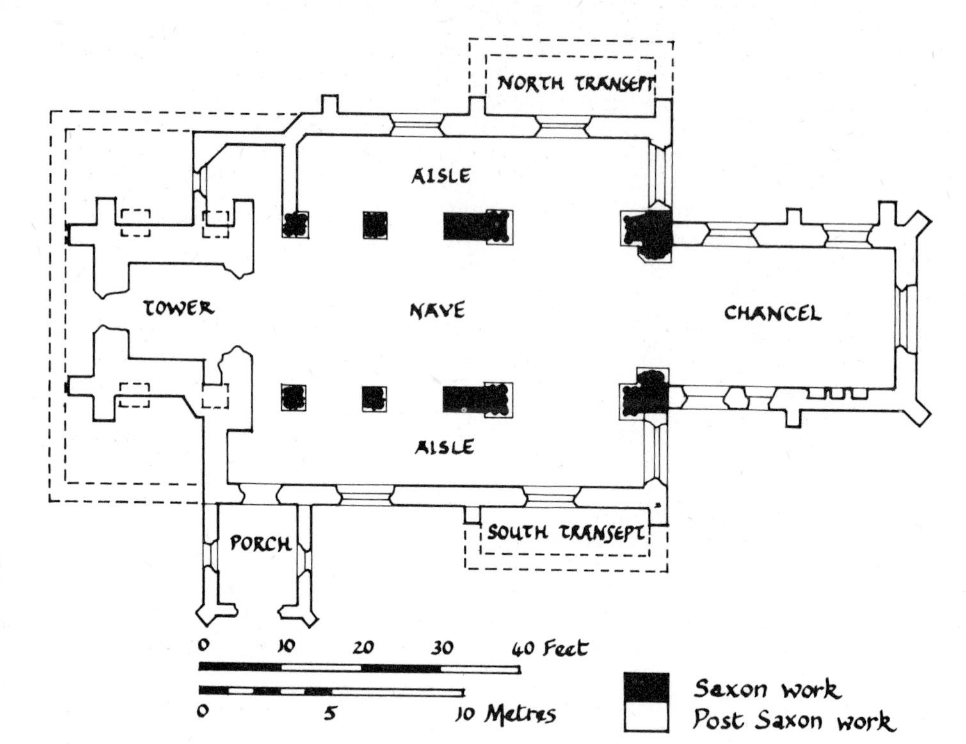

Plan of the church showing the north transept, evidence of which has been recovered by excavation, and a probable balancing transept to the south. Two further bays of the nave arcade are shown in outline below the later tower.

ments have robbed us of the entire late Saxon plan, but sufficient remains for the stylishness of the building to be apparent.

On approaching the church across the neatly kept churchyard, it is clear that the massive bulk of the tower, which is built in paler stone than the nave, is an addition. There may have been a central crossing tower here, as at Breamore in Wiltshire, but if so all trace of it has been destroyed. Instead of the western tower, imagine the nave projecting westwards to cover the same ground. That the row of clerestory windows above the south aisle continued westwards is clear from the way in which the later tower has cut the westernmost of them. There would have been a large transept on the south side which balanced that on the north, for which evidence has been found in excavations. The chancel was probably quite as long as it is today with much the same roof line.

Inside the church, the first impression is one of spaciousness. Looking eastwards towards the chancel, we see that its level is substantially higher than that of the nave. Apart from the various sets of steps, the level also rises eastwards by a slight inclination of the nave floor: everything rises towards the east, thus focusing attention on the sanctuary. At the east end of the nave is a low platform; this is an original feature and was probably occupied by a 'low' altar which was used on weekdays by a priest ministering to the parishioners. The sanctuary would probably have been reserved for Sundays and feast days when the minster clergy would have celebrated the services at the high altar. Such an arrangement of floor levels is highly unusual in Anglo-Saxon England, and it has been plausibly suggested that parallels should be sought in the raised choirs of early German Romanesque churches. This matches the German influence apparent in the contemporary tower at Sompting in Sussex.

The north and south nave arcades are purely Anglo-Saxon, and are on such a scale that they dwarf many a chancel arch elsewhere. Two clerestory windows are visible on each side above the arcade; these again illustrate the advanced design of the building.

On the north side the great arch opening into the north transept has survived, although plaster obscures its detail. The imposts of the chancel arch survive, but the arch itself was replaced during the 13th century. Despite these losses, the surviving arches and imposts in the nave and crossing are of the greatest interest. The bulbous capitals and small foliate details on the nave arcade are unknown elsewhere. It is sad that the proportions of the structure were so drastically altered when the tower was built, since the loss of perhaps as many as two bays at the west end of the nave has robbed us of the long vista up to the sanctuary. But even in its present condition, the church of Holy Trinity is still a remarkable tribute to the Confessor's ecclesiastical zeal.

Map Reference: SP 895830 (metric map 141. 1-inch map 133)
Nearest Town: Kettering
Location: On the east side of the A43 about 3½ miles (5.5 km) north of Kettering the picturesque village of Geddington has a fine Eleanor Cross in the centre. The church stands beside the central square.

Left: *The south face of the north wall of the nave. Here the large Norman arch can be seen to cut through the lower part of the blocked round-headed Anglo-Saxon window. This window cuts through an earlier arcade in its turn which is visible on the north side of the wall.*

43
Geddington: St Mary Magdalene, Northamptonshire

It is impossible to lead the trusting visitor to the fair village of Geddington without due notice that the rather modest Anglo-Saxon features of its church are outshone by the incomparable Eleanor Cross standing nearby! This, the best preserved of Edward I's poignant monuments to his beloved queen, is reward enough for the traveller.

Below: *This sketch of the north face of the north nave wall shows the early traingular-headed arcading which is cut by the later Saxon window, the western jamb of which was removed at the time the Norman nave arcade was inserted.*

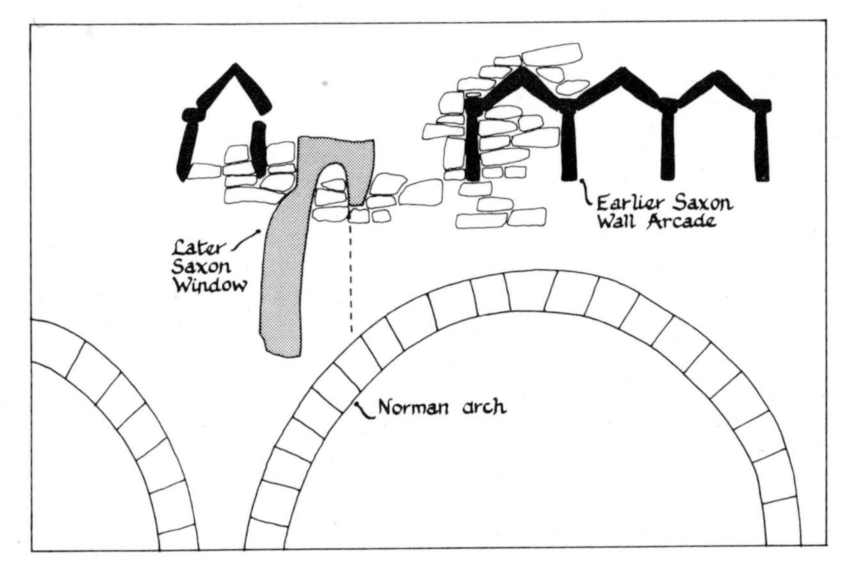

However, we will turn to the pleasant church of St Mary Magdalene, and ponder that part of its fabric which is of our period. It must be straightway said that the nave walls of the church, which are our concern, do not possess rich or unusual features, but rather that they are interesting for their evidence of a developmental sequence.

The chancel of the Saxon church has entirely disappeared, but not without trace since the original pitch of its roof and the positions of its north and south walls can be seen from inside the later chancel above the chancel arch. Further early evidence may be seen in the north transept where again, high up above the nave arcades, a triangular-headed arcade can be seen which is contemporary with the north-eastern long and short nave quoins. Here then is an Anglo-Saxon arrangement which is fairly clear, a simple rubblework nave with a triangular-headed arcade set in its outer northern face, together with indubitably Anglo-Saxon quoining.

The next stage in the sequence is represented by the round-headed window which cuts through the triangular-headed arcade. This is plainly later work, since it pays no regard to the earlier arrangement. The final stage is the round-headed nave arch itself, which cuts through the lower part of the second-stage window. When it is understood that the nave arches are of early Norman date, it will be appreciated that the round-headed window which the arches cut through must itself be Anglo-Saxon. Here at Geddington we see one of the clearest examples of an Anglo-Saxon church which was actually altered during the Anglo-Saxon period.

This realization is important, for there is a great temptation for us to imagine that Anglo-Saxon churches stayed pretty much the same during the whole of the pre-Conquest period, and that no alterations were made until a new architectural style was introduced. In fact we now realize that Saxon churches were just as prone to replanning and alteration as were later ones, and that the story of many of them is a great deal more complicated than was previously thought. This is not particularly surprising, since many churches must have been founded in the 7th and 8th centuries and continued in use for the rest of the Anglo-Saxon period, which might be a total of 300 or 400 years in all. It would indeed be a remarkable building which required no alteration over that time span!

44

Brixworth: All Saints Church, Northamptonshire

Map Reference: SP 747713 (metric map 141. 1-inch map 133)
Nearest Town: Northampton
Location: Brixworth is about 6 miles (9.5 km) due north of the centre of Northampton and is located on the A508 road to Market Harborough. The church is well signposted in the village, and is on the north side, close to open fields.

All Saints church was described by Sir Alfred Clapham as 'perhaps the most imposing architectural monument of the 7th century yet surviving north of the Alps'. Little enough is known of its Anglo-Saxon history, and even the 7th-century date is disputed by some. A 12th-century monk, Hugo Candidus, tells us that the great monastery at Peterborough, called Medeshamstede by the Anglo-Saxons, founded many daughter houses including one here at Brixworth. Hugo provides no actual dates for the foundations, but since they are mentioned in connection with two late 7th-century abbots of Peterborough, Cuthbald and Sexwulf, the origins of Brixworth have generally been traced to this period. This does not necessarily date the building itself, which may have been erected some time afterwards.

Brixworth has also been identified with the site of *Clofesho* where several church synods were held during the 9th century, but there is no direct evidence for this. Even the monastic character of the early church has been questioned, but it is difficult to imagine why else such a huge church was built. At the time of Domesday Book in 1086, Brixworth appears to have been a royal manor, and this connection

The south side of the nave showing the great arches which formerly opened into side chapels, called porticus. The upper windows were perhaps added later: note the horizontal scar just above the heads of the lower arches which marks the height of the original lean-to roof of the Anglo-Saxon aisle.

This detail of one of the southern nave arches shows how the head has been formed from small tiles, but note that the more even work to the right is a modern restoration. Recent scientific analysis of tiles used in the building suggests that most are probably Roman, but that some at least could have been made during the Anglo-Saxon period.

may have existed earlier. Whatever else, there was no monastery at Brixworth after the Conquest, so its Anglo-Saxon monks may have departed at the time of the Danish raids late in the 9th century.

Recently, a programme of research and excavation in and around the church has begun to yield results. In 1972, excavations on the site of the new vicarage west of the church revealed a large ditch which dated to the late 7th or early 8th centuries. This feature has been tentatively identified as a boundary of the monastery in that direction. Adjacent to the ditch were found late Saxon burials, which may have lain in the monks' cemetery. Perhaps more information about Anglo-Saxon Brixworth will be forthcoming in the next few years.

The earliest church had a basilican plan similar to that at Hexham, and this has led some to suggest that the church was built under the influence of St Wilfrid. Similar church plans may be seen in the early Kentish churches, and it is possible that the inspiration came from that quarter. Of the original church, only the nave is now upstanding. The great blocked arches in the side walls led into smaller chapels or porticus like those at Canterbury St Augustine's. At the west end of the nave was a two-storey entrance porch, flanked by a single-storey 'narthex' to north and south.

Later, but still in the Anglo-Saxon period, the side chapels were thrown together to form aisles, and the western bays of the nave may have been raised to the height of the choir in the east. Recent work suggests that the upper clerestory windows in the nave are somewhat later than the earliest fabric, and they may have been added at this time. It is possible that this elaboration of the church coincided with

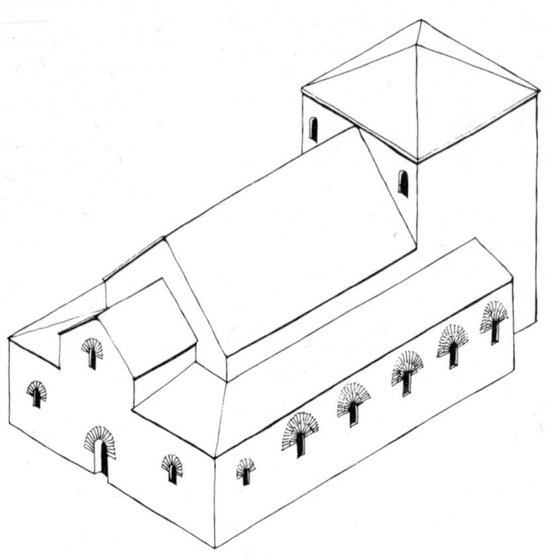

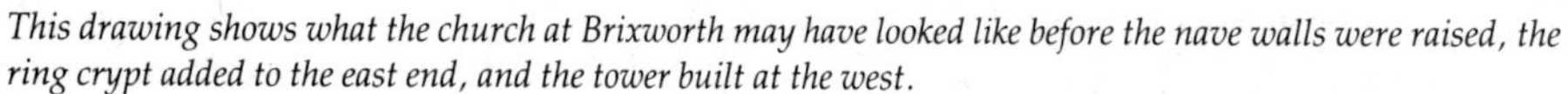

This drawing shows what the church at Brixworth may have looked like before the nave walls were raised, the ring crypt added to the east end, and the tower built at the west.

This highly stylized carving of an eagle owes much to manuscript drawings, it is perhaps the symbol of St John the Evangelist.

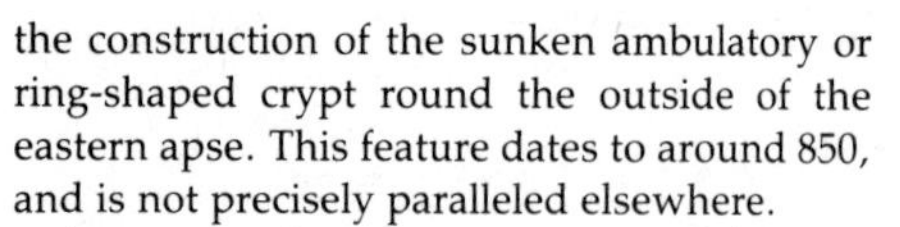

the construction of the sunken ambulatory or ring-shaped crypt round the outside of the eastern apse. This feature dates to around 850, and is not precisely paralleled elsewhere.

Access to the crypt was gained by two doors, the heads of which may be seen just above the floor of the choir to the north and south of the sanctuary arch. The sanctuary itself was largely rebuilt during the last century, and it was then that the ring crypt around its exterior was discovered. The ambulatory may still be seen, though its roof has now gone and it looks like a stone-faced trench round the exterior of the apse. The function of this crypt is uncertain, but it has been suggested that a small chamber containing relics may have opened off to the west, under the sanctuary floor. The sunken walkway would thus have provided access for pilgrims visiting the relics, like the later arrangement at Repton.

The three windows opening from the ringing chamber of the tower into the west end of the nave. Note the finely cut balusters which divide the openings.

In this connection, it is interesting to note that a chapel dedicated to St Boniface existed in the later medieval church on the site, and that a relic which is still housed in a reliquary by the pulpit is said to have come from the saint's body. Some have claimed that this relic of Boniface, who was an Anglo-Saxon missionary to Europe during the 8th century, was originally housed in the ring crypt at the east end, and it has even been suggested that the crypt was built to display the bone. Unfortunately, there is no evidence either way, so we must remain uncertain as to whether this claimed relic of the martyred Archbishop of Mainz in modern West Germany was ever the goal of Anglo-Saxon pilgrims to Brixworth.

It was perhaps also during the 9th century that the west porch was raised to form a tower, as at Monkwearmouth. The fine triple arch opening from the tower ringing chamber into the west wall of the nave was constructed at the same time. The small stair turret on the west side of the tower is probably the latest Anglo-Saxon architectural feature, and might belong to the early 11th century.

The present south doorway by which the church is entered is a Norman insertion into one of the great arches which led from the Anglo-Saxon nave into a side chapel. All the early arches have fine tiled heads which may be made of re-used Roman materials, or it is just possible that they were actually made in Anglo-Saxon times. Just to the left inside the door, notice the small but distinguished carving of an eagle now preserved under glass; this may be the eagle of St John the Evangelist. The careful definition of the feathers together with the rigid pose owe much to manuscript art.

45

Earls Barton Saxon Tower, Northamptonshire

Standing at the centre of the rather humdrum village of Earls Barton is the Anglo-Saxon tower which many a schoolboy must recognize. All save the top of the tower, above the belfry windows, is of the late 10th century. The turrets and top string-course all date from a 15th-century refurbishment of the structure.

There are four main stages, divided by simple string-courses. On the fourth floor, the belfry stage, there are unusual openings consisting of five narrow lights separated by tall slightly bulging circular shafts. Each light has a tight rounded head cut from an individual square stone, and the whole arrangement seems to be a most unsuitable application of stone carving. The pilaster strips begin in earnest on the third stage, and are supplemented by diagonal strips in the lower halves of the main panels which are strongly suggestive of late medieval scissor bracing, as used in timber-framed structures.

Left: *The southern face of the tower. The round-headed window above the south door is a later insertion; the heads of the original windows can be seen above, just below the lower string-course.*

Map Reference: SP 852638 (metric map 152. 1-inch map 133)
Nearest Town: Wellingborough
Location: Earls Barton is about 6 miles (9.5 km) north-east of Northampton, and is a popular commuter town. It can be reached on the A45 Wellingborough road from which it is signposted, about one mile (1.6 km) south on the B573. The church is in an imposing central position.

Left: *The great tower from the south. The stripwork decoration has often been likened to wooden construction and it seems possible that the decorative scheme was inspired by timber prototypes.*

On the second level these 'scissor' strips give way to semi-circular ones which rest quite uselessly on the bases of the panels. The south doorway is a puzzling feature, but it has been suggested that such raised doorways were used for showing relics to the faithful on fsast days – an interesting speculation. Finally, the lowest stage is accentuated by double windows set high up under the string-course. These have strange monolithic heads which bear simple equal-armed crosses. A circular stone bearing a larger version of the same cross is visible beside the southern windows in the photograph. The occurrence of this cross-in-circle motif set apparently at random in the wall is reminiscent of later medieval consecration crosses, which were placed on churches at the time that they were sanctified for Christian worship. The western tower door is a pretty thing, with lightly incised arcading on its massive square imposts. The window over the door is a later insertion since the paired windows above were almost certainly integral to the original arrangement on the south side.

Much discussion has taken place about this mighty tower, and it has even been suggested that it was intended as a place of refuge or defence. These speculations seem unduly dramatic, and it is perhaps better to see Earls Barton as a prodigy example of the 'tower church' plan in which the tower was the main element of the plan, with the eastern extension being a relatively minor part of the construction, as at Barton-on-Humber. There are traces of earthworks in the churchyard to the north, but these are almost certainly the remains of a Norman castle, and thus played no part in the Anglo-Saxon scheme.

As Earls Barton makes such free use of pilaster strips, it is perhaps appropriate to consider briefly their significance. Here as elsewhere, the strips do not appear to play any direct structural part as it is the walling and the well-tied quoins which secure the tower. It has been suggested that the strips were useful during the construction of such buildings, since they helped the builders to 'true up' the faces of the rubble walls, and may also have served to localize structural failure. But they appear largely to be a decorative caprice which reached a greater stage of maturity at Earls Barton than elsewhere. It is difficult to imagine that the exuberance of the stripwork here was dictated by any practical considerations, and rather they illustrate the Anglo-Saxons' love of ornament and decoration on a grand scale.

46

Offa's Dyke: The Anglo Welsh Frontier, Welsh Marches

After the Battle of Dyrham in Gloucestershire in 577, the British inhabitants of Wales were cut off from those of Devon and Cornwall by a Saxon 'wedge'. Attempts to prevent the same

General note: the Offa's Dyke Path is marked by the Waymark Sign. For enthusiasts this can be followed from coast to coast, although the path does not always follow the dyke. Four sections are indicated here where access is easy, and one for Wat's Dyke.

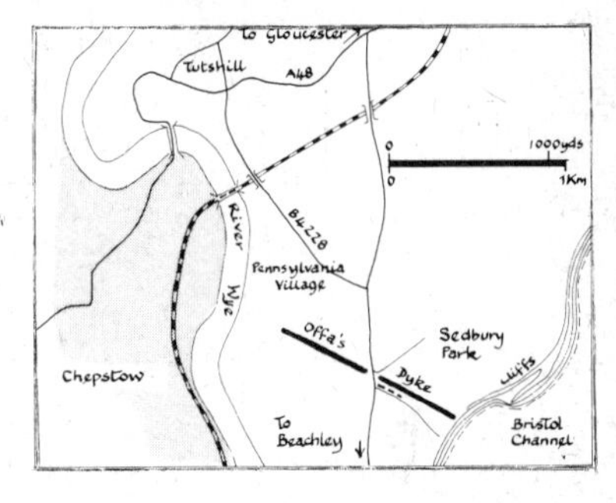

Site A

Map Reference: SJ 548930 (metric map 162. 1-inch map 155)

Nearest Town: Chepstow

Location: A fine section can be seen where the dyke reaches the Bristol Channel. From Chepstow take the A48 to Gloucester. Having crossed the Wye and started the drive up Tutshill, take the right turn signposted to Beachley (B4288). About one mile (1.6 km) before Beachley the dyke crosses the road at an incline, just after Sedbury Park. The path is signposted by the Waymark Sign. The section of the dyke from the road to the cliffs is particularly impressive.

A silver penny of Offa struck by the moneyer Ibba at Canterbury in the late 8th century at a time when the whole of southern England acknowledged Offa's overlordship. The obverse shows a stylized head of Offa with OFFA REX *on it whilst the reverse has a cross fleury with the moneyer's name* IBBA *set between the arms.*

The Welsh side of the dyke in the fine southern section near Chepstow. The great ditch is now silted up, but the bank still stands well over ten feet (3 metres) high.

thing happening in the north were finally frustrated by the defeat of Penda, king of Mercia, at the Battle of Winwaed Field near Leeds. Cadwallon, prince of Gwynedd in north-west Wales, had valued his links with the British kingdom of Strathclyde in south-west Scotland so highly that he had formed an alliance with the pagan Penda against Northumbria. But Northumbria prevailed, and Wales was finally isolated from the other British kingdoms.

Though cut off from the British lands to the north and south, Wales was not invaded by the Anglo-Saxons. The western boundary of Mercia, the people of the 'Mierce' or border, closely follows the modern division between England and Wales, a line which was created as much by geography as by man himself. It was along this boundary that the greatest artificial frontier of Anglo-Saxon England was constructed. It is still called Offa's Dyke in memory of its creator, and the distinction which it marked between English and Welsh is still a reality today.

Offa's Dyke was not the first attempt to stabilize the western frontier of Mercia. From the early 7th century onwards many small dykes were built along the border, presumably to protect Anglo-Saxon settlements in the Marches. Still later, in the first half of the 8th century, a more substantial earthwork was created in the north March which was called

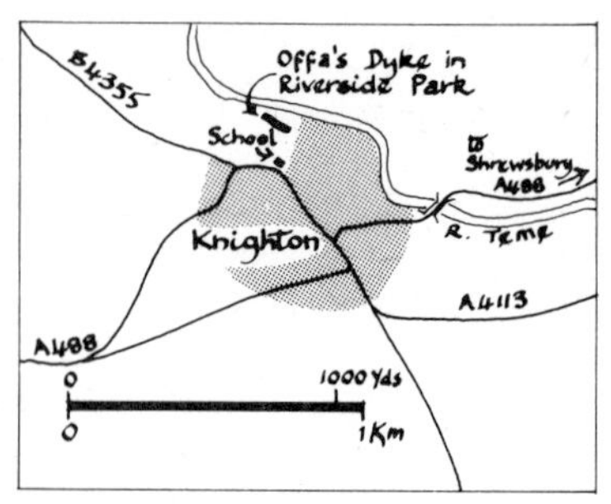

Site B
Map Reference: SO 284727 (metric map 148. 1-inch map 128)
Nearest Town: Knighton
Location: At Knighton, in the Offa's Dyke Riverside Park, a well-preserved section of the dyke can be seen; also the commemorative stone which marks the opening of the path.

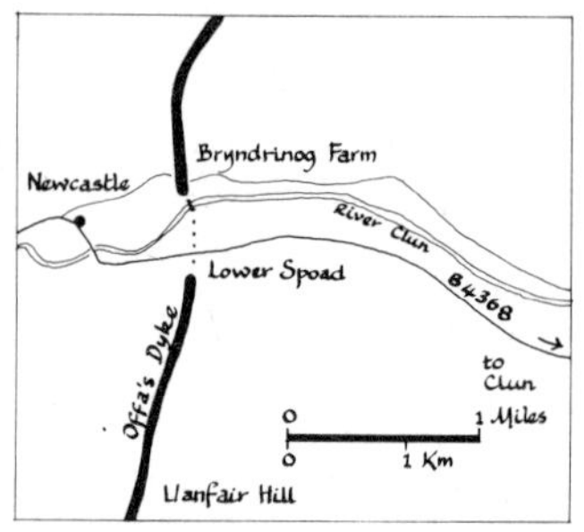

Site C
Map Reference: SO 258870 (metric map 148. 1-inch map 128)
Nearest Town: Clun
Location: Some fine sections of the dyke can be seen either side of the B4368 between Newcastle and Clun at Lower Spoad. Walk south towards Springhill Farm and Llanfair Hill, or north to Bryndrinog Farm.

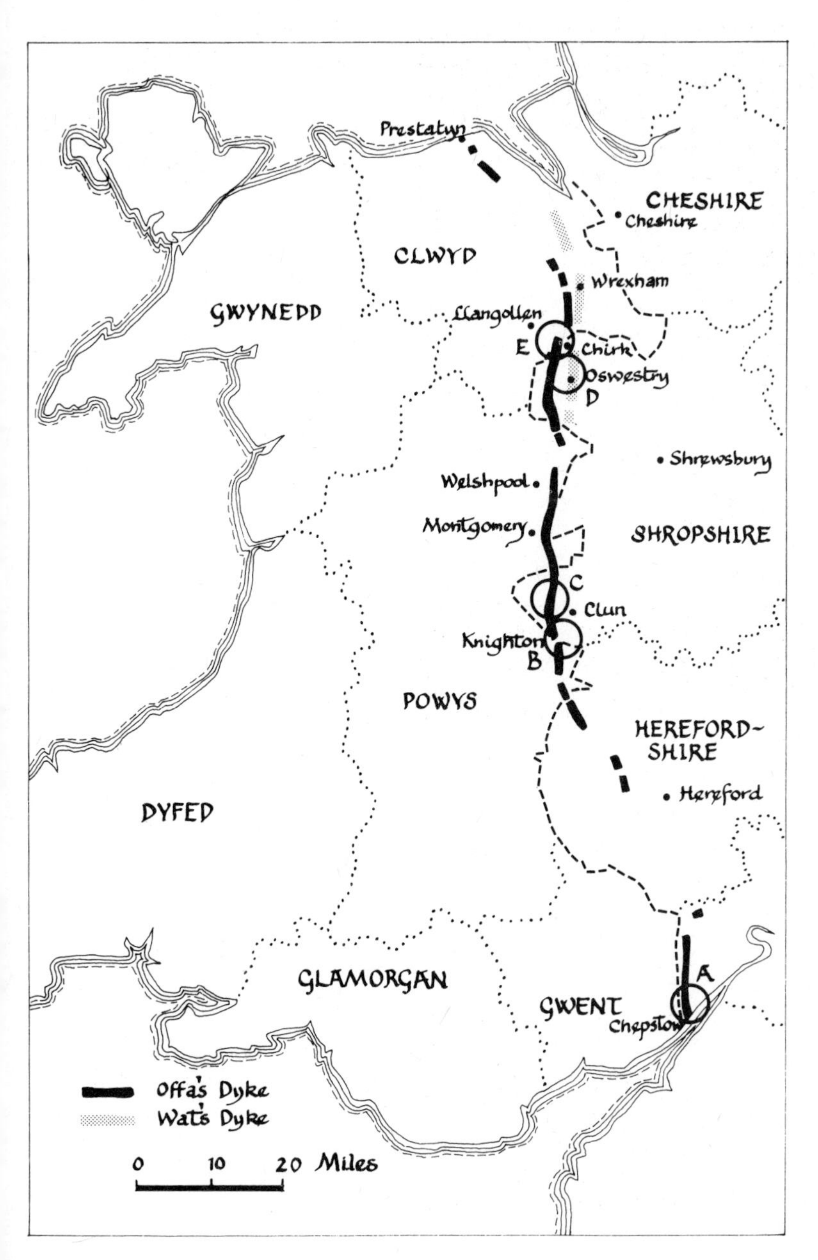

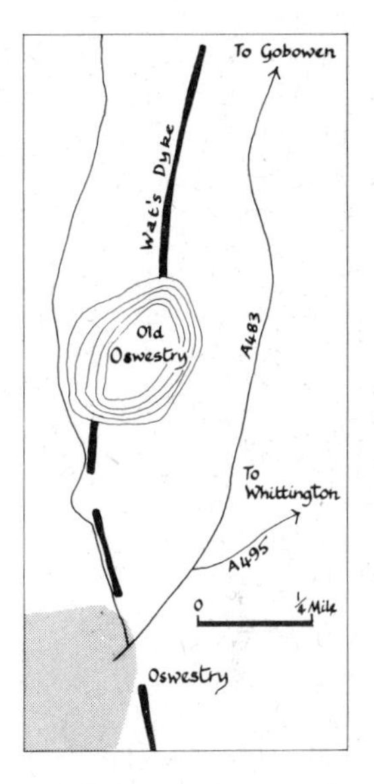

Site D (Wat's Dyke)
Map Reference: SJ 295310 (metric map 126. 1-inch map 118)
Nearest Town: Oswestry
Location: A combined trip can be made to visit Old Oswestry hill-fort (Iron Age) and also to see a fine section of Wat's Dyke. The hill-fort is about half a mile (0.8 km) north of Oswestry, and is sign-posted off the A483. There is room to park at the entrance gates.

Map showing Offa's and Wat's Dykes, together with the sites to be visited. The modern Welsh counties of Gwynedd and Powys correspond with the heartlands of the ancient kingdoms mentioned in the entry. The gaps in the dyke, particularly in the southern section in Hereford and Worcester, were probably filled by dense forest.

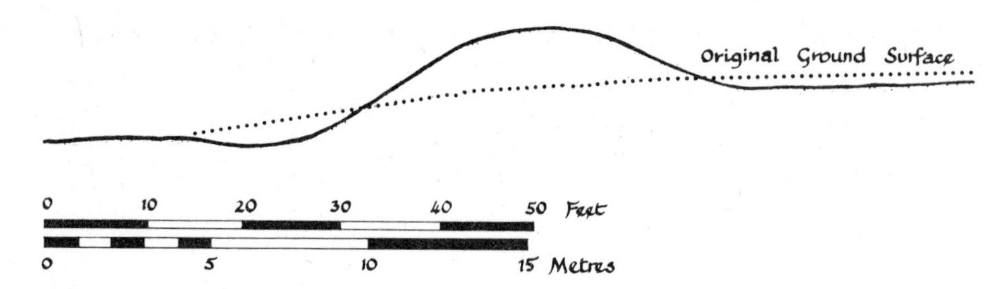

A section through the southern part of the dyke, showing how the natural lie of the land was used to advantage by the dyke builders.

Wat's Dyke. This was less impressive than Offa's work, and was perhaps built by his predecessor, King Aethelbald of Mercia who reigned approximately 716-56.

Evidence for Offa's building of the dyke comes from Asser's *Life of King Alfred*. Asser records that Offa built his frontier *de mari usque ad mare* – 'from sea to sea'. Recent research suggests that this might be somewhat exaggerated, since Offa probably incorporated some parts of Wat's Dyke in the northern section. The total length of the boundary was 149 miles (238 km), but only 80 miles (128 km) or so are known to have been marked by a man-made line; most of the gaps were probably filled by dense forest.

Although the dyke was created by Anglo-Saxons, there are signs that it was sited so as to afford some concession to Welsh interests. In the Wye Valley, for example, the boundary was sited some way to the east of the river, probably to allow Welsh fishermen and timber traders to use both banks of the river. Similarly, further north some of the rich pastures near the headwaters of the Severn fall west of the dyke, presumably so that they could remain in Welsh hands, which as these pastures lay in the old Welsh kingdom of Powys, is probably a tribute to the strength of the earlier resistance put up by renowned leaders such as Eliseg.

The scale of the dyke varies considerably throughout its length, with the strongest defences being provided in the valley bottoms to protect the fertile farmland, and on the high ridges where natural routeways existed. Some parts of the dyke may have been crowned with a wall or timber palisade, but we must imagine that a single bank and ditch was the basic pattern. The boundary was probably intended to function not as a strongly defended 'wall', but more as a brake or barrier to raiding parties, and as an encumbrance to cattle thieves. Mercian lands along the dyke doubtless had to provide sentries to guard the line, but we should not imagine that great standing garrisons were provided along its length. Movement across the dyke was probably controlled at defined crossing points, and we may imagine that opportunities for import levies were not missed!

The dyke crosses much beautiful country, and can be seen to advantage at many different points; the best are included here. The Offa's Dyke Path was opened in 1971 and, whilst this does not follow the line of the dyke the whole way, it provides a fine walk through the Welsh Marches. There is an excellent guide to the path published by Her Majesty's Stationery

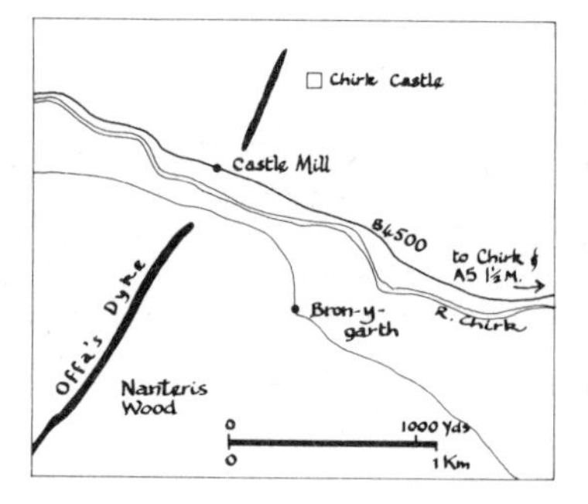

Site E

Map Reference: SJ 264377 (metric map 126. 1-inch map 117)

Nearest Town: Chirk

Location: A good view of Chirk castle as well as a fine section of the dyke can be seen by taking the path south from Castle Mill on the B4500 some 1½ miles (2.5 km) west of Chirk which is on the A5.

Office (*Offa's Dyke Path:* Long Distance Footpath Guide No. 4 by John B. Jones, 1977).

The dyke is a unique personal monument to the greatest of the Mercian kings, a man who not only secured extensive powers in Anglo-Saxon England, but also proved an able statesman on the European stage. In the common speech of our time, England is still spoken of in Wales as the 'land beyond Offa's Dyke', but we must be grateful that any Welshman found on the 'wrong' side of the dyke need no longer fear the amputation of his right hand!

47

Stanton Lacy: St Peter's Church, Shropshire

The church of St Peter is the best of a small group of churches in the southern Marches which have Anglo-Saxon work in them. The early evidence at Stanton Lacy is all external, and comprises the north and west walls of the nave, together with most of the north transept. Large side alternate quoins can be seen at the angles of the Anglo-Saxon fabric.

Originally the church probably had a simple cruciform plan with the chancel being substantially shorter than its medieval successor. The early church was somewhat unusual since it appears that it was entered through the fine doorway on the north side which is now blocked. Southern entrances were more to be expected and, whilst it is possible that a second doorway was demolished on the south side when the aisle was constructed, the elaboration of the north door suggests that it was the principal entrance. The inscribed cross above the door is reminiscent of the northern examples at Middleton and Hovingham in North Yorkshire.

Apart from the doorway, the north nave wall bears nine pilaster strips, one of which rests on a corbel above the door head. The uneven heights at which the strips stop suggest that the upper parts of the wall have been rebuilt at some time. Further pilaster strips occur on the west wall of the nave and on the east and west walls of the north transept. In the north wall of the transept a blocked doorway with cut back facing may be seen, together with a round-headed window. Both are of uncertain date, but the doorway at least may be Saxon.

Map Reference: SO 495788 (metric map 138. 1-inch map 129)
Nearest Town: Ludlow
Location: Stanton Lacy is about 3 miles (5 km) to the north of Ludlow. Follow the A49 from Ludlow towards Shrewsbury; after 2 miles (3 km), take the B4365 to the north. A further mile (1.6 km) up the road, Stanton Lacy lies on a minor road to the east.

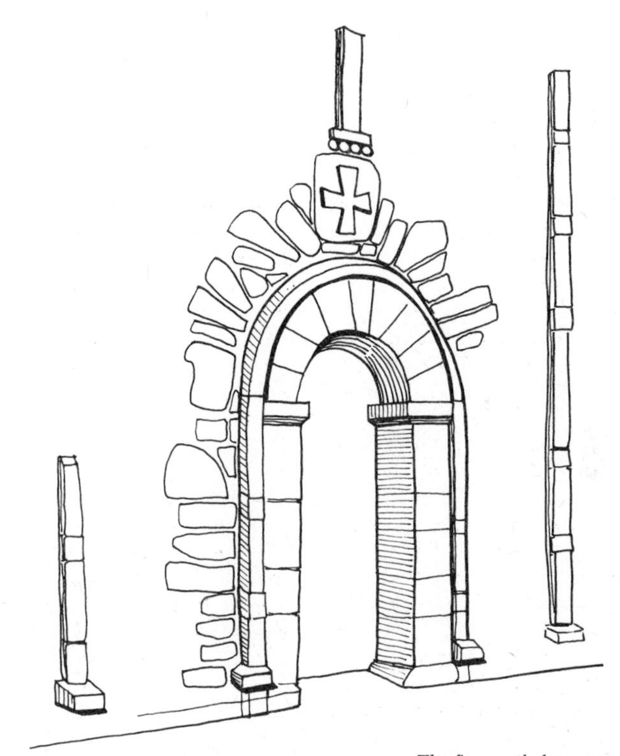

The fine north doorway with its handsome stripwork surround was probably the principal entrance to the original 11th-century church.

48

Ewyas Harold: A Pre-Conquest Motte and Bailey, Hereford and Worcester

Castles were generally a post-Conquest introduction in England, and no certain evidence of an Anglo-Saxon private castle has yet been found, but there is a small group of fortifications which, like all the best exceptions, prove the rule. We know that during the later 10th and early 11th centuries, England and Normandy gradually drew closer together, often because of the common difficulties experienced at the hands of Viking raiders. Under Edward the Confessor, the two states established yet closer connections, and Edward's Norman brother-in-law Ralf, nicknamed 'the Timid', became Earl of Hereford, and therefore ruler of the sensitive military province along the Welsh March.

Edward's friendship with the 'Norman Party' at court was not viewed with equanimity by all his subjects. Earl Godwin of Wessex in particular disapproved strongly of Edward's preferment of the foreigners, and he led a loose confederation of discontented nobles which included his son, the future King Harold. Edward, fearing for the safety of his Norman friends, apparently encouraged them to 'dig in' on their new English estates. This they promptly did, with the result that in 1051

Map Reference: SO 385288 (metric map 161. 1-inch map 142)
Nearest Town: Hereford
Location: Ewyas Harold is only 6 miles (9.5 km) from the Welsh border and is signposted north off the A465, about halfway between Hereford and Abergavenny. Travel on the B4347 then take the minor road through the village, and about 50 yards (45 metres) beyond the centre, look out for some concrete steps on the left-hand side of the road leading to a stile. A rough, rather steep track leads to the site, just to the left of a huge holly tree. Stout shoes or wellingtons are recommended in wet weather.

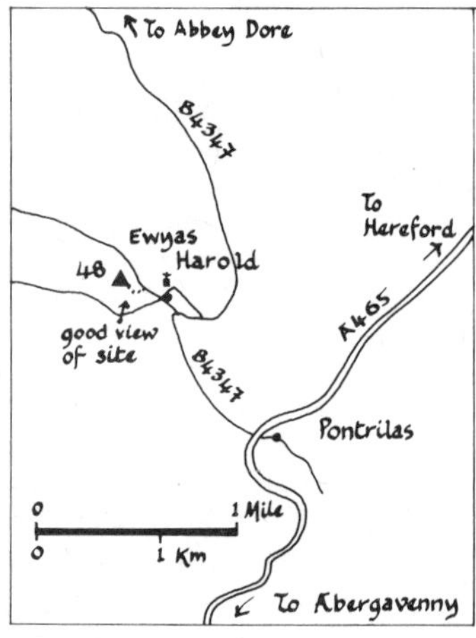

The great motte at Ewyas Harold is now tree-grown, but the great size of the mound is still very impressive.

England saw the first of the motte and bailey castles which were to be such a feature of the post-Conquest landscape. The Anglo-Saxon Chronicle duly records that: 'The foreigners had built a castle in Herefordshire in Earl Swein's territory and inflicted all the injuries and insults they possibly could on the king's men in that region.' The inhabitants were plainly unimpressed by their new neighbours!

During 1051 and 1052, the Norman Party suffered a serious setback at court, and the Norman favourites of the king took horse to their castles. The Chronicle again notes: 'When the Frenchmen learnt this they took horses and some went west to Pentecost's castle and some north to Robert's castle.' There thus appear to have been at least three castles in England by 1052.

The first castle referred to by the Chronicle is thought to have been at Hereford itself; Robert's castle was probably at Clavering in Essex; and Pentecost's stronghold was fairly certainly here at Ewyas Harold. The motte at Ewyas Harold which is over seventy yards (64 metres) in diameter and seventy feet (21 metres) high, has never been scientifically excavated. We know that the site was occupied after the Conquest by William Fitz Osbern, the Conqueror's right-hand man in the west, and that still later it was equipped with a keep and gatehouse built of stone, but that is all. A later source, the chronicler Florence of Worcester

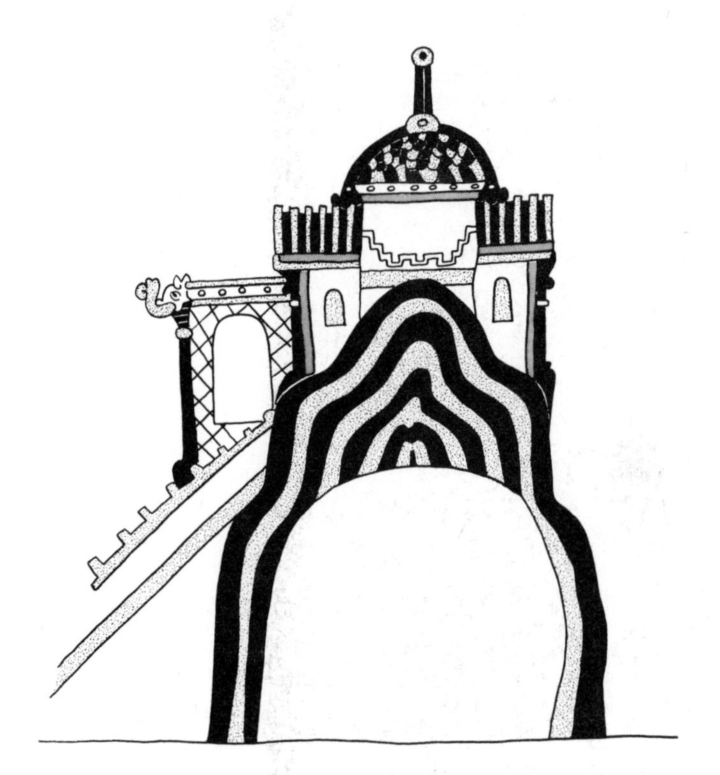

This stylized representation in the Bayeux Tapestry shows the castle at Bayeux itself. Pentecost's castle at Ewyas Harold would have resembled the basic form shown here, with a timber tower atop an earth mound, and a 'flying bridge' or ladder, visible on the left, leading down to the bailey below.

writing in the 12th century, tells us that Osbern, surnamed Pentecost, had to surrender his castle to Earl Godwin after 1052; it would therefore appear that the Saxons enjoyed sweet revenge against the Norman Party before the Conquest!

What would the castle at Ewyas Harold have looked like? The most nearly contemporaneous representations are, of course, in the Bayeux Tapestry which shows several motte and bailey castles. Although very stylized, the tapestry shows the essential features of a timber tower on top of the 'motte' or mound, with a ladder or 'flying bridge' leading down into a defended yard or 'bailey' below. These two elements, of a timber keep atop a motte with a palisaded bailey below, are the distinctive hallmarks of many of the early Norman castles. Ewyas Harold conforms to this general scheme in all save one particular – the bailey ditch did not continue between the bailey and the motte. The reason for this is uncertain, but it is worth visiting Ewyas Harold to see one of the handful of Norman castles built in England before the Conquest.

49

Newent Sculpture and Cross, Gloucestershire

Although nothing of the fabric of the church of St Mary the Virgin is of pre-Conquest date, it houses two very interesting pieces of Anglo-Saxon sculpture. The first of these, the lower part of a 9th-century cross-shaft, is in the south porch. Although Newent lies in the southern marches of Mercia, the details of this shaft, and in particular the splendid beast and the Adam and Eve scene, hark back to Breedon-on-the-Hill in Leicestershire, in the heart of the kingdom.

On the main face is a representation of the Fall of Man. Adam and Eve stand to either side of the Tree of Knowledge about which a wily serpent twines. The sides are decorated with wiry scrollwork, and a panel containing the beast mentioned above. This last is a noble creature with a long curving neck, delicately proportioned body, and interlacing tail. The similarity of this work to the sculpture at Breedon has led some art historians to identify a Mercian tradition of animal representation which is called somewhat dramatically the 'Great Beast'. If this be so, the Newent work is a fine example of the tradition.

The second of Newent's treasures lies within the church at the west end of the nave. Here in a small glass case is a singular stone tablet only a few inches square but richly decorated with carving. The small size of this tablet, together with its rich carving, suggests that it was a small portable altar of the type found in Cuthbert's coffin at Durham. Additionally, the carving, with its imitation nail heads and rounded highlights, might imitate the metal repoussé decorated covers of such altars.

On one side is a panel showing the Cruci-

The Crucifixion scene. The hand of God descends from the clouds above Christ's head.

Map Reference: SO 723259 (metric map 162. 1-inch map 142)
Nearest Town: Ross on Wye
Location: This small market town is in the quiet countryside between the M50 and the A40 Gloucester to Ross road. It is signposted off the M50 at Junction 3, and can also be reached from Gloucester by the A40 and then by the B4215 for some 6 miles (9.5 km) in a north-westerly direction. The church is in the centre of the town to the east of the market hall.

fixion, with Our Lord on a flaring-armed cross set amongst a mass of figures. Those on the bottom left may represent the Resurrection as they seem to show a man lying in a coffin beside another who seems to be waking after the long sleep of death. The Hand of God reaches from the clouds above Christ's head, a feature reminiscent of the great rood at Romsey.

On the reverse is a spirited rendering of the Harrowing of Hell. This legend, which is also depicted on a handsome 11th-century slab in Bristol Cathedral, refers to Christ's descent into Hell after His death and His victory over the Powers of Darkness before His Resurrection. Here He is shown holding the great key of Hell in His left hand, whilst devils and presumably lost souls fall about His feet in misery; an inspiring symbol of Christ Triumphant.

The stone was found in 1912 during excavations for a new vestry. It served as a pillow stone for the head of the body of a priest called Edred, whose name is cut into the Harrowing of Hell face of the stone. This tradition of using stone 'pillows' to support the head of the deceased was common in Northumbria, and it therefore seems possible that Edred himself may have come from the north – we do not know. Apart from his name, those of the Four Evangelists are cut round the edges of the stone. Newent is fortunate indeed to possess this delightful 11th-century gem.

50

Deerhurst: St Mary's Church and Odda's Chapel, Gloucestershire

As with so many of the places in this guide, Deerhurst was much more important in the Anglo-Saxon period than it is today. This little village by the River Severn was the site of major events, and the church of St Mary was

Map Reference: **St Mary's Church:** SO 870299 (metric map 150. 1-inch map 143)
Odda's Chapel: SO 869298
Nearest Town: Tewkesbury
Location: A small, quiet village on the east bank of the Severn, Deerhurst lies quite close to the A38, 3 miles (5 km) south of Tewkesbury. The village is signposted off the main road, on the west side, and is reached on the B4213 and a minor road. The church of St Mary is in the centre of the village, and Odda's Chapel is close by. The chapel is an ancient monument in the care of the Department of the Environment and is open to view free of charge at any reasonable time.

The Deerhurst Angel. This was probably carved during the reign of Alfred in the late 9th century.

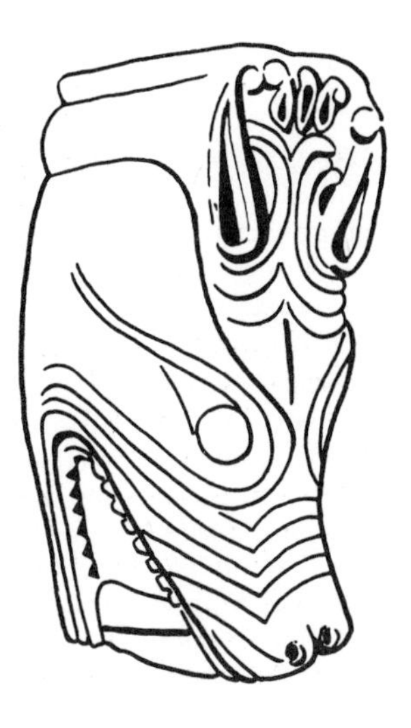

One of the beast-head stops on the west nave door.

Odda's Chapel from the south-west. The round-headed window is original. Note the inward-leaning quoins at the angles of the building which follow the Ancient Greek technique of entasis.

built to serve a major monastery. The earliest reference to the monastery at Deerhurst is in 804, when Aethelric, son of Aethelmund, Earl of Hwicce (Hwicce being the part of Outer Mercia in which Deerhurst lay), made a huge grant of land to the foundation. The size of Aethelric's gift attests the importance of the house, and his wish to be buried here also indicates its favoured status.

Later during the 10th century, St Alphege was a monk here before becoming successively Bishop of Winchester and Archbishop of Canterbury. In 1011 a Danish army besieged Canterbury, and the city finally fell when it was betrayed by the Saxon Archdeacon Aelfmaer. Alphege, together with other prominent men, was captured and the Danes offered them for ransom. Alphege forbade his people to cooperate, though all the other captives were bought back. His conduct so enraged the Danes that

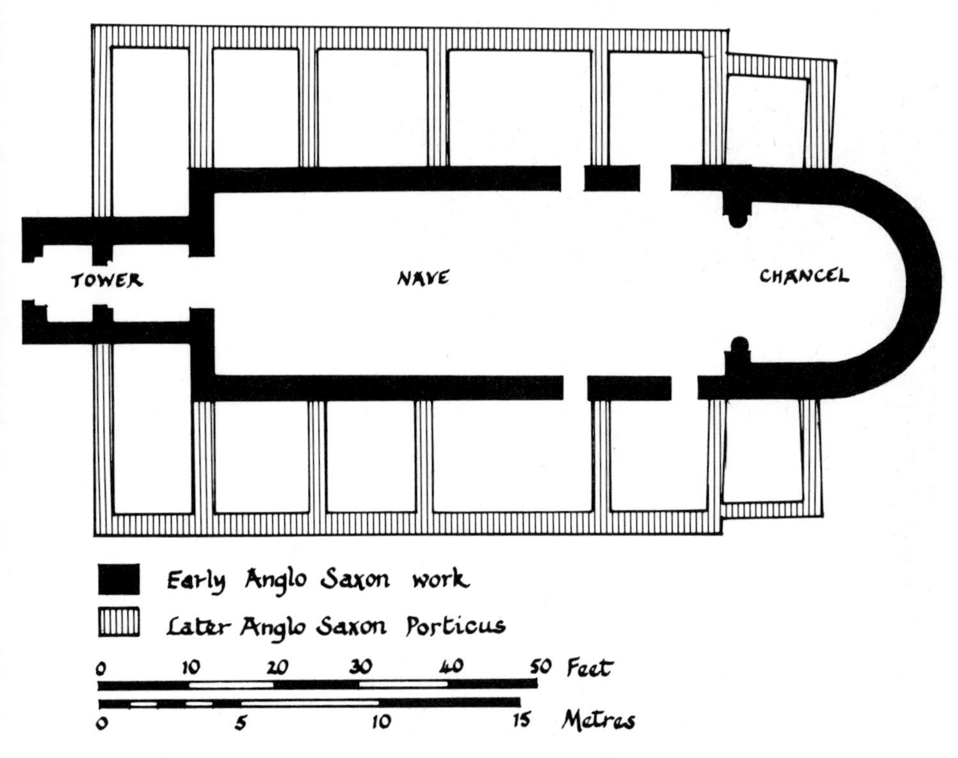

A schematic plan showing the Anglo-Saxon church at the peak of its development. The chancel is now ruinous, and is sealed off from the nave. The church must have been huge, since this whole plan went through two storeys.

after becoming drunk at a feast they battered him to death with ox bones. St Alphege became a national hero, since many Englishmen resented the policy of 'buying off' the Danes with Danegeld.

By a strange chance, Deerhurst was again involved in this story. Five years later in 1016 when Edmund Ironside, King of England, was defeated by the Danes at the disastrous Battle of Ashingdon in Essex, he retreated here with his broken army. The Danish leader Cnut pursued him, and the two men met on an island in the Severn at Alney close to Deerhurst. Here Edmund and Cnut, called 'Canute' by the English, signed a treaty which partitioned England between Saxon and Dane, much as Alfred and Guthrum had done years before at Wedmore. Edmund died the same year, and Canute ruled England. He caused the body of Alphege to be removed to Canterbury cathedral where the saint's cult flourished until it was eclipsed by that of Thomas Becket, the second martyred Archbishop. Indeed Thomas actually referred to the example set by St Alphege in the last sermon he preached before his death.

St Mary's at Deerhurst has retained extensive evidence of its early history as an Anglo-Saxon monastic church. In recent years an intensive architectural and archaeological survey of the site has revealed much new evidence which is not yet published in detail. Dr H. M. Taylor has provisionally identified no less than six major architectural phases in the building, and the following is a brief account of this development.

The first church was a simple rectangle with a porch at the west end. A semi-circular apse was added to the east, followed by the construction of two flanking chapels, or porticus, to the north and south of the east end. Next it seems that the church was considerably heightened, since the upper parts of the nave and side chapels appear to be secondary to the lower walls. We must therefore imagine a 'double decker' church with activities going on at two levels. Later still, the western tower was built, the easternmost chapels were demolished, and the semi-circular apse was replaced by the polygonal structure which can still be seen. Finally, the side chapels were extended westwards to provide a whole row of small chambers; all were of two storeys.

Upon approaching the church, the 10th-century tower is the most impressive feature. The main doorway into the church leads through the tower, although the tower itself is now entered through a later door to the south. A medieval pointed arch has been inserted into the Saxon west doorway, but the round head of the original door can be seen above it. The Anglo-Saxon ground level is over a foot below the modern surface at this point, and the early sill has been found by excavation. Notice the curious beast's head above the doorway which is an original feature. Before going into the nave, look up at the wall facing you just inside the west door where an early carving of the Virgin Mary can be seen. This is a very flat sculpture, and it is likely that it was originally built up in plaster; traces of paint still survive on the surface. There are fine beast-head terminals on the east side of the door into the nave.

The nave is preserved to its full Anglo-Saxon extent, but the chancel has been blocked off. The sanctuary arch is preserved in the east wall of the nave, and it repays careful examination. Fine beast-head terminals decorate the ends of the arch, and traces of early paint may be seen on the arch-head. Looking back towards the west, two fine triangular-headed lights may be seen opening into the tower, in the same position as the belfry lights at Brixworth. Also in the nave are three triangular windows and a blocked door in the west wall at first-floor level. Notice also the handsome font, which is probably of 9th-century date.

From the north and south aisles may be seen an original string-course along the outside of the nave wall. This marks the junction between the earlier single-storey nave and the later two-storey structure. The aisles themselves, which are now continuous, were originally subdivided into side chapels as described above. Several early openings into the chapels through the nave walls are visible in the north and south of the choir.

Since the eastern apse cannot now be entered from the nave, the visitor must leave by the west door and walk round the north side of the church. Although ruined, the facets of the second-phase polygonal apse can still be seen resting on the earlier circular foundation. Only the south-west wall is still standing to its full height, but this survival is very fortunate since it has preserved the carving of the 'Deerhurst Angel'. The Angel was probably one of a series of carvings adorning the upper parts of the walls, which must also have been enriched by the elaborate stripwork which can be seen near the Angel itself. The high quality of the carving, and the elaboration of the plan, attest the importance of Deerhurst during the late 9th century.

Apart from St Mary's church, Deerhurst possesses a second important Anglo-Saxon monument in Odda's Chapel. The chapel is a few hundred yards away to the south-west, next to a farmhouse. Undiscovered until 1885, the chapel had been used as a barn and later a house.

The chapel was a two-cell structure of nave and chancel, presumably served by monks from the nearby monastery. Although later use has somewhat changed the appearance of the building, the nave walls are still visible externally, though the chancel is obscured by the adjoining medieval timber-framed farmhouse. The west end of the nave is of particular interest since apart from having fine long and short quoins, the walls themselves slope gently inwards towards the top, providing slight entasis. This effect, which was much used by Ancient Greek builders, corrects the optical illusion of concavity created by vertical walls.

Inside, the Saxon chancel arch has survived, as well as two double-splayed windows in the nave walls and a mutilated north door. The chapel is rare among Anglo-Saxon monuments in having two inscriptions associated with it. The first of these was found in 1675 in the nearby orchard. It is now in the Ashmolean Museum in Oxford, though a cast is preserved at the site. It reads: 'Earl Odda had this royal hall built and dedicated in honour of the Holy Trinity for the soul of his brother Aelfric which left the body in this place. Bishop Ealdred dedicated it the second of the Ides of April in the fourteenth year of the reign of Edward King of the English' (i.e. on 12 April 1056).

The Anglo-Saxon Chronicle mentions the death of Aelfric at Deerhurst, and that his body was buried at Pershore nearby. Odda, who was described as the 'kinsman' of King Edward (the Confessor) was an important royal official in south-west England for a time. He probably shared Edward's great piety, and the chapel was doubtless built as a thank-offering for his brother's life. The second stone, which is preserved inside the chapel, was found during the restoration of the building: 'This altar was dedicated in honour of the Holy Trinity.'

From all this we can see that Deerhurst, the place in the 'wood of the deer', has a fascinating history which still poses many problems. It is possible there was a Roman settlement here since one field in the parish was called 'Wikeham' in 1424, which incorporates the Old English 'wicham' which often refers to old Roman settlements and a number of Roman finds from the church excavations support this conclusion. Quite apart from all this, Deerhurst is a delightful place to visit, the more so because we can summon to mind the spirits of the Anglo-Saxon kings, lords and churchmen who knew this place a thousand years and more before us.

51

Daglingworth: The Church of Holy Cross, Gloucestershire

Map Reference: SO 994050 (metric map 163. 1-inch map 157)
Nearest Town: Cirencester
Location: A small village church in the Cotswolds, Holy Rood at Daglingworth is about one mile (1.6 km) to the west of the Roman road from Cirencester to Gloucester which is now the A417. The village is about 3 miles (5 km) north-west of Cirencester.

The church stands in pleasant Gloucestershire countryside which has proved resistant to unhappy change. Little is known of the early history of the place, but the great Roman road from Cirencester to Gloucester runs nearby, and a Roman inscription incorporated into the Anglo-Saxon fabric suggests that the good land of the area attracted settlers at an early date.

The nave of the church, in which all the Anglo-Saxon quoins survive, and the chancel rebuilt in 1845-50, provide a clear impression of the original building. Before entering the

The Crucifixion panel.

St Peter holds the key of Heaven in his right hand and a book in his left.

church, the small two-light window in the north wall of the 19th-century vestry should be seen. The openings are cut through a re-used Roman inscription tablet, and the Roman letters are still just visible on the surface. Also outside, high up in the east gable of the chancel, is a small square stone bearing a scene of the Crucifixion. Christ is shown simply clad in a knee-length skirt with a moustached and bearded face.

Upon entering the south porch, look above the Saxon door into the nave at the small sundial above. This is in its original position and is clearly marked with three crossed lines which separated the day into three-hour 'tides'. The bottom vertical stroke represented noon, the horizontal on the left marked 6 a.m., whilst that on the right marks 6 p.m. The extra line of the left hand side which lacks a cross marks 7.30 a.m., which was called *daeg mael* or 'day's marker' and indicated the beginning of morning tide. The hole for the gnomon is clearly visible at the centre of the dial. The door below is Anglo-Saxon, and has delicate 'wheat ear' motifs upon its imposts.

Inside the church, the chancel arch, though rebuilt in the 19th century, is original, and has retained its simple beaded imposts. In the walls of the nave and north aisle are three carved slabs similar in style to the one already noted in the east wall of the chancel; all may have been carved by the same man. Dispute has arisen over the date of the carvings, but it seems likely that they, like the church itself, are early 11th century.

One shows a fine Crucifixion scene, with Christ on an upward flaring cross. Longinus stands on the left with a spear and scourge, and Stephaton on the right with a sponge mounted on a reed which he proffers to our Lord, and what may be a pottery vessel in his right hand containing sour wine in which the sponge was dipped. The two supporting figures are smaller than Christ, doubtless to provide dramatic emphasis.

Another depicts St Peter dressed perhaps as a monk in a long cassock with a simple buckled belt. He holds the key of Heaven in his right hand, denoting his traditional office of heavenly gatekeeper, and a book in his left. The third panel shows Christ in Majesty seated upon a chair, the right hand is raised in blessing whilst the left holds a cross.

Some art historians have dismissed these carvings as being 'ill formed' or 'of little significance', but their very simplicity lends them strength. The Crucifixion in particular is a fine composition and whilst technically unrefined, the figure of Christ commands the attention. Daglingworth church with its simple sundial, doorway and carvings is a unique survival of rural Anglo-Saxon church design. In them we see reflected the simple devotion of their creators and they have a directness which cannot be denied.

52

Bibury: Beage's Church and Sculpture, Gloucestershire

The name 'Bibury' is of considerable interest since it can be traced back to a grant of land made by Bishop Wilfrith of Worcester to a certain Leppa and his daughter Beage in a document dating from 718-45. The lease was granted for the lives of Leppa and his daughter, and it seems likely that when Beage inherited the estate upon her father's death it became known as *Beaganbyrig*, meaning Beage's farmhouse.

This fine 10th-century tombstone was found in the churchyard in 1913.

Map Reference: SP 118065 (metric map 163. 1-inch map 157)
Nearest Town: Cirencester
Location: A popular Cotswold village, Bibury is between Cirencester and Burford on the A433 some 7 miles (11 km) north-east of Cirencester. The church is near the centre of the village.

This extended name did not last long, however, since a charter of 899 refers to 'Bibury', which represented a contraction of the earlier form. It has also been suggested that the element *byrig* used in conjunction with a feminine name might indicate a monastic site. Such an explanation is quite possible, and there are certain features of the site which suggest that it may have been the location of an important Anglo-Saxon foundation, perhaps a nunnery.

Although somewhat obscured by later additions, the Saxon nave and chancel are largely intact. Outside the church, single square-sectioned pilaster strips may be seen on the side walls of the chancel. The pilaster on the north side has a portion of late Saxon tombstone set upon its original base. The stone is decorated with intersecting circles and pellets within a scalloped zigzag border. The stone was dug up in the churchyard, and was set in its present position in 1913. The eastern quoins of the nave are also visible from the east side, the long and short quoins on the north side being better preserved. Moving round to the south side of the nave, a circular double-splayed Anglo-Saxon window can be seen beside the west end of the south aisle.

Inside the church, the first things to notice are the handsome grave slabs near the door. These are casts, the original pieces having been presented to the British Museum in 1913. Dating to the late 10th or 11th century, the stones show strong Scandinavian influence based on the Ringerike style. Four of these slabs have been found at Bibury, and the similarities of their decoration suggest that all were produced by the same school.

The Anglo-Saxon nave, which may have been as long as the present one, had its north and south walls pierced by arcades when the later aisles were added. The Saxon chancel arch was replaced in the 13th century, but the jambs and imposts which are decorated with carved foliage are original. Above the chancel arch are traces of a rood which was supported on the surviving square-sectioned string-course. The rood, which was probably similar to that at Langford in Oxfordshire, has gone, but traces of a figure of St Mary may be seen to the left. High up in the same wall are two blocked windows; these appear to be medieval in their present form but may replace earlier lights.

The interwoven bodies of these two splendid creatures show clearly how Scandinavian influence penetrated into south Mercia late in the 10th century.

The exteriors of the Anglo-Saxon nave walls may be seen from the side aisles above the later arcades. In the north aisle, three pilaster strips are visible above the eastern part of the arcade. A curious blocked round-headed window can be seen a little to the west; it is unusual because it seems to have a transom across it. The south wall is undistinguished apart from a plain string-course which probably marks the top of the Anglo-Saxon nave wall. From the nave, the interior of the circular window may be seen. There are holes drilled in the frame which probably supported a concentric wattle framing which served as a key for plasterwork round the inside of the opening. A similar arrangement may be seen at Avebury in the three surviving windows of the nave.

The church of St Mary is an interesting structure, and probably dates to the 11th century. The comparatively large size of the nave and chancel, together with their structural elaboration and the presence of the carved tombstones, which are unusual in the area, all suggest that the church was an important one. Perhaps this church did indeed serve a nunnery of which Beage was the first leader.

PART III

East Anglia

NORTHUMBRIA
EAST ANGLIA
53
HUMBERSIDE
54
55
Lincoln
56
LINCOLNSHIRE
57
Boston
Grantham
58
59
MERCIA
King's Lynn
60
61
Norwich
NORFOLK
62
63
64
CAMBRIDGESHIRE
65
67
66
Cambridge
SUFFOLK
68
Bedford
Ipswich
BEDFORDSHIRE
72
HERTFORDSHIRE
ESSEX
69
Colchester
Buckingham
BUCKINGHAMSHIRE
St. Albans
Chelmsford
71
70
0
10
20 Miles
73
WESSEX

Introduction

The area called 'East Anglia' in this book is more a reflection of physical geography than of Anglo-Saxon political boundaries. In the north of the area was the kingdom of Lindsey, with its capital at Lincoln. Further south, about the Wash, were a whole series of small tribal lands some of whose names, like the *Spaldingas* – the followers of Spalda – are commemorated in modern place names, in this case Spalding in south Lincolnshire. Southwards again, in Norfolk and Suffolk, we enter the territory of the historical kingdom of East Anglia proper. Essex had independent status during the 6th and early 7th centuries, but none of its kings appears to have been of more than local importance.

The primary areas of settlement in East Anglia were along the river valleys of the Lark, Nene, Ouse and Welland which led inland from the marsh and fenland along the east coast. This pattern is implied by the place names ending in 'ham', such as Elmham and Rendlesham, which have been associated with early Germanic mercenary settlements. These names predominate in the Ipswich area, in north and west Norfolk and in the Breckland. The 'ingas' names like the *Spaldingas* mentioned above, may represent a movement away from these earliest areas of settlement.

The Ipswich area was to become the focus of the East Anglian kingdom. This is supported by documentary evidence that a royal palace was located at Rendlesham, and by the discovery of the royal cemetery at Sutton Hoo nearby. The richly furnished ship burial found there indicates the substantial wealth at the disposal of the early kings, and as the smaller kingdoms became absorbed by those of more powerful rulers, so this wealth increased.

The Welsh monk Nennius writing in the late 8th century records Wenna as being the first king of the East Angles. It was later claimed that he was descended from the god Woden, as was common in early Germanic genealogies. The second ruler was Wuffa, and he gave his name to the East Anglian royal dynasty which was called the *Wuffingas* – the people of Wuffa. By the late 6th century the influence of East Anglia had reached as far north as the River Nene, and westwards to embrace most of southern England. Raedwald, who was probably the king commemorated by the great barrow at Sutton Hoo, thus had control over a large part of southern England at the height of his prestige early in the 7th century.

During the 7th century the power of Mercia was gathering and the impassable marshes and fenlands around the Wash, which had protected East Anglia from northern attack, were now insufficient to stem the Mercian advance. It was perhaps during this period that the Cambridgeshire Dykes were constructed in a vain attempt to reinforce the natural defences of the kingdom. The efforts of the East Anglian rulers were to no avail. Lindsey, the Washlands, Essex and finally East Anglia itself came under Mercian domination. By the end of the 7th century the affairs of East Anglia are so obscure that even the royal succession is not exactly known. We know of one 8th-century king called Aethelberht only because he was beheaded on the orders of King Offa of Mercia, and later canonized as a saint. Traditionally it is held that he died in the defence of his people from the overbearing retainers of his Mercian overlord, but there is no certain evidence of this.

East Anglia languished under Mercian rule until the overthrow of the Mercians by Egbert of Wessex in 825. It is then recorded that the king of East Anglia, who was in revolt against Mercia, asked Egbert for his protection, and shortly afterwards all Mercia and its dependencies were conquered by Egbert. The precise status of East Anglia at this time is uncertain, but the matter was shortly to become academic when the Danes occupied the area during the third quarter of the 9th century. We know that the Danes were well established in eastern England by the time of the Battle of Edington in 878, and under the terms of the treaty of Wedmore between Alfred and Guthrum in 886, the whole area was firmly part of the Danelaw. Lincoln became one of the 'Five Boroughs', and the Danes settled down to enjoy the fruits of conquest.

One of the most dramatic illustrations of the extent of the Danish settlement is provided by the evidence of place names. There are so many villages with names ending in 'by', 'thorpe' and other Scandinavian elements that we must imagine that the initial settlement by the Danish army was quickly followed by large-scale immigration from Denmark itself. In Lincolnshire, Norfolk and Suffolk, in particular, a map of villages with Danish names suggests a severe rash of chicken pox!

The Danes didn't have it all their own way, and by 924 the doughty kings of Wessex had subdued the whole area of the Danelaw. The Danish settlers stayed, of course, but rather than being a self-governing entity they were loyal to the House of Wessex; England was united. From the time of the reconquest of the Danelaw, the fortunes of East Anglia largely followed those of the nation as a whole, though it must be said that when in the late

and has a man's head cut into a stone above it. This slab may originally have been a rood like that at Langford in Oxfordshire, but here the lower parts may have been carved in plaster rather than stone. Standing under the tower, we can imagine the original appearance fairly easily, with a small chancel to the east, probably not much larger than the western annexe, and a higher ceiling above our heads. The place would have been much lighter, with the western annexe windows unblocked and light coming through the tower windows above. Although small, St Peter's retains much of its Anglo-Saxon detail, and it will be fascinating to learn more of this exceptional structure when the present investigation is completed.

The tower from the south. The later upper stage can be distinguished from the 10th-century work below. The small round-headed window in the western annexe to the left is original.

54

Rothwell: St Mary Magdalene, Lincolnshire

Rothwell church has a splendid example of a 'Lincolnshire' bell tower. These western towers are relatively more numerous in Lincolnshire than elsewhere, and are distinguished by their simple vertical rubble walls without batter and stepped stages. They may be either square or rectangular in plan, but they seldom exceed ten or eleven feet (3 metres) along their interior axes. The overall impression is one of grace and elegance, and they provide pleasing examples of the skills of the late Saxon builders.

The village itself is a quiet place set in a deep valley of the Wolds. The church stands a little apart from the houses on the edge of rolling parkland. Built of mellow brownish ironstone, the tower has two external stages separated by a square-sectioned string-course, and rests on

Map Reference: TF 149993 (metric map 113. 1-inch map 104/5)
Nearest Town: Market Rasen/Grimsby
Location: Rothwell is in the Lincolnshire Wolds about 2 miles (3 km) south of Caistor. From Caistor, which is on the A46 between Market Rasen and Grimsby, take the minor road signposted to Rothwell. The church is beautifully situated beside open parkland on the edge of this pleasant village.

Right: *The tower from the south-west. The impression is one of simplicity and restraint, even the tops of the belfry windows have well-mannered cushion capitals.*

Below: *Apart from the rather barbarous modern door, the western entrance must look largely as it did upon the day it was built.*

a bold plinth of two chamfered orders. The parapet is a medieval addition. There are small round-headed windows in the lower stages, and the belfry is lit by paired lights with cylindrical midwall shafts resting on conical bases. The original west doorway is intact, and has a square head with a plain tympanum above outlined in stripwork. The south-west angle of the nave has long and short quoins, whilst the north-western quoin is traceable as a straight joint against the later west wall of the north aisle.

Inside, the originally aisleless nave has been cut through by Norman arches to north and south. The Saxon tower arch has a simple round head of a single square order, the imposts continue as a string-course across the west wall. Little imagination is required to evoke the early interior: St Mary Magdalene is a remarkably unspoilt late Anglo-Saxon church which is satisfying for its very simplicity alone.

55

Stow: 'The Mother Church of Lindsey', Lincolnshire

The prodigious church of St Mary at Stow, traditionally the mother church of Lindsey, is out of all proportion to the little village in which it stands. When during the 19th century the Reverend George Atkinson, the vicar of Stow, undertook restoration of the church, he encountered strong opposition from his parishioners. An action was commenced in the Court of Queen's Bench, and acts of vandalism were committed inside the church itself. This response to the vicar's restoring zeal 'brought the parish into no very creditable notoriety' in the words of the Bishop of Lincoln. The smoke of battle has now dispersed and the Reverend Atkinson lies peacefully in the churchyard. We must thank him for his doughty defence of this

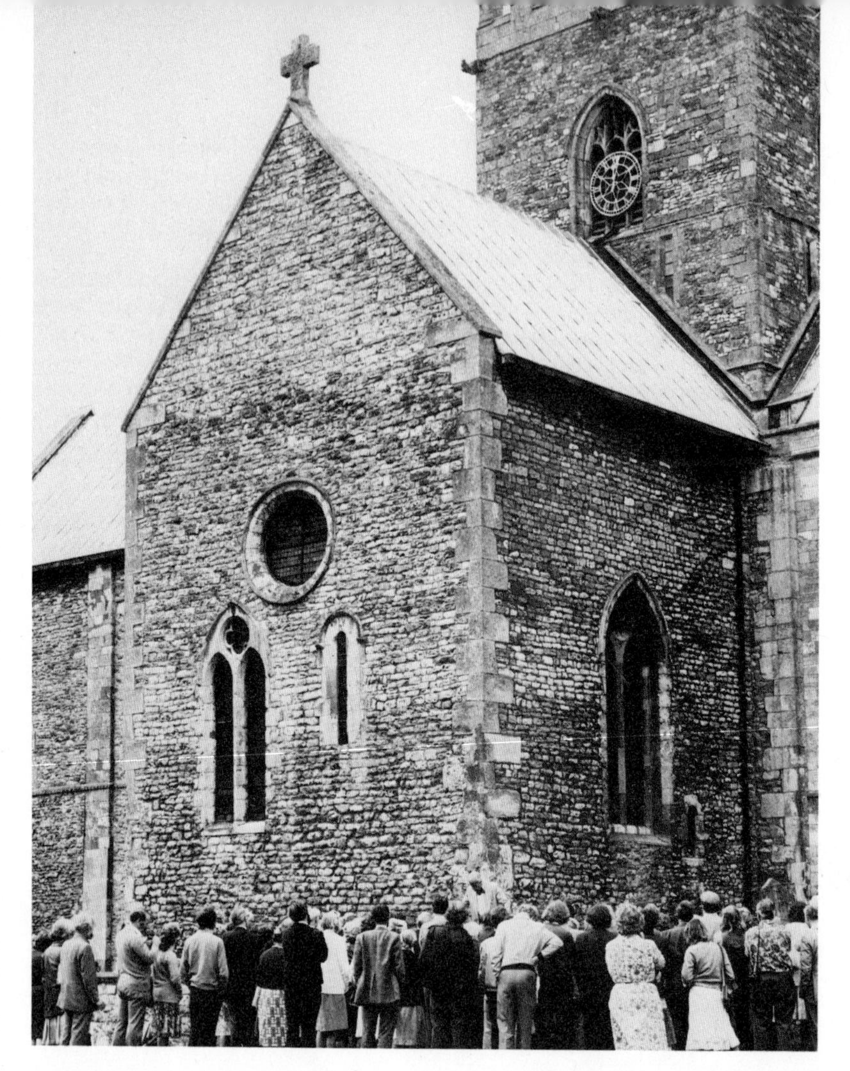

The south transept from the south-west. These people were attending a seminar on the early history of Stow church in 1979. They are listening to Dr H. M. Taylor, who is the figure in a bow tie standing in front of the south-west angle of the transept. This is but one of many such seminars which Dr Taylor has addressed on Anglo-Saxon churches, and his scholarship and erudition mark him out as the [cut off] of Anglo-Saxon architectural studies. Notice h[cut off] the lower quoins are darker and less neatly form[cut off] than those above; they are supposed by some to [cut off] been damaged during a Danish raid on the site [cut off] 870.

great monument to the early kingdom of Lindsey.

The word 'stow' generally means a holy place or a resting place; here it traditionally refers to a place where the saintly Queen Etheldreda rested during her flight from her husband Ecgfrith, king of Northumbria. The Venerable Bede tells us that she was married to Ecgfrith when he was but a boy, and that she preserved her virginity for twelve years. She left Northumbria when her husband wished to consummate the marriage and later went south to Ely where she founded an important monastery.

During her stay at Stow, miraculous happenings took place, the most famous of which concerned the saint's ash stick. Staying one night at Stow, she placed her walking stick in the ground at her head. When she awoke in the morning, it had grown into a great ash tree, reputedly the largest in the kingdom. This event so impressed her husband that he founded a church here in 674, and it was known first as St Etheldreda Stow, and later still as St Mary Stow.

Little is known of Ecgfrith's foundation; the Danes destroyed a church here in 870 which was probably his. Early in the 11th century, Eadnoth I, Bishop of Dorchester, founded a college of canons here. The college was evidently a successful foundation, for in 1055 Leofric, Earl of Mercia, and the Lady Godiva his wife, of Coventry fame, gave land to the church for the maintenance of its priests and to ensure the continuance of divine services. One wonders what their reaction would be if they knew that divine service is continuing 900 years after their pious gift.

The Anglo-Saxon work at Stow is confined to the great central crossing, which may originally have been surmounted by a tower, and to the transepts. Nave and chancel are Norman, but their majestic scale doubtless reflects that of the earlier work. The walls of the transept rest on their original plinths, and the Anglo-Saxon quoins with their massive side alternate stones are easily distinguishable from the smaller Norman work above. About nine feet (2.7 metres) above the ground, both the crossing and transept quoins undergo a change. Below they are cracked and burnt, and it appears that the building may have been restored after a fire. Note the interesting window in the south wall of the south transept, which apart from its pleasing palmette decoration also has dowel holes for shutters in its outer face. An original window also survives on the north side of the north transept, and a

The early doorway in the north transept.

Map Reference: SK 882819 (metric map 121. 1-inch map 104)
Nearest Town: Lincoln
Location: Stow is north-west of Lincoln. From the city take the A57 Worksop road; just before Saxilby take the B1241 north; Stow is 4½ miles (7 km) up this road. The huge church dominates the village.

further one to the west.

Internally, the church is dominated by the mighty crossing arches which are the tallest and widest to survive in any Anglo-Saxon cruciform church. The work is awesome in its scale; the arches are formed of great moulded voussoirs resting on simple chamfered imposts. The great piers, which are over fourteen feet (4.3 metres) apart, are somewhat obscured by the later medieval work, but their rectangular and half-round pilasters can still be seen. Only the outer face of the western arch has any decoration, and this is limited to the outer hood moulding which has simple debased palmettes or 'jew's harp' ornament. In the west wall of the north transept is an Anglo-Saxon doorway; there was a balancing door to the east. This arrangement may have been repeated in the south transept, since traces of a similar west door have been noted there. Such auxilliary entrances may have opened into side chapels, but the configuration is somewhat unusual here.

Much argument has raged about the dating of the various parts of Stow church, and the architectural evidence is very complex. Some have claimed that because the lower parts of the transept and crossing show fire damage, they must date from before the Danish raid in 870. Such things are notoriously difficult to prove, and fires can happen at any time. If these lower parts were indeed some part of Ecgfrith's church, it must have been a very large and advanced 7th-century structure. The upper parts are certainly of 11th-century date, and reflect the wealth and prestige of the college of canons to which Leofric and Godiva made their gift. Stow church is a fine monument to Anglo-Saxon Christendom, and it has been rightly hailed as one of the greatest surviving Anglo-Saxon churches.

56

Lincoln: St Mary-le-Wigford and St Peter-at-Gowts, Lincolnshire

The Venerable Bede, writing in the 8th century, tells us that St Paulinus, Bishop of York, went south to the kingdom of Lindsey in order to convert the inhabitants. He went first to Lincoln itself, site of a great Roman city, which suggests that the place was the capital of the kingdom. His first convert was Blecca, who was probably the chief magistrate or leader of the town council. Having converted Blecca and his household, Paulinus then: 'built a stone church of remarkable workmanship; its roof has now fallen either through long neglect or by the hand of the enemy, but its walls are still standing and every year miracles of healing are performed in the place, for the benefit of those who seek them in faith.'

The traditional site of the church which Paulinus built in 628 was St Paul's-in-the-Bail, and when redevelopment threatened in 1978, the archaeologists set to work. They found the outline of a simple nave and apsidal chancel which might well be Paulinus' church. It was built upon the worn surface of the Roman forum courtyard, and a beautiful bronze bowl from a grave inside the structure dates to the 7th century. Nothing positively links the structure with Paulinus, but it seems likely that this early stone church in the very centre of the city is indeed the very place where the 'miracles of healing' were performed.

But the visitor to Lincoln will see nothing of this site: it is buried beneath a modern building, and plans and photographs in the Museum must suffice. Instead visitors must console themselves with two fine late Saxon church towers. They are unusual since they stand less than half a mile apart along the main southern access road to the old city. The churches were not inside the city itself, but served the suburb of Wigford, which stretched

Map Reference: **St Mary-le-Wigford** SK 974708
St Peter-at-Gowts SK 973703
St Benedict's SK 975711
(metric map 121. 1-inch map 113)
Location: The easiest way to find St Mary-le-Wigford is to follow the signs to the station. The church stands in the angle between the main railway line and the High Street (A15 Sleaford road) by a level crossing.

About half a mile (0.8 km) further down High Street, the old Roman Ermine Street, St Peter-at-Gowts stands on the left hand side.

St Benedict's stands at the north end of the High Street, on the west side close to the Brayford Pool behind the war memorial gardens.

The western tower of St Mary-le-Wigford. The dedication slab with its triangular-shaped head may just be seen to the right of the west door behind the fine 15th-century conduit in the foreground.

below the walled area. This suburb grew up during late Saxon times, and its name incorporates the element 'wik' which indicates that it was the 'street of the traders'. These two churches evidently provided a focus for the spiritual life of this thriving industrial community, and they are interesting monuments to Lincoln's late Saxon prosperity.

The first of these, nearer the city, is St Mary-le-Wigford, which name neatly records its original associations. Beside the head of the west door, a stone built into the fabric records that: 'Eirtig had me built and endowed to the glory of Christ and Mary.'

The stone is of interest apart from the inscription since it is a re-used Roman tombstone, and the lower part retains a Latin memorial inscription. The tower is of rubblework with fine ashlar side alternate quoins. The belfry stage is lit by tall double lights with elegant mid-wall shafts topped by simple cushion capitals.

The western doorway has been somewhat mangled by later restoration, and all the decorative details are suspect, but the tall narrow form and chamfered imposts proclaim its Anglo-Saxon pedigree. Before entering the church, which is now a 'church centre', note the quoins at the angles of the west nave wall which show that it too is Saxon. Inside, the large tower arch bears chequer ornament similar to that on the west door. Although the exterior of the west door has been recut, the worn condition of the internal ornament suggests that it is original. High above the tower arch is a round-headed doorway, one stone of which has a curious beast's head cut into it, as well as interlacing ornament. These details will

St Peter-at-Gowts. The small decorated slab is just visible above the head of the lower window; it perhaps depicts St Peter, the patron saint.

only be appreciated by the well-equipped visitor, however, since a pair of field glasses is required to see them well!

The second church, St Peter-at-Gowts, has a tall simple tower of 'Lincolnshire' type like St Mary's. Its walling and quoining are closely similar to its neighbour, though the capitals of the belfry mid-wall shafts are more elaborate. There is no dedication slab here, but in compensation there is a weathered carved slab above the west belfry light which bears a carving either of Christ in Majesty or of St Peter, since the figure appears to hold a key in his right hand, as at Daglingworth in Gloucestershire; a figure of St Peter would also fit the dedication. It may be that this church is slightly the later of the two, since St Mary's is both closer to the city and also claims to serve Wigford by its title, suggesting primacy. Moreover, the capitals of St Peter's are of a somewhat later character.

Before leaving Lincoln, the visitor should see the little church of St Benedict which has a rebuilt Saxon tower. The church stands near the Brayford Pool which was a Roman harbour and doubtless saw much traffic in Anglo-Saxon times. Finally, the cathedral, which is Lincoln's undoubted glory, retains a link with the Anglo-Saxon past. Although the magnificent fabric is all of Norman and later date, there is a great frieze across the west front which bears scenes from the life of St Guthlac, the monk of Repton in Derbyshire, who was sorely tried by devils in the fenny lands of south Lincolnshire where he lived his solitary life in praise of God.

57

Hough-on-the-Hill: All Saints Church and Loveden Hill, Lincolnshire

In the parish of Hough, at a site called Loveden Hill, was a very large pagan Anglo-Saxon cemetery. The site was totally excavated by the authors in advance of destruction by deep ploughing, but the grandeur of the setting can still be appreciated by the visitor. Perched high on a hill-top, the name of which means 'Hill of the Loved Ones', we can imagine sombre mourners toiling up the hill from the valley below bearing the last remnants of the deceased. Hills were often chosen as cemetery sites by the Saxons, probably to enable the dead to watch over the activities of the living. But Loveden also illustrates a further aspect of this belief; it is virtually surrounded by minor streams, and it was believed that the souls of the dead could not pass over running water. Hence, the dead could oversee the living, but could not interfere with them.

The cemetery was in use from the time of the earliest Saxon settlement during the early 5th century to the conversion to Christianity in 700 or thereabouts. It contained over 2,000 burials, mostly cremations which had been placed in pottery urns. Other burials were unburnt, and were simply placed in shallow graves marked by piles of stones. Since the people were pagan they were often buried with elements of their worldly wealth about them. Gravegoods recovered have included glass vessels, ivory bangles, amber beads, bronze bowls, glass beads, bone combs, iron knives, bone counters and much else besides. Loveden Hill was plainly an important cemetery which served a wide area. The discovery of a carved whetstone in the parish rather like the 'sceptre' from the king's barrow at Sutton Hoo shows that Hough may have been an early royal centre.

The church of All Saints in Hough village

Hough-on-the-Hill
Map Reference: SK 923463 (metric map 130. 1-inch map 113)
Nearest Town: Grantham
Location: Perched on the Lincoln Edge, Hough is reached by minor roads from the A607 Grantham to Lincoln road. At Barkston, 4 miles (6.5 km) north of Grantham, take the minor road to the north on the northern edge of the village; it is signposted to Hough. The church is at the centre of the village.

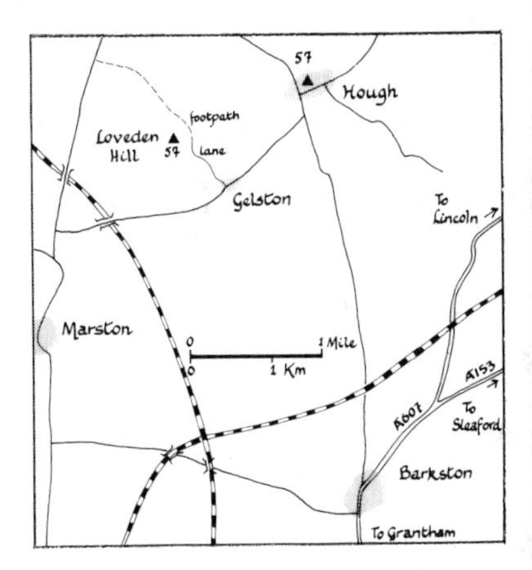

Loveden Hill
Map Reference: SK 908458
Location: To reach Loveden Hill from Hough church, go back to the cross roads by the Brownlow Arms, turn left and then first right to Gelston. In this hamlet park your vehicle and proceed on foot along the lane which leads downhill north-west from the green. Loveden Hill is the eminence to the left of the track, crowned by a plantation. The pagan cemetery was located on the flattish ground on the near side of the plantation. The hill-top site is typical of pagan cemeteries since the dead were believed to watch over the activities of the living.

A warrior burial from the Loveden cemetery. The iron boss of the warrior's shield lies beside his head, and it is likely that the wooden shield board, which has since rotted away, acted as a pillow. The corpse, which was that of a man of about forty-five years of age, had the feet cut off before burial. They were placed behind his legs, where the metatarsals may still be seen. The reason for this mutilation is uncertain, but it is possible that it was done to prevent his spirit walking.

Most of the pottery cremation urns had been crushed by the weight of earth above them, as in this example. Apart from ashes, the pots contained a wide variety of burnt material which accompanied the corpse on the funeral pyre.

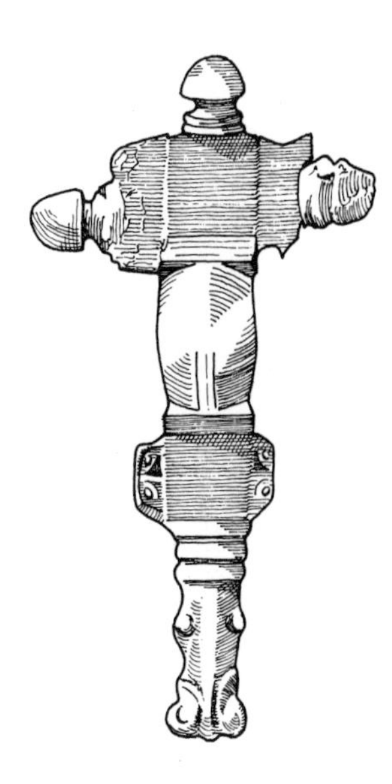

This handsome bronze brooch with its foot in the style of a horse's head came from one of the female graves excavated by the authors in 1972.

Right: *The 10th-century stair turret at Hough church. Each of the small windows is made to a different design.*

provides a contrast to the pagan cemetery at Loveden. Although no part of the present church dates back to the 8th century, we may be fairly certain that a church was built here shortly after the area had been converted to Christianity. The focus of religious attention moved away from Loveden Hill to the new church in the village, and pagan burials ceased. But old habits die hard; Loveden Hill still retained some importance in the local community since we know that the moot or local council met on the hill-top, and that the Wapentake, Church of England Rural Diocese and even the local telephone exchange are all

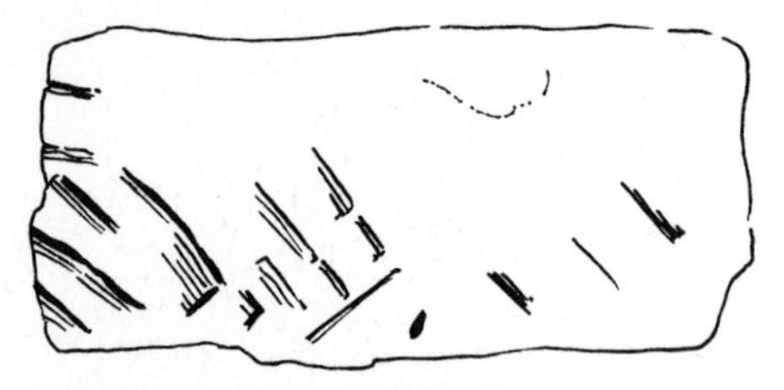

A building stone near the base of the tower which still shows the adze marks made on it by the Saxon builders.

Details of two windows in the stair turret.

named after the pagan site of Loveden rather than the modern village of Hough-on-the Hill!

The interest of Hough church is immediately apparent on approaching it along the path beside the rectory. The tower and stair turret bear unmistakable signs of Saxon work, the turret in particular with its arched, diamond and porthole-shaped windows set between huge pillow-like stones is a strange sight. The three lower courses of the 10th-century tower have good long and short quoins and square string-courses. Above is a 15th-century belfry, the stone of which is smoother and more regular than the Saxon work below. The early nave has almost disappeared under later work, but the north-east angle is still visible outside.

58

Edenham: St Michael's Church and Cross, Lincolnshire

Map Reference: TF 062218 (metric map 130. 1-inch map 123)
Nearest Town: Bourne
Location: The small village of Edenham is 2½ miles (4 km) north-west of Bourne on the A151.

Edenham lies in pleasant country which is gently broken into hill and dale, wooded by a remnant of the old Kesteven Forest, and watered by the Eden stream twisting southward to join the River Glen. The church stands on a raised site in the centre of the village, and contains interesting remains of the 9th century, before the Danish invasion of the county. The first of these is a portion of cross-shaft, somewhat battered, but bearing images of St John and what might be a seated representation of the Virgin Mary. Above her head are complicated interlacing motifs, the leaf-shaped terminals of which bear a close resemblance to the other Saxon carving in the church.

The major remains at Edenham are visible in the south aisle, where on the south face of the nave wall, above the Early English arcade, elements of an interesting decorative scheme are preserved. These consist of a plain square-sectioned string-course with two carved roundels set above it. This arrangement is

The western roundel.

highly unusual and if, as is likely, it was carried right round the church, the effect must have been very rich. Each roundel is approximately two feet (61 cm) in diameter and stands proud of the wall. They contain relief patterns of stems and leaves within a simply moulded border. The leaves on the western roundel closely resemble those on the cross-shaft, and it seems probable that all shared a common origin.

59

Creeton Crosses, Lincolnshire

This piece of Anglo-Saxon cross-shaft provides a rare instance of a monument recut in the Norman period. Originally, the cross was decorated on all sides with interlace panels, one of which is illustrated here. Later, probably in the 12th century, one of the broad faces was cut back, and the characteristic Norman 'star' pattern added. There is a marked contrast between the two, the later work having a sharper and more regular appearance.

There is another, smaller decorated cross fragment in the north-west corner of the churchyard re-used as a grave marker.

Photograph of the south face of the stone. The later Norman work is on the west side of the shaft. Note how the border of the design is narrower on the left-hand side, showing that the stone was cut back to a new lower face before the new design was added.

Map Reference: TF 014199 (metric map 130. 1-inch map 123)
Nearest Town: Bourne
Location: Creeton is just off the B1176 between Stamford and Corby Glen, 8 miles (13 km) north of Stamford. Turn into the village and, as parking is restricted by the church, park by the green and walk.

Drawing of the interlace decoration. The flaccid interlace on the Anglo-Saxon parts of the shaft indicates that it is late work, perhaps of the 11th century.

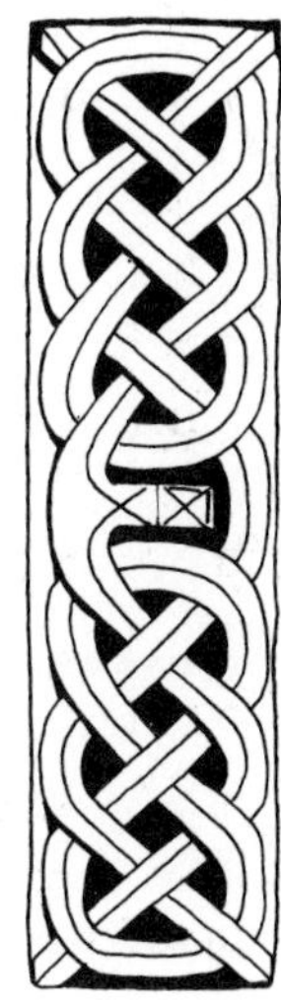

60
North Elmham Cathedral Church, Norfolk

The Venerable Bede tells us in his *History* that after the Synod of Hertford in 673, Bishop Bisi of the East Angles fell ill and that two bishops called Aecci and Badwin were consecrated in his place, and that 'from then until the present day this province has had two bishops'.

Much controversy has surrounded the question of the locations of the two bishopseats, but it is now generally accepted that Bisi's seat, which was called 'Dommoc' by Bede, was at Dunwich, whilst the second, perhaps newly created for Bishop Badwin, was at North Elmham. Since Dommoc was located in Suffolk, the new church at Elmham was doubtless intended as a focus for the religious life of Norfolk. Later, after the Danish raids, Elmham was to become the principal church of East Anglia when the province was united under a single bishop.

The Saxon cathedral lies within a later moated enclosure, and owes its survival to its subsequent use as a medieval manor house. Since nothing of the present structure appears to pre-date the early 10th century, it must be

Map Reference: TF 988217 (metric map 132. 1-inch map 125)
Nearest Town: East Dereham
Location: North Elmham lies 5 miles (8 km) north of East Dereham and is reached by the B1110. The site is an ancient monument in the care of the Department of the Environment, and is well signposted. It is open during standard hours, and there is a small entrance charge. Guidebooks and postcards are on sale.

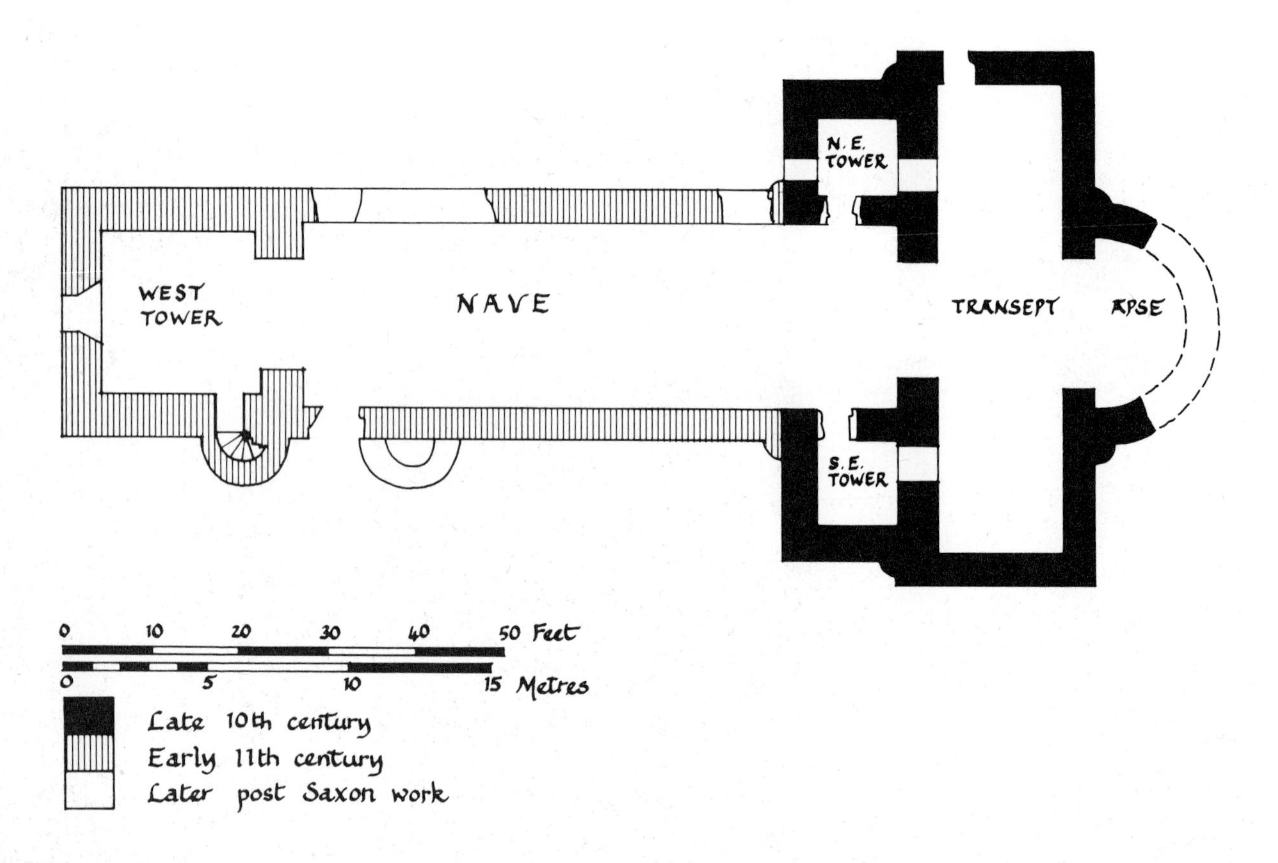

presumed that the earliest church lay elsewhere on the site. Excavations have revealed the presence of earlier timber phases below the present structure, but none of these belongs to a period as early as the 7th century. This is a matter of some importance, since the failure to find early evidence on the site means that the difficult question of the site of the pre-Danish cathedral, which could perhaps have been at South Elmham, is not resolved.

This comparatively small church, only a little over 100 feet (30 metres) in length, consists of an aisleless nave with a 'T'-shaped transept and an eastern apse. Originally there were only two small towers in the angles between the transept and nave, but a more substantial west tower was added in the 11th century. The flint walls have generally been robbed of any freestone work, but at the east end the plinth is adorned with quarter shafts in some of the angles.

Excavations near the parish church at the north end of the village have revealed a fascinating series of timber buildings dating from both before and after the Danish raids of the 9th century. Large halls and smaller huts, together with boundary ditches, fences and an impressive well demonstrate the importance of the early settlement.

View across the east end of the cathedral church. The foundations of the apse are marked in the foreground, whilst in the background may be seen the grassy defences of the castle which was built here after the see was transferred to Thetford and thence to Norwich after the Conquest.

61

Great Dunham: St Andrew's Church, Norfolk

Map Reference: TF 873147 (metric map 132. 1-inch map 125)
Nearest Town: Swaffham
Location: Great Dunham can be reached by minor roads from the A47 between Swaffham and East Dereham. About 4 miles (6.5 km) east of Swaffham take the road north to Little Dunham, and thence to Great Dunham itself.

The little church of St Andrew belongs to the very end of the Anglo-Saxon period, and may even be post-Conquest. Dunham was presumably the centre of two Anglo-Saxon manors, since, as at Bywell in Northumberland, there were originally two churches here, the other being dedicated to St Mary. St Andrew's is a remarkably perfect Anglo-Saxon church, intact apart from a later chancel and south porch. The scar of the early chancel roof can be seen on the east wall of the tower, cresting about six feet (1.8 metres) above the present ridge.

The original entrance to the church was through the now blocked triangular-headed west doorway. This opening is most curious, and now has an 18th-century escutcheon set into its recut head. The exterior of the tower is very fine, with knobbly flints and honey-coloured mortar. It has neat long and short quoins, their narrow stones reflecting the paucity of local freestone. The belfry lights, with their tall, narrow mid-wall shafts and capitals, demonstrate the late Saxon date of the structure. Roman tiles may be seen above the blocked south window of the nave and the lowest south tower window.

Internally the church is tall and light and the nave is dominated by the two great tower arches decorated with diamond and cable work. The most notable feature is the Anglo-Saxon arcading on the north and south walls. Enough remains to convey an impression of the original appearance. The Barnack stone capitals of the arcades are decorated with simple chevrons, diamonds and rolled mouldings; the heads and bases of the arches are formed of Roman bricks which are similar to those visible outside. All in all, St Andrew's church is a pleasing and stimulating place to visit.

The church from the south-east. Note the fine long and short quoins on the tower, and the scar of the early chancel roof above the present roof ridge.

62

Haddiscoe Thorpe: St Matthias Church, Norfolk

The two Haddiscoes together make an interesting visit; this tower is similar in some respects to that at Haddiscoe, but there are also important differences. Whereas Haddiscoe tower is perhaps all of the late Saxon period, the belfry stage at Haddiscoe Thorpe is certainly of Norman date. Here, therefore, we may feel fairly confident in describing the lower portion of the tower as Saxon.

Despite the loss of its topmost stage, the tower has several features of interest. There are three Anglo-Saxon storeys separated from the top stage by a chamfered off-set of dressed stones. Rather than being truly circular, the tower is slightly faceted, particularly on the south side; this impression is heightened by the shallow pilasters of the third stage. There is no doorway on the ground floor, and the west window is post-Saxon. The second stage has three small original windows, and the south and west windows have crudely carved animal heads above them. Apart from the ten pilaster strips, the third stage has four windows, and above is the Norman belfry.

The west wall of the nave is earlier than the tower, since the face of the wall is carried on inside the lower stages. This means that the tower was built against an existing wall, which could only have happened if the wall was standing before the tower was constructed. Further evidence of this sequence is provided by the circular window high up in the west wall of the nave. This must originally have opened to the sky, but it was blocked off when the tower was added. As the tower is probably late Saxon rather than Saxo-Norman, in view of the added belfry stage, it seems likely that the nave belongs to the early 11th century.

The topmost belfry stage is a Norman addition, but all below is Saxon work. The shallow pilasters on the third stage are most unusual; note the blocked round-headed window in the same stage.

Map Reference: TM 436981 (metric map 134. 1-inch map 137)
Nearest Town: Beccles
Location: Thorpe is about three-quarters of a mile (1.2 km) north of Haddiscoe, close to the Thorpe and Haddiscoe marshes. It can be reached by a minor road running north-west from Haddiscoe.

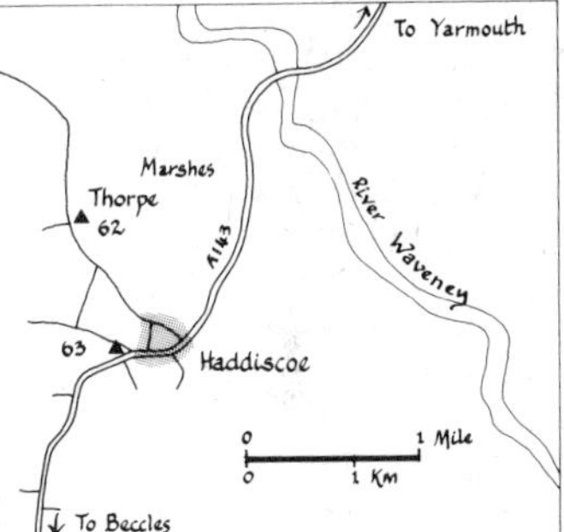

63

Haddiscoe: An East Anglian Round Tower, Norfolk

The circular tower of St Mary's church is a good example of an East Anglian round tower. These distinctive towers vastly predominate in Norfolk, where there are 129, and in Suffolk where there are forty-one. Occasional examples are known elsewhere, but they are basically a phenomenon of the two eastern counties. Perhaps the most important reason for the shape of these towers is not any aesthetic predilection but quite simply a dearth of good building stone.

That stone was transported around Anglo-Saxon England is evident from the pieces of Barnack (Cambridgeshire) stone built into distant churches, such as St Andrew's at Great Dunham in Norfolk, but this was plainly an expensive business. In the area of the round towers, flints from the chalk and beach pebbles were the available materials, and the round towers with their absence of quoins and other features requiring good freestone were the answering design.

St Mary's church, which lies on a hill above a tributary of the River Waveney, is a classical flint-built church with a round western tower. Only the tower is of our period and, in common with many such towers, it is impossible to be more accurate than to say 'late Saxon'. Some at least of these flint towers are fairly certainly of Norman date, and others have been claimed as being even later. Haddiscoe tower is of four stages separated by string-courses; it is surmounted by a medieval chequerwork parapet. The ground floor has no doorway and only one small window; the middle stages are each lit by three small round-headed windows. The uppermost belfry stage has four double windows with triangular heads and cylindrical mid-wall shafts. The shafts have cubical scalloped capitals; angle shafts in the jambs are outlined by billeted stripwork of very late character.

The nave of the church, which has tall, thin walls, might also be of Anglo-Saxon date. There is no doubt about the tower arch which is tall, narrow and typically Anglo-Saxon with a round head and single square order.

Above the blocked Norman north doorway of the nave is a curious figure carved in low

Map Reference: TM 439969 (metric map 134. 1-inch map 137)
Nearest Town: Beccles
Location: From Beccles take the A146 Norwich road, and in about 1½ miles (2.5 km) take the A143 east towards Yarmouth. Haddiscoe is 4 miles (6.5 km) along this road, just where it dips into the Waveney Valley.

This picture shows the elevated position of Haddiscoe church, which overlooks a tributary of the Waveney. The chequerwork parapet is 15th century, but all the work below, including the handsome triangular-headed windows, is late Saxon.

relief which is shown seated and clad in elaborate vestments, the hands holding sceptres or perhaps keys. This may be Anglo-Saxon since a dove or hand of God is dimly visible above the figure's head, rather like the one in the Crucifixion at Newent in Gloucestershire. This doorway, indeed the whole church, speaks eloquently of the overlap between the Anglo-Saxon and Norman styles.

64

South Elmham: Earthwork Enclosure with a Ruined Church, Suffolk

Standing in a mysterious and overgrown earthwork enclosure, the ruined church at South Elmham has been the subject of much controversy over many years. It has been claimed as one of the two Anglo-Saxon bishop-seats in the kingdom of East Anglia; the earlier being at a place called 'Dommoc' which the Venerable Bede mentions. This was for long thought to be at Dunwich on the Suffolk coast, but recently it has been argued that it lay at Walton Castle near Felixstowe. Early records mention only the Bishop of Elmham, and from the mid-9th century, documents definitely refer to North rather than to South Elmham as being the site of the cathedral. But as no pre-10th century remains have been found at North Elmham, some still incline to the view that this was the original site, and that only later was it removed to North Elmham. Certainly the plan of the building, with its simple

Map Reference: TM 309826 (metric map 156. 1-inch map 137)
Nearest Town: Bungay
Nearest Village: St Cross South Elmham
Location: Many an enthusiast has given up trying to find this site, roaming disconsolately about the nine parishes all with South Elmham names! One is not helped by the fact that the site is somewhat remote and screened by trees. We found this the easiest route; take the A143 signposted to Diss from Bungay; about 4 miles (6.5 km) from Bungay take the B1062 on the left, signposted to Homersfield. Follow the Homersfield sign at first right and then into the village following the sign to the South Elmhams. Past the church on the left take the road to St Cross; in that village, take the second right turn with a signpost to St James (this is a V-fork in the road). About three-quarters of a mile (1.2 km) along this road, look out for farm buildings on the right which you can see on the horizon beyond a hedge. Pull up off the road and follow the hedge-lined footpath. At the stream, follow the footpath to the left alongside the stream. The moated enclosure in which the site lies will be seen beyond the second field.

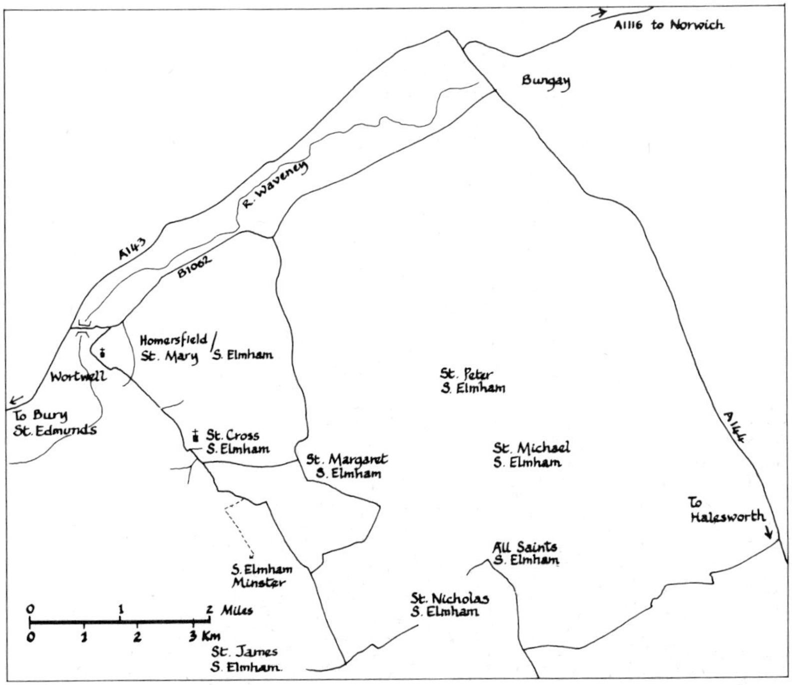

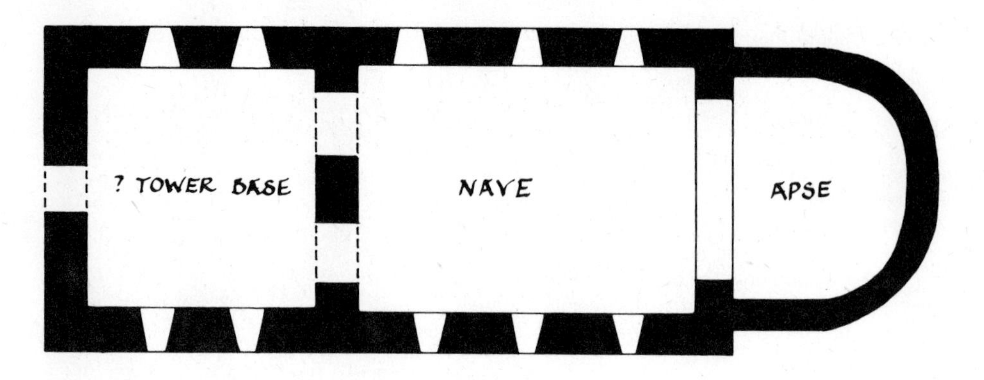

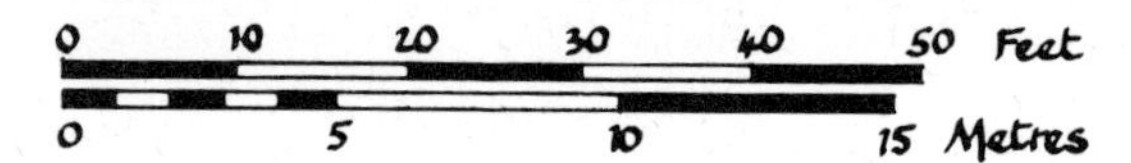

Plan of the Church.

eastern apse, rectangular nave and what has been interpreted as a late Saxon western tower base, suggests the structure is early, and an early 9th-century date had been proposed. In 1963-4, excavations were undertaken which resolved some of the problems. When the south-east angle of the nave was investigated, a fragment of carved tombstone was found built into the structure, which could hardly be earlier than the 9th century. As the stone was somewhat weathered, it is unlikely that it was re-used before the 10th century. This discovery has rather upset the advocates of the primacy of South Elmham, but difficulties remain since the 9th-century tombstone might suggest the existence of an earlier church on the site.

Although ruined, the church at Elmham is a fascinating place to visit. The walls are built of uncut flint, and stand to a maximum height of 15 feet (4.5 metres) at the west end of the nave. Apart from the western doorway and single-splayed windows, there are curious triangular holes in the walls which probably supported scaffolding during construction. The presence of the holes on the insides of the walls has led to suggestions that the church was never finished, but it is more likely that they were

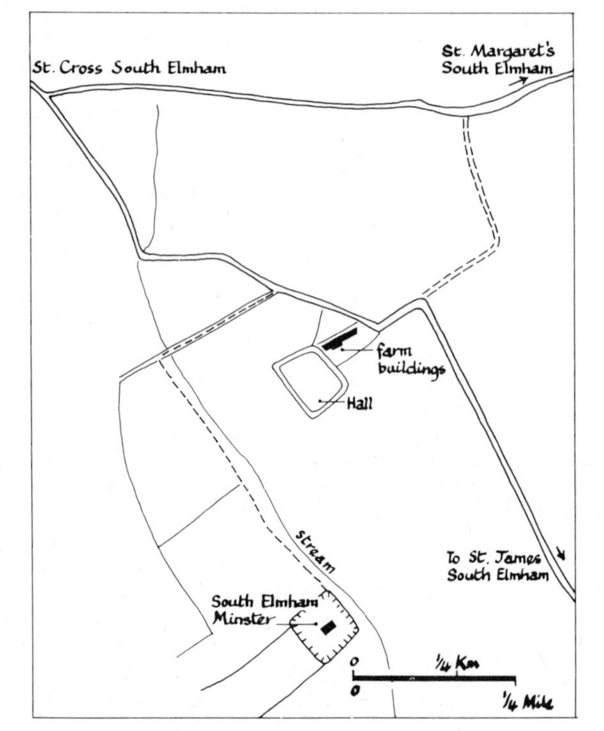

originally filled with loose rubble which has since fallen out.

The enclosure in which the church stands may be of Roman date, and sherds of Romano-British pottery have been found within it. Advocates of the early origins of South Elmham have suggested that the bank and ditch may have been created as a defence against the Danes, or alternatively that the church may have been sited within an old enclosure to provide protection from the same enemy. Excavation alone can resolve these difficulties, and it is to be hoped that more work will take place in due course. Many questions remain unanswered, including one 19th-century description of the site which mentions 'urns filled with burnt bones and ashes'. It is therefore possible that there was a pagan Saxon cemetery here before the church was founded. Mysterious Elmham in its green wood will continue to be the subject of controversy for many years yet.

65

West Stow: Reconstructed Timber Houses, Suffolk

Here at West Stow a remarkable discovery was made. On a low sandy ridge by the River Lark, on the edge of the Breckland, a whole village was excavated which dated back to the very earliest days of the Anglo-Saxon settlement of East Anglia. Traces of eighty timber buildings were found, which spanned the period from the end of Roman rule in the early 5th century to the introduction of Christianity in the mid-7th. Two hundred and fifty years of early Saxon village life were investigated here, and West Stow has provided us with a unique insight into the lifestyle of the earliest Englishmen.

Here were found their pots, jewellery, weaving equipment, combs, food bones and much else. We know they kept dogs and cats, used sheep for wool and meat, herded cattle and pigs, and probably prepared linen from flax. They hunted wildfowl and deer in the woods nearby, and caught fish in the river. The village had fields about it in which were grown a variety of cereal crops, and where animals were grazed. Judging from the quantity of finds associated with the spinning and weaving of wool, and the various working huts with evidence of weaving frames within them, we must imagine that wool was the economic staple. With the proceeds from the wool, bronze brooches, amber beads and other finery were purchased, as well as many commodities like skins and furs which have left no trace for archaeologists to find. In the village cemetery nearby, many everyday objects have been found with the burials, for like Loveden Hill in Lincolnshire, this was a pagan cemetery in which people were buried as they had lived, surrounded by their wealth.

The modern visitor will be disappointed if he expects to see all these things, for they are in the Museum at Ipswich, but West Stow is worthy of attention because an interesting experiment has been tried here. The excavator of the village, Mr Stanley West, decided to 'try out' his interpretations of the excavated buildings by reconstructing them. The reconstructions are carefully based on the evidence recorded on the site, and the resulting structures provide a unique opportunity to see what an early Saxon house was like.

The village houses were of two types, 'huts' and 'halls'. Much controversy has arisen about the appearance of the smaller huts in particular. They were unusual because they had either a sunken floor or an under-floor space, which was excavated into the ground before the hut walls were built around it. Traditionally they have been interpreted as 'pit dwellings' in which the inhabitants lived on the earth floor with a simple tent-like structure above. But at West Stow, evidence was found which

Map Reference: TL 808710 (metric map 155. 1-inch map 136)
Nearest Town: Bury St Edmunds
Location: The site can be reached from the A1101 some 4½ miles (7 km) north-west of Bury at Flempton, follow the signs to West Stow. Go past the church and turn left into the village. Take the next left turn to Icklingham and Mildenhall and follow this road for half a mile (0.8 km) through a conifer plantation. At a group of three cottages on the right of the road, pull in to the left. Go through the gate, following the track to the right; the reconstructed houses will soon be visible. The Anglo-Saxon village is supported by a trust, and although there is no entry charge, donations would be appreciated.

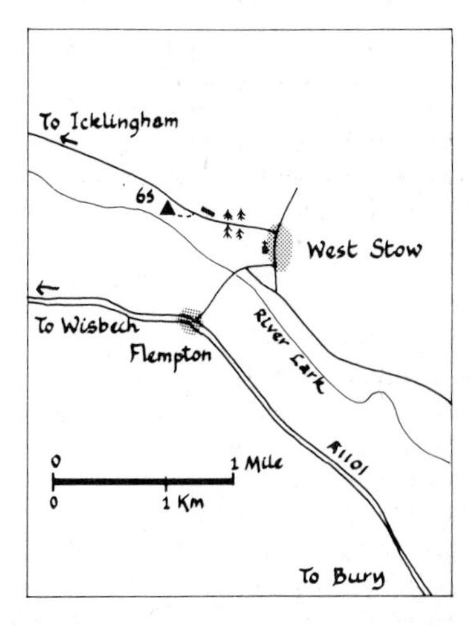

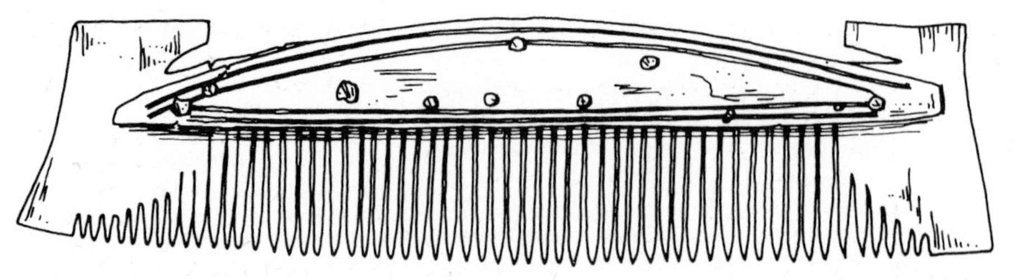

One of the many fine bone combs from the village. Some of them may have been used for carding wool.

The final touches being given to the thatched roof of one of the rectangular halls. The walls are built from split tree trunks with clay packed into the joints to stop draughts.

suggests that the holes were used not as living floors but as storage or air spaces below suspended wooden floors. The upper parts of the huts were also more substantially built than the earlier tent hypothesis allowed. Although it is still not entirely clear why the early Anglo-Saxons adopted this form of construction, it has been suggested that the air space below the wooden floor would have kept the huts drier, and by providing air-circulation around the floor timbers, prevented them from rotting.

The larger halls had plain earth floors with walls constructed of single posts set close together. This form of construction is easier to interpret and, as there were fewer of these structures, it seems likely that they may have been the living quarters of the people who used the smaller huts for weaving and other activities. The West Stow houses are surprisingly spacious, and the timber structures must have been very cosy in winter.

66
Cambridgeshire Dykes: An In-Depth Defence System

Between Cambridge and Newmarket are two of the greatest and least-known earthworks of the Dark Ages, the Devil's Ditch and the Fleam Ditch. Much argument has taken place about the identity of their builders and their actual date of construction. Whatever else, it appears that these two great earthworks, together with the Brent Ditch and the Bran Ditch to the south-west, were a comprehensive system of defence or demarcation between two great powers. Some argue that they are relics of the dim days of the 6th or 7th centuries, when this was 'debateable land' between the great kingdoms of Mercia and East Anglia. Others hold that they are older, and that they represent an attempt by the Romanized Britons to halt the Anglo-Saxon advance westwards during the 5th century.

The Devil's Ditch, the name of which probably derives from the old pagan god Grimr who was castigated as a devil after the Christian conversion, is the strongest of the works. Its mighty ramparts dwarf those of Offa's Dyke in some sections. As this was the 'front line' of the system, that is the easternmost of the lines, its scale is not perhaps surprising. Cutting across the chalk belt, its ends lie on marsh to the north and on clay land to the south. The latter would almost certainly have been thickly wooded, and thus would have hindered the passage of an invading force as effectively as the Ditch itself. The lines behind are of a declining scale, with the Fleam Ditch, the name of which means the 'dyke of the fugitives', being more powerful than the lesser works behind.

Here then is an 'in-depth' defence plan, created by men who expected their boundary to remain static for some time to come. It cuts

Map References: **Devil's Ditch** TL 620605 (metric map 154. 1-inch map 135)
Fleam Ditch TL 548541
Nearest Town: Newmarket
Location: Devil's Ditch is almost 7 miles (11 km) long and is of huge proportions along parts of its length. A very good section can be seen by taking the B1061 from Newmarket. Three-quarters of a mile (1.2 km) after the level crossing, a line of woodland can be seen on either side of the road, just before a bend. Park in the layby and take the public footpath towards Reach and Burwell, towards the railway embankment. Wellington boots are advisable, as a stream has to be crossed.

Fleam Ditch: From Newmarket take the A11. About 1½ miles (2.5 km) after the dual carriageway ends there is a white house on the right-hand side, followed by a layby. The ditch is cut by the road, and follows the line of a footpath to Balsham and Fulbourn.

This map shows the dykes in what may have been their original setting, with dense woodland on the higher ground to each side of the lower chalkland across which they are cut. Note that the Brent Ditch has its bank and ditch reversed. (After Fox)

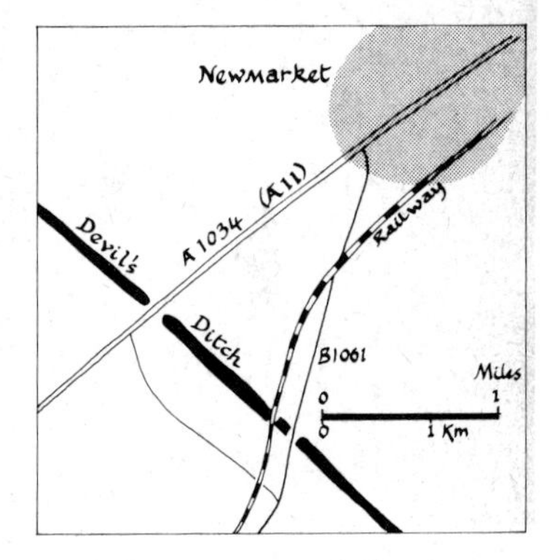

across one of the prime natural routeways from East Anglia into Middle England, and uses the natural boundaries of rivers, marshes and woodland as integral parts of the system. The parallel with the 8th-century Offa's Dyke is compelling, but we should recall that the Romans could build artificial frontiers where necessary, as the northern Walls indicate. Perhaps the Cambridgeshire Dykes are best seen as an attempt by the romanized Britons to contain the Anglo-Saxon advance after their victory at Mount Badon in 500 or thereabouts. But nothing is really certain about these strange features; excavation alone might provide the answers we seek.

The great bank and ditch of the Devil's Ditch, the 'front line' of the system. Snow was still lying in the ditch when we visited on a bright winter's day.

67

Cambridge: St Bene't's Church, Cambridgeshire

The tower of St Bene't's church – the name is a contraction of St Benedict – is a well known landmark in the city of Cambridge, and is a good example of late 10th-century work. Fewer people realize that the upper parts of the nave of the church are probably of the same date and that all four Saxon nave quoins are still visible from the outside.

The tower is built of rubblework and has fine long and short quoins rebated to take plaster as at Barton-on-Humber. It is in three stages separated by simple square-sectioned string-courses, the lowest stage being taller than the others. Short pilaster strips may be seen on the topmost stage, and there are no scars to show that they ever existed lower down. It has been plausibly suggested that the upper strips indicate that the tower once had a 'helmed' roof like that at Sompting, Sussex. The belfry has double openings in all four sides, with single arched lintels and banded balusters which are set unusually far back into the windows. There are two tall round-headed windows set to each side of the belfry lights.

Internally, the nave is dominated by the superb tower arch. This has through-stone voussoirs laid with radial joints, the whole providing a massive yet well-modelled effect. The imposts of the arch are enriched with complex mouldings, and continue as a string-course across the west wall. The eastern face of the arch is enlivened by the addition of singular beasts which cavort at each end of the hood-mould above the imposts. Above the tower arch is a Saxon doorway, which is too low to have opened into the roof-space, and so may have served some liturgical purpose, perhaps for the display of relics. Alternatively, it may have opened into a wooden gallery as at Wing in Buckinghamshire. The church of St Bene't exhibits some unusual features, and the

Map References: **St Bene't** TL 449583 **St Giles** TL 445591 (metric map 154. 1-inch map 135)

Locations: St Bene't's is right in the centre of Cambridge in Benet Street, a turning off Trumpington Street almost opposite King's College.

St Giles church is at the bottom of Castle Hill.

St Bene't's Church from the south-east.

splendid tower arch in particular, which bears comparison with that at Barnack, is a fine example of the skill of the late Saxon builder.

Before leaving Cambridge, the visitor should also try to see in St Giles church the rebuilt chancel arch, which now stands at the east end of the south aisle. Do not be deceived by the fact that St Giles is a brick-built Victorian edifice, or by the fact that the arch has been re-erected with the decorated face towards the east. The imposts are richly adorned with cable moulding and diaper patterns; it must be very late Anglo-Saxon work, and came from an ancient church which stood beside the later building.

68

Sutton Hoo: Royal Cemetery of East Anglia, Suffolk

On this headland above the River Deben was the royal cemetery of the ancient kings of East Anglia. In the largest mound was discovered a mass of grave goods which has been described as the richest treasure from British soil. All this finery has long since been removed to the British Museum, where it is displayed to wondering visitors, but here, on the site itself, we can allow the mind to roam freely over its secrets.

Three of the barrows were dug in 1938, and various impressive objects were recovered from them, but it was not until 1939, on the eve of World War II that the king's barrow was assailed. The burial deposit had been laid in a ship propelled by thirty-eight oars. The ship's timbers had perished, but the iron nails survived to show the lines of the great craft. A wooden chamber had been built amidships, and this contained a rich panoply of objects.

These included a solid gold buckle decorated with rich interlace ornament, a gold and garnet-mounted purse lid, a gold and garnet sword pommel and mounts for a sword harness, a pair of gold shoulder clasps, various small gold and garnet strap ends, buckles and fittings, a Byzantine silver dish, a set of ten silver bowls, parts of a lyre, a decorated shield, a gilt bronze helmet, an ornamental whetstone which was perhaps a 'sceptre', bronze hanging bowls, cauldrons, drinking horn mounts, drinking vessels and a pair of silver spoons inscribed 'Saul' and 'Paul'. There were many other iron objects, and a purse contained thirty-seven Merovingian coins and a single piece of gold. The only thing which the grave lacked was a body; no trace of one was found during the original excavation, and later work on the site has failed to clarify the matter.

From the dating evidence supplied by the coins, it is generally accepted that the burial deposit commemorated King Raedwald, who died in 625 or thereabouts.

He fits the bill not only because of his death date, but also because he was a relatively new convert to the Christian faith. This might explain the occurrence of Christian objects in the burial. Early Christians, like their modern counterparts, believed that they could not take their worldly wealth into the afterlife, so there was little point in burying offerings with the dead. This was directly contrary to pagan beliefs, and the Sutton Hoo burial is undoubtedly of pagan inspiration. But the occurrence of the 'Saul and Paul' spoons in particular, which commemorate Saul's renaming after his baptism, have been claimed as evidence that the owner of the wealth was in fact a Christian. Raedwald is an even more likely candidate for this admixture of rituals since there is evidence that he renounced Christianity before he died in favour of the old religion. But this doesn't explain the absence of a body. Raedwald died in East Anglia as far as is known, so why was he not buried with his treasure? This is but one of the many problems which has arisen out of the discovery of the

Map Reference: TM 288487 (metric map 169. 1-inch map 150)
Nearest Town: Woodbridge/Ipswich
Location: The site of Sutton Hoo lies on the east side of the Deben estuary, opposite Woodbridge. It can be reached by taking the A12 north out of Woodbridge and turning east to Melton. Cross the River Deben and then turn south down the B1083. Within half a mile (0.8 km) at the end of the golf course, park off the road and take the trackway leading to the west, opposite a V junction with a minor road. The cemetery can be seen almost half a mile down this track. The track which runs along the north side of the site is a public footpath, but the site itself is private property, and should not be entered without prior permission from the owners.

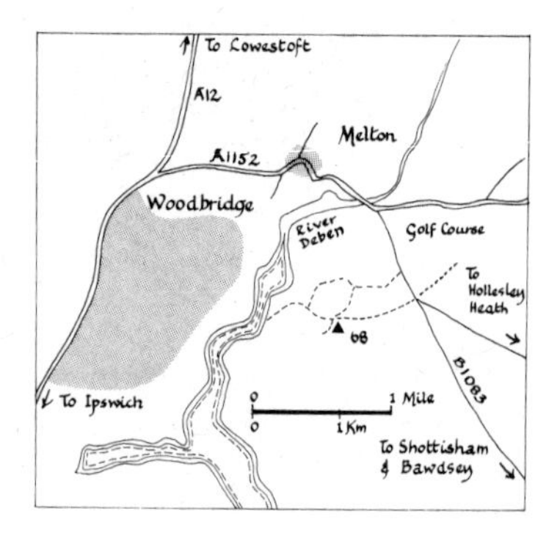

The great gold buckle decorated with interlacing animal ornament.

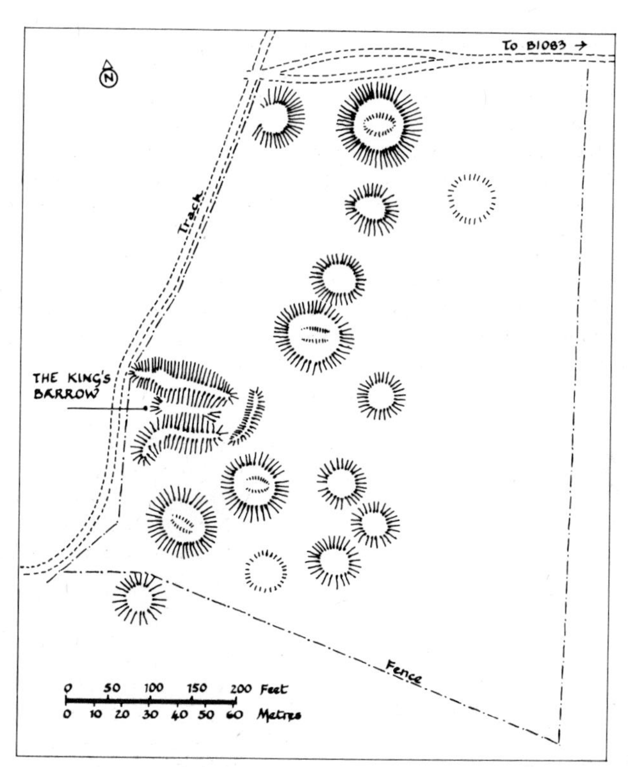

Plan of the cemetery.

burial, and it is likely that the Sutton Hoo burial will provide archaeologists with plenty of discussion material for many years to come!

A side effect of the Sutton Hoo discovery is that it has led to a reappraisal of the great Anglo-Saxon poem, *Beowulf*. This is heroic verse and it was formerly thought that its descriptions of treasure hoards and the like were mere poetic licence, but now we realize they may be quite factual. It is even possible that the poem was composed in East Anglia at about the time that Raedwald was buried. There is a description in the poem of Beowulf the hero's burial which echoes in our minds as we stand in the royal cemetery of East Anglia. Raedwald's burial must have been just like this:

Then the Geats built a barrow on the headland —
it was high and broad, visible from far
to all seafarers . . .
They buried rings and brooches in the barrow,
all those adornments that brave men
had brought out from the hoard after Beowulf died.
They bequeathed the gleaming gold, treasure of men,
to the earth, and there it still remains,
as useless to men as it was before.
Then twelve brave warriors, sons of heroes,
rode round the barrow, sorrowing . . .

(Trans. K. Crossley-Holland)

69

Great Tey: Saxo-Norman Tower, Essex

The lower three stages of St Barnabas's tower are Anglo-Saxon, dating to the first half of the 11th century. The original tower must have been extremely handsome with its quoins and string-courses formed in bright red tiles which were also used to emphasize the heads of the windows and recesses. As at Brixworth in Northamptonshire, we are moved to wonder whether all these tiles were really recovered from a derelict Roman site, or whether they were made by the Anglo-Saxons themselves. Technical analysis of the sort applied at Brixworth might provide an answer to this fascinating question.

Nothing of the Anglo-Saxon nave and chancel now survives, but it is fairly clear that the tower occupied an axial position between them. That is to say that the tower, which now has later medieval openings in its north and south walls, originally had only two openings to the east and west, and formed a link between nave and chancel. Only one bay of the later nave survives after 19th-century demolition; the later chancel now provides the main accommodation.

The lower stages of the tower are of roughly dressed rubblework and are separated from each other by plain string-courses formed of double thicknesses of tiles. In the third stage are two broad windows in each face, with heads and jambs formed of tiles. Below are six round-headed blind recesses in each face. On the lowest floor are two round-headed windows in each face which have plain stone jambs in contrast to those above.

Inside, the tower opens into the nave and chancel through large round-headed arches which have a single square order to the east and two similar orders on the western faces. Hollow chamfered imposts are continued along the east and west walls as string-courses. Traces of vertical stripwork survive on each side of the eastern arch. This slight trace of stripwork is a familiar Anglo-Saxon touch in a building which otherwise shows the general ponderousness and unsplayed windows more characteristic of Norman work.

The topmost belfry stage is Norman work, but all below is of late Anglo-Saxon date. The later Essex brick vernacular tradition is foreshadowed by the lavish use of tiles in this building where freestone would have been employed elsewhere.

Map Reference: TL 891258 (metric map 168. 1-inch map 149)
Nearest Town: Colchester
Location: Great Tey can be reached by minor roads from either the A120 Colchester to Braintree road, or by the A604 Colchester to Halstead road. It is some 6 miles (9.5 km) west of Colchester, and lies about half way between these two major roads. The church has a pleasant, open aspect and an attractive well-maintained churchyard.

70

Bradwell-on-Sea: The Church of St Cedd, Essex

Bradwell is one of those remarkable sites where past and present seem very close. Standing on the windswept Essex coast just above the marshes, the church of St Peter-on-the-Wall straddles the line of the western defences of the Roman fort of Othona. This fort, built during the dark days of the late 3rd century, was a base from which the commander of the Roman Channel fleet sailed against Saxon pirates from free Germany beyond the Roman frontier. Its great walls with their circular bastions and massive facing stones may be seen here and there around the site, and local people say that the submerged outlines of the Roman naval harbour can be glimpsed in the marshes to the east. Long after the Romans had departed and the Saxons had settled eastern England, the influence of Rome was again felt in this remote place, but this time it was a peaceful rather than a military presence.

The Venerable Bede tells us that in 652 or thereabouts St Cedd was consecrated bishop of the East Saxons at his home monastery of Lindisfarne. Sigebert, king of the East Saxons, gave Cedd the old Roman site at Bradwell for his church, and it was from here that Cedd and his monks began the work of conversion.

Cedd was an intelligent man and, coming from Lindisfarne, was a member of the Celtic church. At the Synod of Whitby in 664, he acted as interpreter for the Celtic party, but he accepted the ways of Rome thereafter and applied them in his own diocese. As may be seen from the church at Bradwell, Cedd had already encountered Roman influence, since the plan of the structure closely follows the early design at Canterbury. This has led to some doubt as to whether or not this really was Cedd's church, but it seems likely that he used Kentish masons who were schooled in the Roman traditions.

Using building materials taken from the old fort, Cedd's masons built a small church consisting of a nave, eastern apse, small north and south chapels, and perhaps a western porch. Only the nave stands today, but the stubs of the apse walls can be seen at its eastern end

St Cedd's lonely chapel at Bradwell. It was perhaps sacked by the Danes before the great Battle of Maldon in 991 for the Anglo-Saxon Chronicle records: 'In this year Anlaf came with ninety-three ships to Folkestone and ravaged the neighbourhood . . . and overran the whole area, and so to Maldon. And there Ealdorman Bryhtnoth and his fyrd [army] came to meet him, and fought with him. And they killed the Ealdorman and the battlefield was theirs . . .'

Map Reference: TM 031082 (metric map 168. 1-inch map 162)
Nearest Town: Maldon
Location: Seemingly on the edge of England, Bradwell is on the promontory between the Blackwater and Crouch estuaries. From Maldon it can be reached by the B1018 and thence by minor roads for some 10 miles (16 km) from Latchingdon. Alternatively, the B1021 north of Burnham-on-Crouch may be used. The chapel is on bird watchers' territory in the Essex marshes. Do not be confused by the parish church in the village; the chapel is signposted and is about 2 miles (3 km) from the village, towards the sea. It is eventually reached by a straight footpath past World War II defence installations.

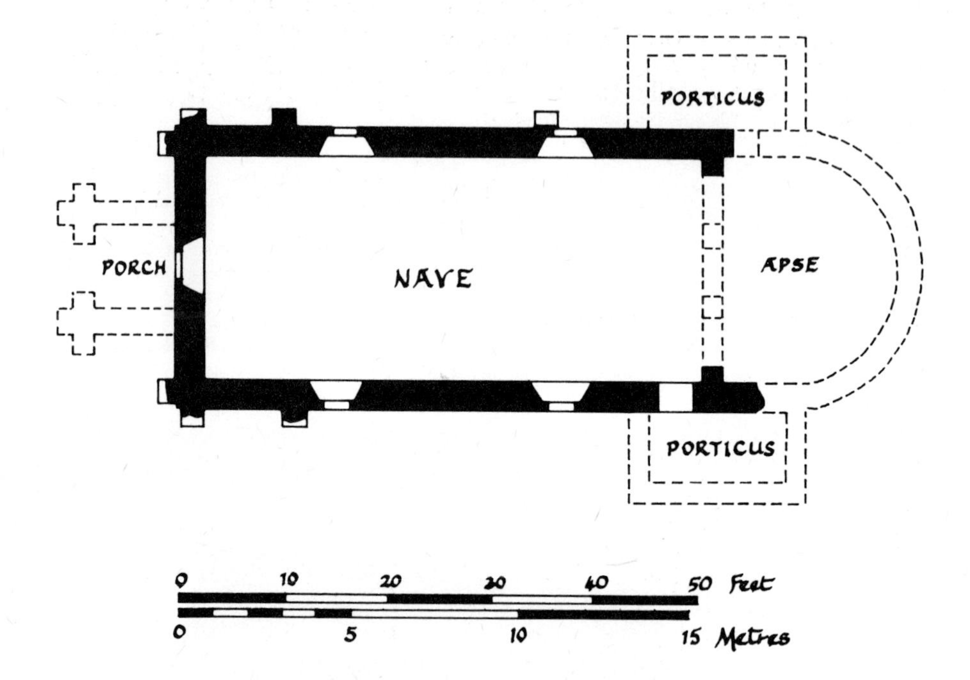

and, inside, the heads of three tall arches which opened from the nave into the apse may still be seen. There is a blocked door into the south porticus. The northern transept was apparently entered from the chancel since there is no corresponding disturbance in the north nave wall. Many Roman tiles are re-used in the fabric, particularly in the pilasters, and despite the great doors which were cut through the nave walls during its extended use as a barn until 1920, much of the original work survives.

This place, called *Ythanceaster* by Bede, was a place of pilgrimage during the Anglo-Saxon period. It is recorded that upon learning of Cedd's death, thirty monks walked here from Lindisfarne and lived here on God's providence until all save one boy had died, so great was their devotion to the saint's memory. Cedd's feast day, which commemorates the date of his death on 26 October 664, is still honoured and an annual pilgrimage takes place.

These wide Essex marshes saw not only the Romans and Christian Saxons, but also the ravages of the Vikings. It was near this place that the great Battle of Maldon was fought in 991 which gave rise to an immortal Anglo-Saxon poem, some lines from which are quoted in the entry for Battle (No. 101).

71

Greensted: Timber Church, Essex

No guide to Anglo-Saxon England would be complete without reference to the freakish survival of the unique timber nave of this church. Here at Greensted we can see something which must have been a common sight in many parts of England where stone was scarce – a church built in wood, that most fugitive of constructional materials. Countless references tell us that timber churches were common during the early days of Christianity all over England, and not merely in those areas where stone was unavailable. The first church at York was of timber, as was that at Lindisfarne, and traces of timber phases have been found under the stone cathedral at North Elmham and in many other excavations of church sites.

This church at Greensted, which probably dates from the 11th century, may have served as a resting-place for the body of St Edmund, king and martyr, which was conveyed from Bury St Edmunds to London in 1013 when the Danes landed in East Anglia. Edmund had been king of East Anglia in the 9th century before he was captured by the Danes. They murdered him, traditionally by shooting him with arrows and then beheading him, when he refused to deny his faith.

The nave walls are made of large vertically split logs which were morticed at top and bottom into wooden beams. Each log was joined to its neighbour by a 'tongue and groove' technique. The north-west angle clearly shows how a single log was used to turn the corner; it merely had a quarter of its circumference removed rather than being split in half like the wall members. The present brick sill is Victorian, but the wooden members at top and bottom follow the original pattern.

By analogy with Scandinavian timber churches of a similar date, it is likely that Greensted originally had a simple square chancel. In looking at the Scandinavian churches, we are reminded that not all timber structures were as simple as that at Greensted: there must have been English parallels to the complicated aisled plans and other variants which have been found by excavation in Norway and Denmark. Here at Greensted, for example, we

Map Reference: TL 538030 (metric map 167. 1-inch map 161)
Nearest Town: Epping/Chipping Ongar
Location: Greensted lies three-quarters of a mile (1.2 km) west of Chipping Ongar on a minor road which is signposted from the town centre.

Greensted church with its timber nave.

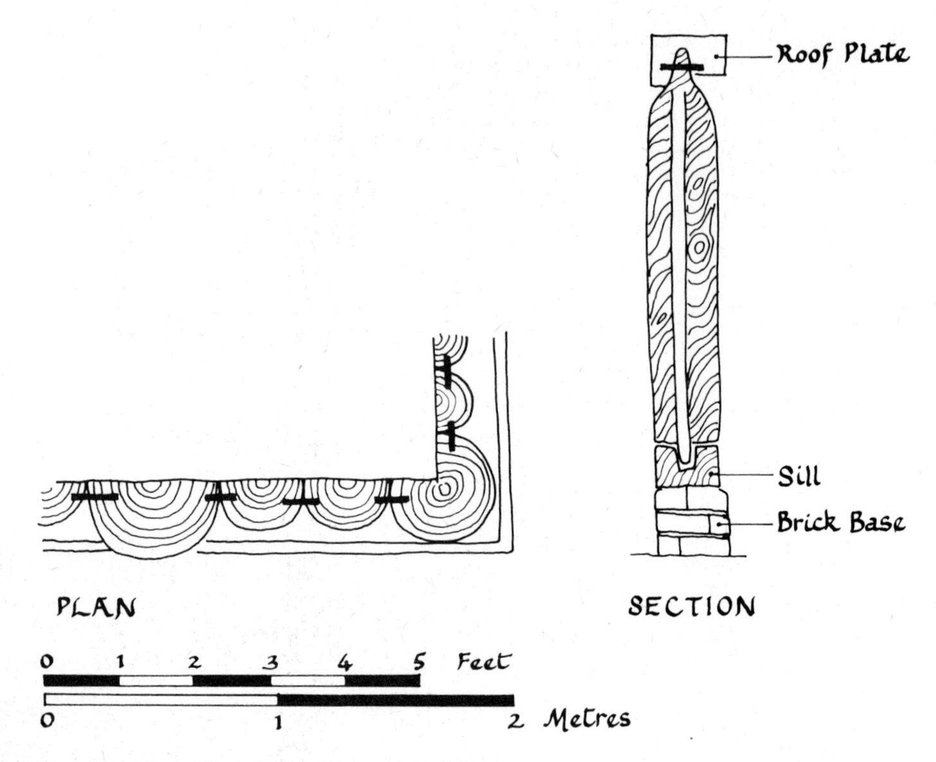

Plan and section of the timbers in the nave wall. (After Taylor)

know from excavations in 1960 that this was not the first timber church on the site; how many other complicated sequences lie beneath our parish churches? Excavation alone will provide the answers.

72

Wing: All Saints Church, Buckinghamshire

The remarkable church at Wing must originally have resembled that at Brixworth in Northamptonshire; both shared a basilican plan, together with an apsidal chancel with a crypt beneath. The similarities between the two plans suggest that both are of similar date, perhaps as early as the 7th century. Later, during the 10th century, Wing church underwent some alterations, but the basic elements of the plan – the wide nave and narrower side aisles – remained constant throughout.

Upon approaching the church, the most notable feature is the splendid seven-sided chancel. This has an unusual decorative scheme consisting of vertical pilasters linked by arches. Above are round-headed windows set in triangular stripwork panels. At the bottom of the chancel walls to the north, south and east are round-headed windows which light the crypt beneath. The crypt is entered

Map Reference: SP 880225 (metric map 165. 1-inch map 146)
Nearest Town: Aylesbury
Location: Wing is on the A418 road to Leighton Buzzard, some 3 miles (5 km) south-west of the town. The church stands in a fine churchyard, behind the main street.

through an adapted window on the south side down a short flight of steps. Access was originally provided by two flights of stairs which led down from the east end of the nave, as at Repton.

The crypt is octagonal in plan, and may have had a timber roof in the first phase. Later, during the 10th century, the outer walls were thickened and the great piers which now support the barrel vault were added. It is probable that the chancel above was also rebuilt at this time, since it resembles the chancel at Deerhurst in Gloucestershire in its use of pilaster strips. The rectangular recesses below the windows may have accommodated burials, as at Repton.

Before entering the church, a blocked Anglo-Saxon doorway in the east wall of the north aisle should be seen. This doorway is not set in the centre of the wall, but is displaced towards the south, perhaps in order to accommodate an altar to the north, as in the north transept at Bradford-on-Avon. The east wall may itself be of Anglo-Saxon date.

Inside, the three great bays of the nave survive intact. They are relatively plain with simple stepped imposts. The later pointed arches at the east end of the nave do not reflect the original arrangement: the walls would have been uninterrupted in front of the chancel arch. The huge chancel arch is now somewhat obscured by a wooden screen; it is almost certainly Anglo-Saxon, though it may have lost some of its inner orders since it is unusually stark for such a large span. Above is a handsome double window with a central turned baluster shaft which shows it to be a later insertion, perhaps of the 10th century. At the west end of the nave, two doorways should be noted high up in the side walls; they led to a wooden gallery which has since been demolished. The gallery must either have been entered by ladders, or else the north and south aisles may have been two storeys high, as at Deerhurst.

The chancel from the south-east on a misty winter's day. The faceted plan and elaborate stripwork scheme closely resemble the 10th-century work at Deerhurst. One of the round-headed windows which light the crypt is visible low down in the south wall.

Why such a large and important church should have been built at Wing is something of a mystery. Nothing is known of the 7th-century history of the place to account for the foundation. Not until the 10th century, the period of the later alterations, is there any indication of major patronage.

The estate of which Wing formed part was held during the 10th century by Lady Aelfgifu, who was probably the sister-in-law of King Eadred of England. Her will has survived, and she left her estate at some time before 975 to the king. In her will she refers to a shrine and relics at Wing, and it may be that she ordered the refurbishment of the crypt in order to display these precious objects. By the terms of her will, the relics were removed to Winchester where she was buried. Wing, thus deprived of its royal patronage, presumably sank into obscurity thereafter. But this tells us nothing of the earliest history of the place; we can only conjecture that Wing must have been one of the many nameless early Christian centres from which the conversion of England was accomplished.

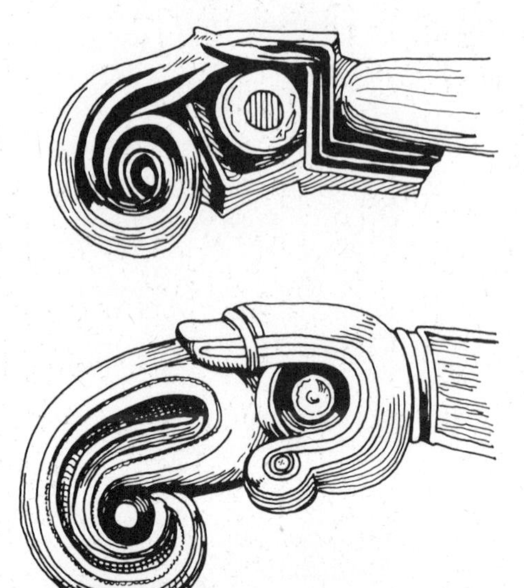

The silver gilt drinking horn mounts. These fitted on to the ends of great horns, perhaps culled from the mighty aurochs, a form of ferocious wild cow, the hunting of which was a celebrated heroic pursuit. The horns from the Sutton Hoo burial are estimated to have had a capacity of around six quarts (7 litres) – a mighty draught indeed!

73

Taplow: Taeppa's Burial Mound, Buckinghamshire

Map Reference: SU 903822 (metric map 175. 1-inch map 160)
Nearest Town: Maidenhead
Location: Taplow can be reached from the A4 about a mile (1.6 km) east of Maidenhead by taking the B476 northwards. The barrow is in the grounds of Taplow Court, a fine Victorian mansion in the Tudor taste. Keep on the B476 road in the village and up a hill; the court is on the left hand side opposite Taplow Cricket Club. Access to the barrow is by the Tradesmen's Entrance to the left of the house itself. It is situated in the old churchyard.

Before the great discovery at Sutton Hoo, Taplow was the richest Anglo-Saxon burial known in England. The name Taplow derives from the Anglo-Saxon *Taeppa's Low*, with *Low* meaning a burial mound. So the place name comes from the burial site itself, and we can be as sure as may be that the man buried there was called Taeppa. He was certainly an important man, as the wealth of his gravegoods indicates, and he was doubtless at least a chieftain of the area, if not actually a king.

Taeppa was laid under a great earth mound which can still be seen. It is 15 feet (4.5 metres) high, with a diameter of 80 feet (24 metres) at the base. The grave lay at the centre of the mound, and was dug 6 feet (2.8 metres) into the ground below. Taeppa was laid in a planked coffin within a large grave pit, surrounded by his weapons and gear. His arms comprising a sword, spears, knife and two shields were found, together with his solid gold buckle set with garnets and lapis lazuli, gilt bronze clasps, a bronze mounted mead bucket, drinking horns with silver gilt terminals, precious glass vessels, wooden cups, a set of bone playing pieces, a harp and a bronze bowl imported from Egypt. These finds are eloquent of the chief's life in both war and peace.

Apart from these surrounding objects, de-

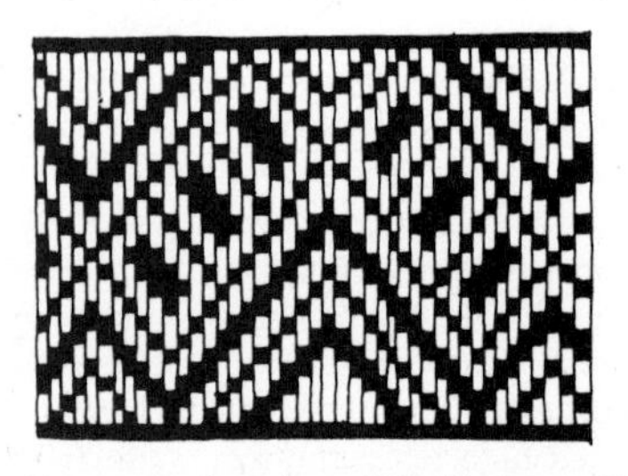

Reconstruction of one of the Taplow gold braids. The pattern has been assembled by reference to the 'pressure points' on the gold threads, which show how they were originally woven. (After Crowfoot)

The 7th-century burial mound in the grounds of Taplow Court. This was the burial place of Taeppa, who may have been a king. A plaque records that the mound was opened in 1883 by the parish clerk. The contents are now in the British Museum.

cayed cloth was found on the body, together with a large quantity of gold threads. The gold threads were originally thought to have come from a cloak, but it now appears that they belonged to a golden baldric from which the sword was hung, and perhaps from the neck of a tunic. The sheer quantity of this precious stuff demonstrates Taeppa's importance, and some have claimed him as a 7th-century king. Sadly we will never know for sure, since no documents survive recording Taeppa's deeds or station. But we can imagine him selecting this imposing site for his great barrow, looking out over the Thames Valley which he must have known well, and perhaps ruled, when England was yet to be born.

PART IV

Wessex

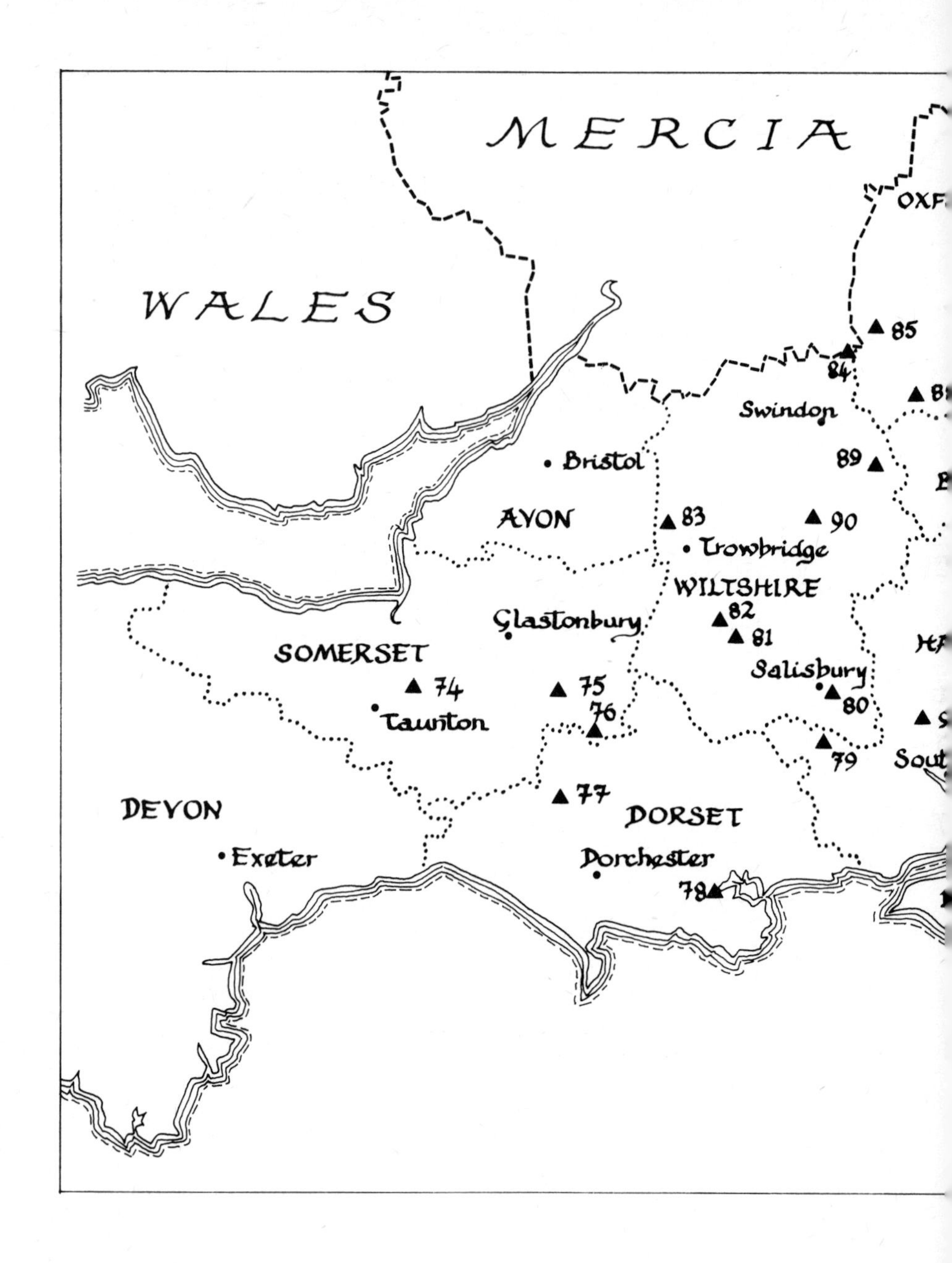
MERCIA
OXF
WALES
85
84
Swindon
Bristol
89
AVON
83
90
Trowbridge
WILTSHIRE
82
81
Glastonbury
SOMERSET
Salisbury
74
75
76
80
Taunton
79
77
DEVON
DORSET
Exeter
Dorchester
78

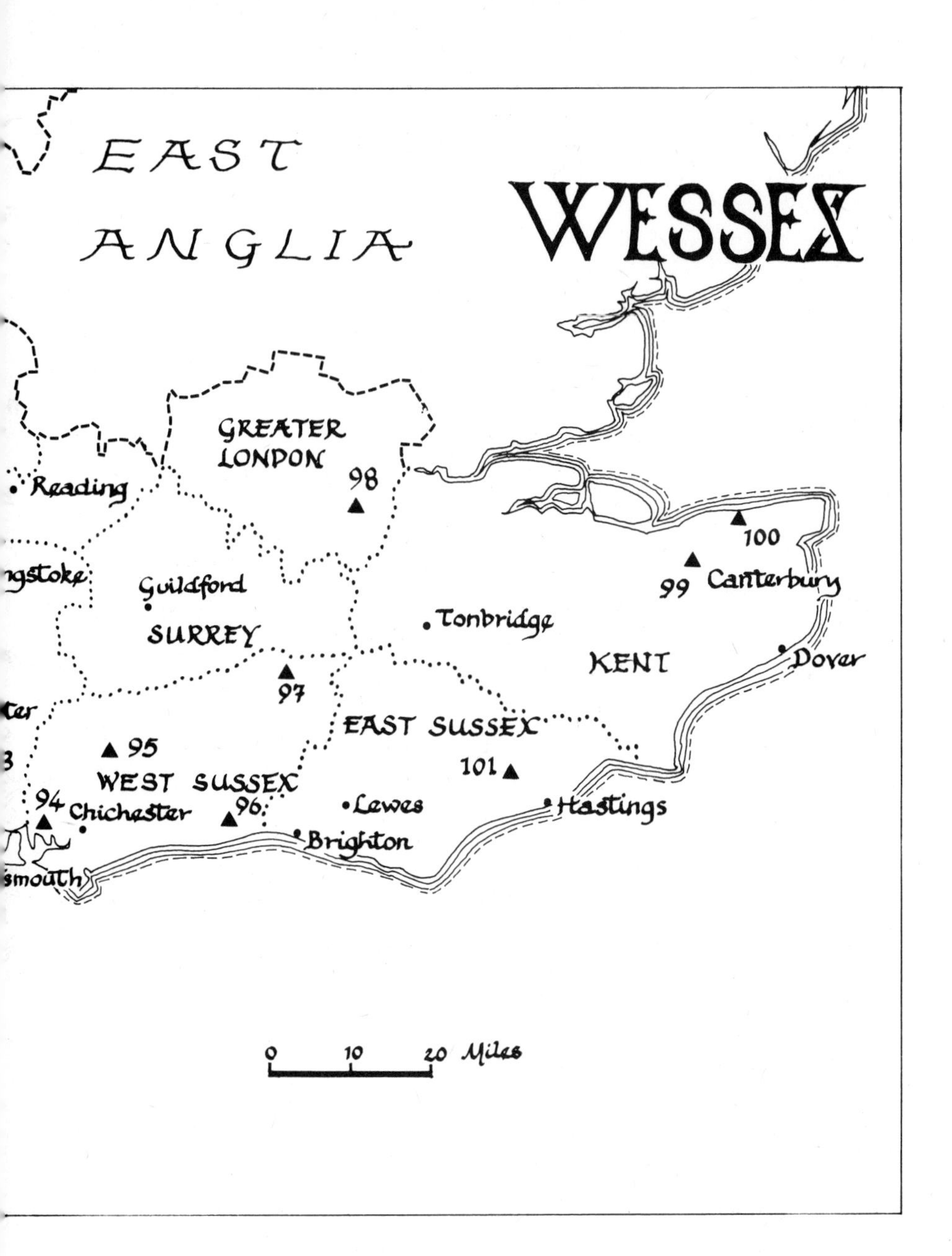
EAST
ANGLIA
WESSEX
GREATER
LONDON
98
Reading
100
gstoke
Guildford
99 Canterbury
Tonbridge
SURREY
KENT
Dover
97
ter
EAST SUSSEX
95
WEST SUSSEX
101
94 Chichester
96
Lewes
Hastings
Brighton
smouth
0 10 20 Miles

Introduction

The Saxon settlement south of the Thames emerges in history as the kingdoms of Kent, Sussex and Wessex. Of these, Kent was the earliest kingdom to attain a degree of stability. The traditional story of how the British ruler Vortigern invited the Saxon leaders Hengist and Horsa to defend the area from their fellow countrymen suggests an early settlement by mercenary soldiers. Canterbury was an important centre, as its Anglo-Saxon name Cantwarburgh which means 'fortress of the dwellers of Kent', indicates. The excellent communications which Kent enjoyed with the Thames estuary and the Channel ports led to strong trading links with the Continent, and a subsequent increase in wealth and prosperity.

The reign of Ethelbert, who is attested to have ruled over the whole area south of the Humber during the later 6th century, marked the apogee of Kentish fortunes. Kent began to fall into insignificance during the 8th century when the expansion of Wessex absorbed the lesser kingdoms.

Sussex, the territory of the 'South Saxons', was founded by a powerful leader called Aelle late in the 5th century. There is little historical record for the early kingdom of Sussex until the early 7th century when a series of charters locate a Saxon cathedral at Selsey. At this time it is also recorded that many kings were reigning simultaneously in Sussex. These were probably local dynasties whose rivalry militated against the development of the kingdom as a whole.

The Anglo-Saxon Chronicle tells us that Wessex was founded by Cerdic and Cynric who arrived on the south coast in 495. In the following years they captured the Isle of Wight and consolidated the coastal areas. The British victory at Mount Badon in 500 or thereabouts presumably had some effect on the Saxon expansion, but in 577 the Saxons won a great battle at Dyrham, north of Bath, after which they took control of the country south of the lower Severn.

Unfortunately there is a conflict between the Chronicle's version of the origins of Wessex and the archaeological evidence. Finds in the Upper Thames Valley demonstrate that Anglo-Saxons were living peacefully there at least by the middle of the 5th century and perhaps before. This is reinforced by the location of the royal seat at Dorchester early in the 7th century; it was only later moved to Winchester because of Mercian pressure in the 640s.

Wessex was the last of the English kingdoms to attain national ascendancy, and it was not until the reign of Egbert that it became a power in the land. He became king in 802, and had extended his rule over the whole country south of the Thames by the time of his death in 839. Sporadic Viking attacks occurred from the time of Egbert onwards, but only in 865, with the arrival of a Danish army bent on conquest and settlement, did things become really desperate. The victory of Alfred over the Danes at Edington in 878 preserved the independence of Wessex, but he was forced to make a treaty with the Danish leader Guthrum in 886 by which the Danelaw recognized the Danish occupation of large areas of north and east England.

The succeeding kings of Wessex built strongly upon Alfred's heroic defence of the kingdom, and during the 10th century Edward, Athelstan and Edgar won back much of the land settled by the Danes. Edgar's reign marked the high point of the house of Wessex, and with it the kingdom of England, for Wessex was by now the leading power in the land. Edgar received homage from most of the rulers of Wales, Scotland and the Irish Sea area at Chester in 973, and the Danish-settled parts of England were now loyal to the House of Alfred.

All went well until the disastrous reign of Ethelred II, who was bitterly remembered as Unraed: literally 'wise counsel – no counsel'. His was the policy of Danegeld, a new and shameful attempt to 'buy off' the Danes rather than fight them. During his reign and that of Edmund Ironside who briefly succeeded him, the Danish king, Cnut, anglicized as 'Canute', fought his way to the throne of England. After the English defeat at Ashingdon in Essex, Canute ruled an empire which stretched from the Baltic to the Irish Sea. But on his death the empire fell to pieces, and Ethelred's son Edward, who had been exiled in Normandy, claimed the throne.

This Edward, called the 'Confessor' because of his piety, was of the Wessex royal line, but he alienated much English sympathy by his friendship with the Normans. Godwin, Earl of Wessex, and Harold his son were particularly opposed to the Norman Party at Edward's court, but it was not until 1052 that they managed to turn the tables on them. But before this, in 1051, William of Normandy had visited Edward, and always claimed that the king had promised the English crown to him on his death. In this lay the seeds of the conflict which was to culminate in the Battle of Hastings.

Harold had become the most powerful noble in the land by the time of the death of Edward in January 1066, and was popularly acclaimed king. He dealt first with the immediate threat to his kingdom, the landing of Harold Hardrada, King of Norway, in

Yorkshire. He then marched south and came close to resisting the Conqueror's forces at Senlac near Hastings. The fate of England was decided on that field, and when Harold died the old Anglo-Saxon order passed with him.

Much of what remains from Anglo-Saxon Wessex is bound up with Christianity, which was the driving force behind most of the artistic and architectural enterprise. St Augustine's fine monastery at Canterbury, built by the powerful King Ethelbert, is a major monument of early Christianity and in its classical plan and advanced construction displays the Roman influence which Augustine brought with him. The little church at Reculver carries on this tradition, and marks the success of the Kentish conversion. Later churches reflect the prosperity of the region and its relatively peaceful conditions. The 10th century, when Wessex alone was preserved from the turmoils of Viking raids and settlement, has been called a 'renaissance', in which the Church and State together made great strides towards civilization.

Continental contacts encouraged the production of manuscripts and sculpture at the monastic centres, and the famous 'Winchester School' set the pace. The fine carvings at Britford, Codford St Peter and Bradford-on-Avon attest the flourishing of the arts in Wessex, and clearly reflect European influences. Another strain is embodied in the Scandinavian-influenced designs at Ramsbury; it marks the existence of the Danish settlement, but their achievements never rivalled those of the 'Winchester School'. From the late Saxon period comes a fine group of churches, of which Worth, Breamore and Bradford-on-Avon are particularly notable for their completeness, whilst Sompting, Knook and Melbury Bubb have important individual features.

Not all the Wessex monuments are derived from the church, however. The mighty Wansdyke defended the nascent kingdom from the Mercian onslaught, and a series of monuments commemorates the fight against the Danes. The strange Blowing Stone at Kingston Lisle, with its traditional function as an alarm signal for the fyrd (army), is a fascinating enigma. The impressive remains of Alfred's defended burghs at Wallingford and Wareham, as well as the forlorn site of his exile in the Somerset marshes at Athelney are redolent of those troubled times. Later still, Ethelred Unraed allowed the Danes to overrun his kingdom, and the great fort at South Cadbury was pressed into service as an emergency burgh.

The last site in Wessex, and in this book, is Battle near Hastings. Here, where Harold and his huscarles (bodyguard) were overwhelmed by the Norman host, the old Anglo-Saxon kingdom came to an end. No more fitting end for the last of the English kings could have been devised than that warrior's death.

74

Athelney: Alfred's Refuge, Somerset

Engle hirde, Engle derling – shepherd of the English, Englishmen's darling – was the affectionate title by which Alfred the Great was to become known to his countrymen. He was a symbol of hope and eventual freedom for all those Englishmen who lived in the areas conquered by the Danes. In the words of the Anglo-Saxon Chronicle: 'all the English people submitted to Alfred except those who were under the power of the Danes.' But this later national recognition was hard won, and we know that at Athelney he faced his darkest hours. Standing today on the windswept hill at Athelney, we can still appreciate the remoteness of this site to which Alfred came when the Danes invaded his kingdom.

The Viking menace had first appeared at Lindisfarne late in the 8th century. To begin with they confined themselves to 'hit and run' raids, brief summer affairs, but in 850-1, a Danish army 'wintered' in England for the first time, and quickly established a firm grip on northern and eastern England. By 868 Alfred and his brother Ethelred were fighting in Mercia in a vain attempt to save that kingdom from collapse, and in 878 the Danes made a surprise attack on Wessex itself. In the words of the Chronicle:

> In this year the host went secretly in midwinter after Twelfth Night to Chippenham, and rode over Wessex and occupied it, and drove a great part of the inhabitants oversea, and reduced the greater part of the rest to submission, except Alfred the king; and he with a small company moved under difficulties through woods and into inaccessible places in marshes . . . And the Easter after, King Alfred with a small company built a fortification at Athelney, and from that fortification, with the men of that part of Somerset nearest to it, he continued the fighting against the host.

Alfred probably chose Athelney as his base because he knew the place and its people well. He must have hunted in the area as a boy, since the West Saxon royal palace was located not far away at Cheddar. The Somerset marshes, with their swamps and reed beds, remnants of which can still be seen around Athelney today, must have been a wild place in Anglo-Saxon times. The king was safe here from an enemy who did not know the ground.

It was during Alfred's stay at Athelney that the famous incident of the cakes occurred. Asser, Alfred's chronicler, tells us that a country-woman, the wife of a cowherd in whose hut he was resting, was baking some cakes whilst Alfred 'sat before the fire repairing his bow and arrows and instruments of war.' When the woman saw that the cakes were burning, 'she ran up in great haste and scolded our invincible king after this fashion – "Look, man, the cakes are burning, and you do not take the trouble to turn them; you are active enough when the time comes for eating them!"' This tale is one of the lighter moments in what must have been desperate times. Men looked to Alfred for hope, and he did not fail them. By his persistent harrying of the Danish army, he showed that resistance was still possible.

After seven weeks at Athelney, he was strong enough to do battle with the main Danish army. We do not know the details of Alfred's communications and intelligence network, but it must have been efficient. He marched to a pre-arranged meeting place on the edge of Selwood, south of Warminster, and the men of Somerset, Wiltshire and Hampshire west of Southampton Water were there to meet him. With careful understatement, the Chronicle tells us that they 'received

Map Reference: ST 346293 (metric map 193. 1-inch map 177)
Nearest Town: Taunton
Location: The Isle of Athelney is on the opposite side of the River Tone from the village of Athelney, about 8 miles (13 km) north-east of Taunton. The hill can be viewed from the layby on the A361 about half a mile (0.8 km) north-east of Lyng. To visit the site and monument, it is necessary to call at the farm on the minor road between Lyng and Athelney and ask permission to enter the field behind the farmhouse.

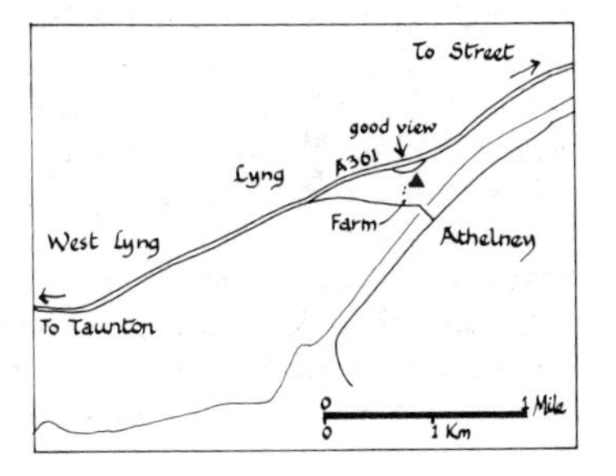

The peaceful Isle of Athelney from which Alfred, still the only English king called 'Great', led the desperate resistance against the Danes which was to culminate in the triumph of Edington.

The front and back of the Alfred Jewel, perhaps the most famous Anglo-Saxon treasure of all. The inscription on the edge of the mount reads + AELFRED MEC HEHT GEWYRCAN *– 'Alfred ordered me to be made'. This was found in the marshes near Athelney, and forms an enduring link with the first king of the English. It is now preserved in the Ashmolean Museum at Oxford.*

him warmly'. Alfred met the Danes at Edington on the northern edge of Salisbury Plain, 'there he fought against the entire host, and put it to flight.'

The Danish leader Guthrum, together with his shattered army, retreated to his base at Chippenham; the Danes surrendered a fortnight later. Three weeks afterwards, Guthrum accompanied by thirty of his chief men came to the little church at Aller near Athelney. There Guthrum was baptized a Christian, and received the English name of Athelstan from his godfather Alfred. The two leaders feasted together, and in the autumn Guthrum and his host marched out of Wessex into Mercia and East Anglia. Alfred had saved his kingdom from the Danes, and the royal House of Wessex would in the future win back all the territory which the Danes had settled in the north and east.

Nothing remains of Alfred's fortification at Athelney, which was probably only a fairly makeshift affair in any case. The low hill in the marsh has a monument recording the monastery which Alfred founded on the site as a thank-offering for the deliverance of his kingdom, and a causeway linking the island with nearby Lyng probably dates from Alfred's time. Asser tells us that one of Alfred's fortified towns was created at Lyng, and this formed a link in the chain of refuges which surrounded the kingdom.

This quiet Isle of Athelney irresistibly reminds us of other dark times in England's history. Could not Alfred have said: 'We shall not flag or fail . . . we shall fight in the fields and in the streets, we shall fight in the hills; we shall never surrender.'

75

South Cadbury: Hill Fort, Somerset

South Cadbury, traditional site of Arthur's Camelot, is a mighty hill-fort which looks north and west over the Somerset basin to the Bristol Channel and the hills of Wales beyond. We do not know for sure whether Arthur and his knights ever admired this view, or whether they fought the Anglo-Saxons over the neighbouring terrain, but legend does not doubt these matters. South Cadbury is associated with Arthur, the Once and Future King, and he waits still, with his knights about him in the hollow hill of Cadbury, until his nation needs him again.

Arthur was not the only leader who sought sanctuary at Cadbury; its ramparts were already ancient when he knew them, having

Chapel Cross
To Wincanton
A303
To Ilminster
South Cadbury
75
0 km 1
0 Mile ½

Map Reference: ST 627250 (metric map 183. 1-inch map 166)
Nearest Town: Yeovil
Location: The distinctive free-standing hill of South Cadbury can be seen from some distance across the flatlands of Somerset. The village is to the south of the A303 between Wincanton and Ilminster and about 9 miles (14.5 km) north of Yeovil. The hill-fort can be reached by a rough track, which is signposted, close to the village pub.

A small piece of carved bone work dating from the Ethelredan occupation of the site. Finds were naturally sparse since the later use of the site only lasted for around six years.

Below: *Plan of the great fort of Cadbury. Most of the ramparts are of Iron Age date. Ethelred's wall ran round the inside of the innermost defence line.*

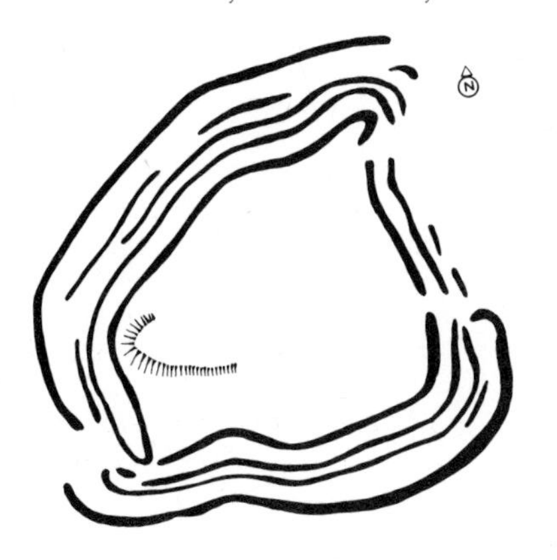

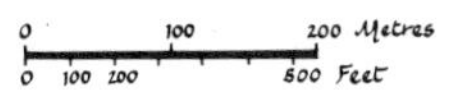

Parts of the defences are now tree-grown, but fine views may be had from the crown of the hill.

been built in the Iron Age, centuries before. During excavations on the site in 1966-70, Professor Leslie Alcock also found evidence of a later, Anglo-Saxon, use of the hill-top.

This later occupation relates to the troubled times during the reign of Ethelred, called the Unraed, in the early years of the 11th century. After Alfred's defence of Wessex against the Danes, southern England had lain largely undisturbed. But in 1009 Thorkell the Tall and his army harried large areas of the kingdom. Shortly after, perhaps in 1010, Ethelred founded an emergency citadel or 'burgh' at Cadbury. This was a fortified town, and it meshed in with the earlier system of strongholds established by Alfred after the Battle of Edington, of which Wallingford and Wareham formed part.

During the excavation at Cadbury, remains of the great stone wall which Ethelred had built on top of the old defences were uncovered. This was a massive affair with a fine mortared face and a great bank behind. Parts of it can still be seen around the top of the hill. The south-western fort gate was also rebuilt at this time, and the great stone wall encircling the hill-top must have been an impressive site.

Although no traces of it were found during the excavation, we know that there was a mint at Cadbury during Ethelred's reign since coins bearing the name CADANBYRIG, the Anglo-Saxon name for Cadbury, have been found elsewhere. It seems that the occupation of the site was short-lived, and that after King Canute acceded to the throne in 1016 the old fort at Cadbury was again deserted. The stone wall seems to have been carefully demolished, and much of its stone carted away. This was doubtless done to deny the men of Somerset a refuge in any future revolt against their Danish overlord.

76

Milborne Port: St John's Church, Somerset

Map Reference: ST 676186 (metric map 183. 1-inch map 178)
Nearest Town: Sherborne
Location: Milborne Port is 3 miles (5 km) east of Sherborne on the A30 Shaftesbury road.

Milborne was an Anglo-Saxon burgh or town, and the presence of a mint here during the 10th century indicates its former importance. The name, which means the town or 'port' of the mill on the stream called 'borne', suggests the presence of a water mill, perhaps of the type excavated at Tamworth, Staffordshire. At the time of the Domesday Book in the later 11th century, Milborne had six mills, suggesting that its earlier economy had continued.

The parish church of St John the Evangelist retains interesting Anglo-Saxon work which indicates that it was a substantial structure. Stripwork traces on the chancel and the west wall of the south transept suggest an elaborate scheme which, though now less well-preserved, was originally more delicate and highly decorated than that at Bradford-on-Avon.

Inside, all four piers of the Anglo-Saxon crossing have survived and the large high crossing space provides an impression of the scale of the early church. The pier capitals bear interlacing foliage ornament, some of which is a 19th-century plaster restoration. Within the chancel, traces of original windows may be seen in the side walls.

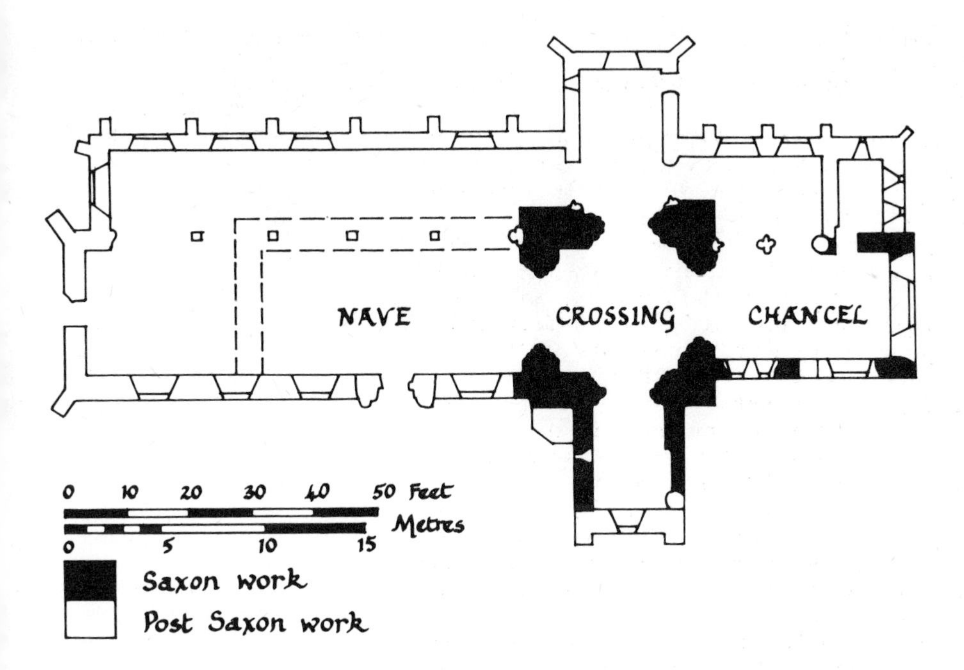

One of the elaborately carved capitals of the crossing piers at Milborne Port.

77
Melbury Bubb Font, Dorset

Nothing of the fabric of the delightful country church at Melbury Bubb is known to be of Anglo-Saxon origin, but it is the possessor of a first-class piece of 10th-century sculpture.

The font at the west end of the church is formed from an inverted section of a circular cross-shaft which has been hollowed out for its later use. The shaft is enriched with a frieze of animals including a noble stag, a lion, a wolf and small gambolling creatures, one of which appears to be a dolphin. The tails of these beasts curl round and about themselves in order to form abstracts which fill the spaces between the figures. This example of the Anglo-Saxon dislike of unoccupied space is particularly pleasing, since there is no feeling

Map Reference: ST 596065 (metric map 194. 1-inch map 178)
Nearest Town: Yeovil
Location: From Yeovil take the A37 south towards Dorchester. After 7 miles (11 km) take the east turn to Stockwood, carry on for one mile (1.6 km), then turn south at the T-junction. Melbury Bubb is a dead end to the west of this minor road.

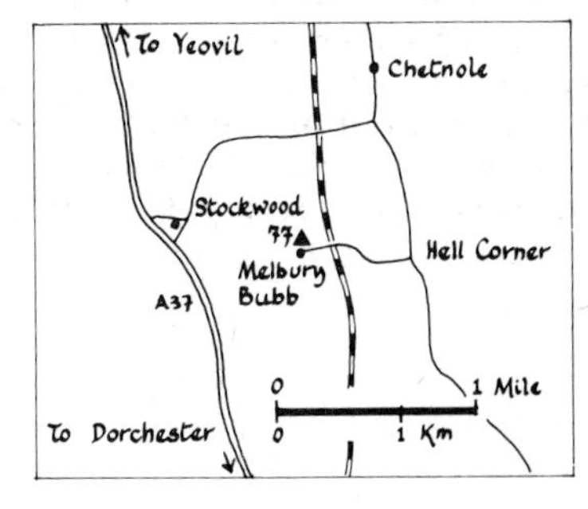

The splendid carved frieze from the font at Melbury Bubb.

of cramping or over-elaboration, but rather of liveliness and delicacy. The curving bodies of the beasts owe something to Scandinavian styles, but the relief carving and well-formed bodies are more akin to early Northumbrian work.

78

Wareham: Town Defences and St Martin's Church, Dorset

Wareham, like Wallingford, was part of the great system of defences erected against future Danish attacks by Alfred after the Battle of Edington in 878.

The fortifications at Wareham are the best preserved of all the towns in the 'Burghal Hidage', the nature of which is explained in the entry for Wallingford (No. 87). Alfred's chronicler Asser described Wareham as having 'the safest situation in the world, except on the west side where it is joined to the mainland.' This assessment of Wareham's defensive potential is perfectly accurate, as the River Frome lay to the south, with marshes and the River Piddle to the north and east. No bank was built along the river frontage, and the entry in the Burghal Hidage takes account of this since it assesses Wareham at 1,600 hides, which in turn gives a length of 2,200 yards, closely approximating to the extent of the three banks.

The 9th-century town was not the first use of the site for in Lady St Mary church are preserved five early Christian inscribed monuments. Four of these date from the 6th to the 8th centuries and bear British names. The stones are evidence of the existence of a British church on the site before the Anglo-Saxon invasion in the 7th century. The church was rebuilt by the Saxons in 700 or thereabouts, and became an important nunnery. Pictures of the church before its lamentable destruction in the 1840s show it to have been a large and impressive structure somewhat similar to the church at Brixworth in Northamptonshire.

Apart from the mighty ramparts which attest Wareham's strategic role as one of the Wessex frontier fortresses, there is evidence that it was an important centre in its own right.

Map Reference: **St Martin's Church** SY 923877 (metric map 195. 1-inch map 178)
Location: Wareham is delightfully situated near Poole Harbour between the Rivers Piddle and Frome. The splendidly preserved ramparts are particularly fine on the west side and a large car park has been conveniently, if rather insensitively, located beside the ramparts on the western edge of the town. It is well worth walking along the defences to visit St Martin's church, which stands on the line of the ramparts beside the site of the north gate.

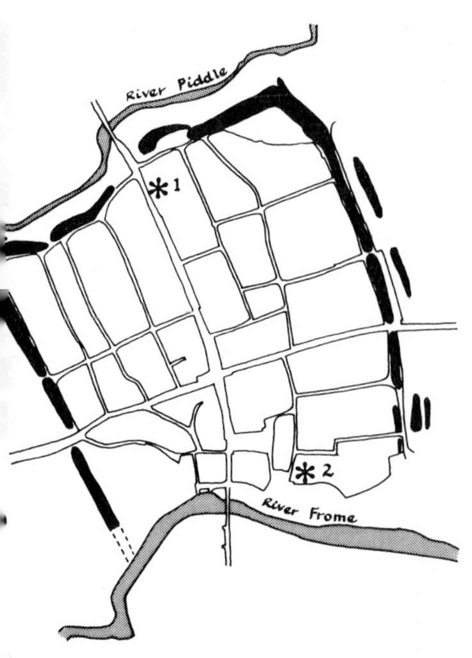

1 St. Martin's Church
2 St. Mary's Church
Defences

0 200 400 600 Metres
0 1000 2000 Feet

The great west bank of the defences.

St Martin's church, beside the site of the old north gate. The early nave and chancel plan is largely unaltered apart from the later south porch and a small north aisle which contains an effigy of Lawrence of Arabia, who lived nearby.

The nunnery was a prestigious foundation, and at least one Wessex king, Beorhtric, who died in 802, was buried there. William of Malmesbury, writing in the 12th century, also tells us that Wareham was a bustling seaport with a thriving cross-Channel trade. Elements of the 'grid-iron' street plan may well date from the 9th century, and we may imagine that their frontages were quite as busy then as they are today.

During the late 10th century, the little church of St Martin's was built beside the north entrance to the town on the line of the burgh bank. The high walls of the structure proclaim its antiquity, and the eastern nave and chancel quoins as well as the original plinth have survived. One round-headed Saxo-Norman window may be seen in the north wall of the chancel, and the chancel arch itself with its simple roll-moulding is an original feature.

The little town of Wareham can thus show a long occupation stretching back to Roman times. The great defensive banks have protected the town for 1,100 years, and they were put in readiness as recently as 1940, but this time as a defence against Hitler's tanks rather than the Vikings!

79

Breamore: The Minster Church of St Mary, Hampshire

In the parish of Breamore is a place called Charford, which legend connects with the site of one of Cerdic's battles during the foundation of Wessex. The battle is supposed to have occurred in 519. Some 5,000 Britons as well as their king 'Natan-Leod' were slain by the Saxon invaders. Modern research is now providing a complex picture of the origins of Wessex, but the tradition might contain a core of truth.

The church of St Mary is large and spacious

Map Reference: SU 153188 (metric map 184. 1-inch map 179)
Nearest Town: Salisbury/Fordingbridge
Location: Further down the A338 from Britford (see No. 80) is the village of Breamore. Turn off the main road into the village and fork right at the far end of the village green. The church is about a quarter of a mile (0.4 km) down this road, next to Breamore House. It stands in a fine churchyard, surrounded by beautiful parkland.

Detail of the doorway and window in the east wall of the south porticus.

The church from the south-east. The central timber tower, although not original, is thought to reflect the Anglo-Saxon design.

and contains a number of important early features. It probably dates from the late 10th century and its size suggests that it may have been a minster, a conclusion which is reinforced by the large size of the parish and early evidence of royal patronage.

The Anglo-Saxon nave, central tower and south porticus all survive, together with portions of the chancel walls and slight remains of a north porticus. Externally the flint walls have freestone long and short quoins, as well as pilaster strips. Three of the tower windows are Saxon, and others can be seen in the side walls of the nave and in the walls of the porticus. The timber superstructure of the tower is post-Saxon, but it probably reflects the early arrangement.

The church is entered through the later south porch. Above the inner door are the horribly mangled remains of a rood. The figures of St Mary and St John can be seen below the cross, and the original composition must have resembled that at Romsey. The

The doorway into the south porticus. Above is the famous inscription which still bears traces of red paint which might be original. Note the fine cable decoration on the impost.

hand of God descends from a cloud above, and the paint, although it is almost certainly medieval, reminds us of the colours with which the carving was originally decorated.

Inside, it is the length of the building which creates the strongest impression. The east and west tower arches were replaced in the 15th century, which has doubtless altered the proportions somewhat, but 19th-century records suggest that the Saxon arch was at least seven feet (2 metres) wide, which was a very substantial opening.

Mercifully the doorway into the south porticus has escaped serious alteration. On the head of the arch is a unique inscription formed of capital letters which retain what might be their original red pigment. The inscription has been interpreted as meaning 'Here is manifested the Covenant unto thee.' Comparison of the form of the letters with those on coins suggests that they must date from before 1020. The rather cryptic nature of the inscription has raised doubts as to whether it is complete. It is possible, in view of a stone from the chancel arch which bears the letters DES, that it was part of a longer passage which was continued over the heads of the other central arches. The south porticus could have been a baptistry, which function the inscription might describe, or alternatively it may have been used for the reservation of the Host. As with so many aspects of early liturgical practice, we may never know the answer.

80

Britford: St Peter's Church, Wiltshire

The manor of Britford was held by Edward the Confessor, and the Anglo-Saxon Chronicle tells us that he and his brother Tostig were staying here in 1065 when word reached them of a rebellion in Northumbria. Tostig was the Earl of Northumbria, as the inscription at Kirkdale in North Yorkshire records, and we must imagine that these tidings occasioned him considerable alarm.

The earliest fabric of St Peter's church reaches well back before Edward's time to the 8th century. When we look at the fine carving on the arch into the north porticus, it is interesting to speculate that Edward himself may have admired its quality. In view of the richness of the work at Britford, it seems highly probable that the church had benefited from royal patronage well before the 11th century.

The lower parts of the nave walls below the level of the windowsills, are Saxon, and at the east end of the nave are two original openings in the side walls. These arches led into small side chapels or porticus, which has been proved by excavation on the north side. The

Drawing of the decoration on the eastern jamb of the doorway into the north porticus.

Map Reference: SU 163284 (metric map 184. 1-inch map 167)
Nearest Town: Salisbury
Location: Britford is an attractively situated village 2 miles (3 km) south-east of Salisbury. It is signposted off the A338 road to Fordingbridge and Bournemouth.

Anglo-Saxon church probably had transepts, the west walls of which followed the present line.

The northern opening is a most elaborate affair with an inner lining of dressed stonework. The eastern jamb has two vertical stones with rich vinescrolls having leaf-shaped bunches of grapes at their centres. This work is of outstanding quality, and bears comparison with that produced during Northumbria's 'Golden Age'. Between the vertical slabs are square panels decorated with knotwork and rosettes, again of the highest quality. The extensive use of tiles in this doorway as well as in the simpler work round the southern opening, together with the fact that the tiles appear to have been made to fit the composition, suggest that they are Anglo-Saxon rather than re-used Roman material.

81

Codford St Peter: The Dancing Man, Wiltshire

Codford church has no surviving Anglo-Saxon fabric, but it has a splendid and highly unusual piece of sculpture. Built into the north wall of the chancel, the extraordinary 'dancing man' is a puzzling piece. The stone formed part of a cross-shaft, and tapers noticeably towards the top. If, as seems likely, this cross served as a memorial, it could commemorate a jester. Certainly the stance of the man, with his head thrown back, glancing up at the fruit-laden branch balanced in his right hand, suggests a fairly lighthearted activity. The object in his left hand has been identified as a mallet or a musical instrument, but nobody knows for certain.

The details of the man's dress, such as the narrow fillet which holds his hair in place, together with the 'tiptoe' stance and the lobed leaves on the sides of the shaft all indicate a close connection with manuscript art of the late 8th century. Closest similarities lie with books from Canterbury, which were themselves influenced by Continental Carolingian art styles. This suggests that the Codford man belongs to the great artistic revival of the early 9th century. Some have claimed it as being later in the 9th century, perhaps dating from the reign of Alfred. Either of these theories is quite possible; but in any case it is a tantalizing example of the work of Wessex sculptors of which all too few pieces survive. It has recently been suggested that the figure on the stone might be a bungled 'archer', like the earlier Northumbrian examples at Bishop Auckland and elsewhere but this seems to us to underestimate the quality of this work. The Codford man may not yet be explicable, but we may rest assured that he does not represent some half-remembered theme, but rather a subject which was perfectly familiar to the wealthy patrons who commissioned the work.

Map Reference: SU 966399 (metric map 184. 1-inch map 167)
Nearest Town: Warminster
Location: Codford is on the main A36 road between Warminster and Salisbury, 6 miles (9.5 km) south-east of Warminster.

This carving of the 'Codford Man' must rate as one of the masterpieces of 9th-century Wessex art.

82

Knook Tympanum, Wiltshire

Map Reference: ST 937418 (metric map 184. 1-inch map 167)
Nearest Town: Warminster
Location: Close by the River Wylye, Knook church is at the end of a short spur off the main A36 Warminster to Salisbury road, about 5 miles (8 km) south-east of Warminster.

Although close to a busy road, the little church of St Margaret at Knook stands in an oasis of quietness beside the River Wylye. Heavy restoration has removed much of the early fabric, but a remarkable doorway has been preserved in the south wall of the nave. The doorway has a round head enriched with roll-mouldings in a similar style to those on the tower at Langford in Oxfordshire.

Between the square head of the door and the arch above is a fine tympanum which has been the source of some debate. Some authorities have dismissed it out of hand as being of post-Conquest date, but Sir Alfred Clapham pointed out its similarities to Anglo-Saxon manuscript art of the late 10th or early 11th centuries. This correlation appears compelling, and the Knook tympanum can thus be accepted as an important example of West Saxon architectural sculpture. It is interesting in this connection to note the correspondence between manuscript and sculptural styles which was a marked feature of the 'Winchester School' tradition.

The carving is in very low relief, and resembles a line drawing more than a sculpture. Two opposed animals form the basis of the design: a lion on the right and a griffin on the left. They bite at a central tree stem, the branches of which curl about the beasts' bodies in such a way that every part of the tympanum is uniformly filled with scrollwork. Unlike the font at Melbury Bubb, where the Anglo-Saxon horror of wasted space does not detract from the quality of the design, the effect here is one of muddle. Indeed, it is difficult to perceive the various elements of the design at first glance, the more so because the absence of any relief renders the work flat and toneless. But this aside, the carving is well executed, and the symmetry of the design very pleasing.

Inside the church is a remarkable wooden chancel arch of Norman date in which two Anglo-Saxon stone capitals are re-used. Behind the altar in the east wall of the chancel a short section of Anglo-Saxon interlace work is built into the wall; however, part of this stone is a modern copy.

At first sight this panel looks like a confused jumble of animals and scrollwork, but well-formed beasts appear from the swirling scrolls when the eyes have adjusted to the low-relief carving.

83

Bradford-on-Avon: St Laurence's Chapel, Wiltshire

The 12th-century chronicler William of Malmesbury made the following reference to Bradford: 'to this day at that place there exists a little church which Aldhelm is said to have built to the name of the most blessed Laurence.'

St Aldhelm was Bishop of Malmesbury from around 675 to 709. He was a noted writer and poet whose verses, which were sung to a harp accompaniment, were later admired by King Alfred. He is said to have founded monasteries at Bradford and Frome, but the chapel to which William refers appears to have been an independent venture.

The little church at Bradford has, even for an Anglo-Saxon building, been the source of more than usual controversy. Before Canon Jones, then vicar of Bradford, realized the true nature of the building in 1856, it had been used as a cottage and a chapel. Upon recognizing its Anglo-Saxon character, Jones hailed it as the long-lost chapel to which William had referred, and it was promptly restored and rededicated to St Laurence. Since then, it has become apparent that the architecture of the building belongs to a later period than the time of Aldhelm, and hot argument has arisen as to whether any part of the structure dated from the early 8th century. The latest opinion of Dr H. M. Taylor suggests that the building is in fact entirely of the 10th century, and that it need have no relevance at all to the church described by William of Malmesbury.

Having disposed of one theory, another must be erected in its place. We know that during the 10th century Aldhelm's body was translated to Bradford, and it is suggested that this chapel may have been built to house it. A crypt is known to exist under one of the porticus, and this may have contained the saint's body. It is likely that the chapel was built within the precinct of the monastery earlier founded by Aldhelm, and it is suspected that the early monastic church was on the site of the present parish church. St Laurence's chapel may therefore have been built as a mortuary chapel, perhaps dedicated to

The chancel from the south. Note the three reeded pilasters in the eastern gable of the nave above the chancel roof and the fine arcaded decoration on the upper parts of the walls. It is a handsome building.

Map Reference: ST 824609 (metric map 173. 1-inch map 166)
Location: Bradford is a busy bridgepoint on the Avon downstream from Bath, about 6 miles (9.5 km) south-east of the city. The now famous chapel of St Laurence is on the north side of the Avon, opposite Holy Trinity church. It is well signposted in the town. There is a convenient car park beside the library from where a footbridge over the river leads directly to the church and chapel.

The chancel arch. The reeded moulding round the head closely resembles the pilasters at the east end of the nave, indicating that the elements of the building were carefully planned in a single scheme.

One of the Bradford Angels. They probably hovered above the arms of a Crucifixion scene in positions similar to the angels on the smaller rood at Romsey.

Aldhelm himself. This would account for the building of a new chapel during the 10th century which, to judge from its architectural elaboration, was plainly of considerable importance. So much for theory; the only certainty which attaches to this building is that it will be a bone of contention for many years to come!

Upon approaching the chapel, the tall narrow proportions of the structure are very much apparent. Loftiness is a marked feature of much Anglo-Saxon architecture, whether it be in entire buildings as here and at Escomb (No. 11), or merely in details, as with the doorways at Ledsham (No. 23) and Worth (No. 97). The plan of St Laurence's is of the simplest, comprising a small nave and chancel, together with a surviving north porticus and a balancing structure to the south which has since been demolished. The outside walls bear a pleasing decorative scheme of pilaster strips which spring from a high plinth and terminate in a bold string-course which forms a base for blank arcading above. Traces of pilaster strips with reeded decoration occur in the eastern gable of the nave and in the gable of the north porticus. The completeness of this scheme is in refreshing contrast to the many fragmentary examples elsewhere, such as that at Milborne

Port. There is evidence that some of the windows were enlarged during the later Saxon period and this is particularly noticeable on the west wall of the north porticus where a window jamb cuts across the line of a pilaster strip.

Inside, the height of the building is very striking; the roof vanishes into darkness, and the atmosphere is one of dark holiness. The chancel arch is a robust no-nonsense affair, with square imposts and simply reeded head. Fragments of fine Anglo-Saxon friezework are incorporated into the frontal of the modern altar. High above the chancel arch the Bradford Angels may be seen; superb examples of 'Winchester School' carving which in the delicate folds of their garments and stiffly posed wings owe much to manuscript art. They were probably originally positioned lower down the wall above the arms of a Crucifixion which has now disappeared. The north porticus doorway resembles the chancel arch, but note how the northern door is off-set to the west, probably to accommodate an altar to the east.

The Virgin sits in a chair and the Child holds a book; MARIA *is carved into the upper frame. The later sundial cut into the stone below the figure of the Virgin indicates that the stone was originally built into the exterior of the south wall.*

84

Inglesham: The Virgin and Child, Wiltshire

Map Reference: SU 205984 (metric map 163. 1-inch map 157)
Nearest Town: Highworth
Location: Inglesham is tucked into a spur of Wiltshire close to both the Wiltshire and Oxfordshire boundaries. The hamlet is beside the River Thames about a mile (1.6 km) south of Lechlade just to the west of the A361. The church stands between two large farms. There is no other settlement in the vicinity.

The little church of St John the Baptist is an extraordinary place. It was beloved of William Morris, doyen of the Arts and Crafts Movement, and he succeeded in staying the hand of the Victorian church restorers. The result is a charming village church which retains many ancient features. The nave is of early character, and may well be late Saxon. The south door by which the church is entered is perhaps the original south door of the nave, re-erected in its present position when the aisle was added.

But the principal interest of Inglesham resides in the carving of the Madonna and Child in the south wall of the south aisle. This carving is a good example of 11th-century West Saxon work: the technique is undistinguished, with shallow relief and poorly executed detail, but the overall effect reveals the artist's tender feelings towards his subject. The figure of the Virgin bends protectively over the Child, and the hand of God descends powerfully above the Child's head. There is no artistry in the drapery as there is at Barnack in Cambridgeshire, but the placing of the figures subtly emphasizes the poignancy of the scene. In the words of Sir Thomas Kendrick: '. . . though the panel was never a great sculpture, . . . it is significant as a truthful translation into stone of the essential virtues of the finest English drawing of the age.'

85
Langford Tower and Roods, Oxfordshire

The church at Langford is a somewhat puzzling structure, not least because its original dedication is unknown. It appears to have formed part of a royal estate, and this doubtless accounts for the high quality of its sculpture and its advanced design. The early church consisted of three cells – a nave and chancel linked by a central tower but the tower alone survives. Langford makes up for the loss of its nave and chancel by the intrinsic interest of its remaining fabric.

At first sight, it might appear that the topmost belfry stage of the tower is Norman, for the windows with their impressive roll-mouldings and decorated imposts are very advanced. The corbel table at the top of the tower with its little beast heads is unmistakably Norman, but all the work below is late

Map Reference: SP 249025 (metric map 163. 1-inch map 157)
Nearest Town: Burford
Location: Langford is in the Upper Thames Valley close to the Cotswolds. The church is in a delightful rural setting. The village is between Lechlade and Burford, on a minor road to the east of the A361.

The smaller of the two Langford roods.

Saxon. The middle stage has more familiar Saxon features in its round-headed windows and pilaster strips. The strip in the centre of the south wall has a decorative plaque set half way up which shows two figures bearing aloft a sundial. The weathered tide lines can just be made out upon its face if the light is kind. The southern aspect of the tower, with its finely dressed quoins and neat stripwork, is a noble sight. Inside are two majestic tower arches, the eastern relying for its effect on the skilful balance of its mouldings.

The church is very fortunate in possessing two late Saxon roods which are now built into the later south porch. The larger of them, in the east wall, is a marvellous piece of work with the folds of the garment delicately drawn, and a moving elegance in the composition. The flowing lines seem surprisingly modern, and the figure has the same forceful quality as the Epstein Christ in Llandaff Cathedral. It is a thousand pities that the head of this masterpiece has been lost; a few curls of the beard are left below the neck to attest the quality of the original, which must have rivalled the York Christ.

The second rood is built into the gable over the south door; it is cruder than the other, but intact. Christ hangs from the cross whilst St Mary and St John look sorrowfully away. The figures are all nimbed, and Christ's nimbus bears a cross, as is usual in Anglo-Saxon art. In contrast to the image of Christ Triumphant depicted in the great rood, he appears in agony here. These two carvings, one showing the death of the mortal man and the other the triumph of the Son of God together illustrate the subtlety of the Anglo-Saxon religious experience.

86

Oxford: St Michael's Church, Oxfordshire

Map Reference: SP 513063 (metric map 164. 1-inch map 158)
Location: The church is in the heart of Oxford in Cornmarket Street, which leads off Broad Street.

St Michael's church stands just inside the old north gate of the city, and must have been a well-known landmark. Only the west tower of the Saxon church survives; an example of sturdy late Saxon workmanship.

St Michael's tower from the south. The quoins at the south-west angle are a modern restoration. Note the fine turned baluster shaft in the lower double window.

The rubble fabric of the tower is tied in with long and short quoins at the northern angles, but those to the south are finished with irregular blocks; perhaps the northern aspect was considered the more important since it faced a main entrance to the city. On the ground floor is a blocked round-headed western doorway; the jambs have been robbed but the plain dressed stone head and square imposts remain. On the first floor are windows to the north and west, the latter having been enlarged to form a door. On the north side is a second-floor doorway which is seemingly original; perhaps this was for the display of relics or banners during triumphal entrances into the city. The fourth floor has good late Saxon double belfry windows with pleasing turned baluster shafts between the lights. The bell-chamber above has original double lights in all save the east face which are of similar character to those on the floor below. Within, the tower arch has been replaced and there are no further Anglo-Saxon features extant.

87
Wallingford Town Defences, Oxfordshire

After Alfred's defeat of the Danes at Edington in 878, which is described under the entry for Athelney (No. 74), he set about strengthening the defences of Wessex in order to resist further Danish attacks. He introduced a seaborne force to counter the Danes before they landed, and thereby earned for himself the title of 'Father of the English Navy'. The army was reorganized in such a way that troops were always available to meet an invasion, and he also established a chain of fortified 'burghs' or towns in the kingdom, of which Wallingford and Wareham are examples.

A remarkable document recording Alfred's defensive strategy has survived. It is now known as the 'Burghal Hidage', and the towns or burghs mentioned in it are generally called the 'forts of the Burghal Hidage'. The basic idea was that a chain of strongpoints would be established round the borders of Wessex together with some in the central areas. No subject was further than 25 miles (40 km) from a 'Hidage' fort, and many were closer; the forts would serve as refuges in case of Danish attack. From the borders of Kent and Sussex in the east to the fort at Lydford in Devon, the Burghal Hidage provides a blueprint of Alfred's defensive strategy.

But the system was more complex than this. Apart from listing the forts, the Burghal Hidage also states how many 'hides' – which were traditionally the units of land which would support one free family and its dependants – belonged to each burgh. Each hide was expected to contribute one man for the defence

Map Reference: SU 610890 (metric map 174/5. 1-inch map 158)
Location: The attractive town of Wallingford is beside the River Thames 12 miles (19 km) south-east of Oxford. The Saxon defences can best be seen in the park on the south-west side of the town.

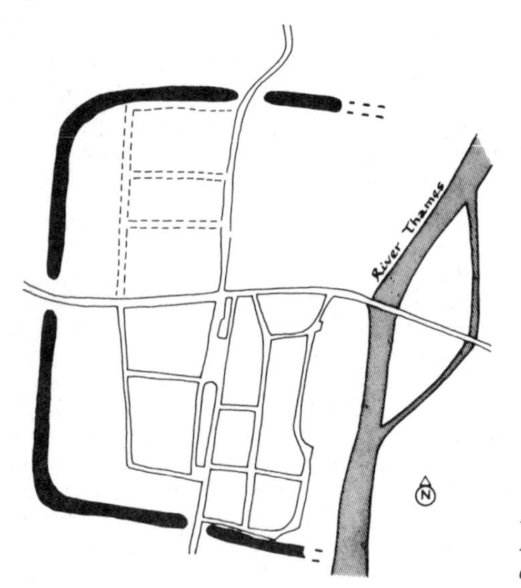

Plan showing the surviving Anglo-Saxon defences together with elements of the original grid-iron street plan. The stream on the opposite side of the Thames perhaps marks the line of an outwork on that side which was designed to prevent an attacker rushing the bridge across the river.

The bank and ditch in the south-west quadrant of the town where they are best preserved. This section of the defences has had gaps cut in it later; they may date from the time of the Civil War when Wallingford was again defended, and may have been used as cannon loops.

of the burgh to which it was allocated. The defences of each burgh were then laid out in such a way that four men could guard every 5½ yards (5 metres) of wall. So this was a remarkable system indeed – a home defence plan which ensured that an adequate garrison would be available to man each strongpoint in the event of a Viking attack, and the reasonable probability of safety for every man and his family. In this careful plan, which was unsurpassed elsewhere in Anglo-Saxon England, we perceive the cool logic of Alfred, who sought not only to strengthen the Church and to educate his subjects, but also to protect them from the wrath of the Northmen more effectively than any other Anglo-Saxon monarch.

Wallingford was set on a royal estate and commanded a bridgepoint of the River Thames. It was therefore a strategic site, and the scale of its defensive works is second only to that at Wareham. Wallingford has 2,400 hides allocated to it in the Burghal Hidage, giving a force of the same number of men who in turn could defend a circuit 3,300 yards in circumference. This figure tallies closely with the total length of Wareham's defences including the river frontage. It is possible that the eastern boundary actually crossed the river at one point, in order to guard the bridge across the river. The modern council boundary swings across the river and follows the line of a ditch which might mark the old defence line.

Excavations have shown that the great banks were originally faced with timber, and that they were restored on several occasions; perhaps the last was during the reign of Ethelred when the old fort at South Cadbury was added to the network of strongholds. Little is known of the life of the inhabitants of Anglo-Saxon Wallingford, but it must have been a thriving place, acting as a market centre for the country round. As you walk through the modern town, notice how many of the streets meet at right angles. This grid-iron street plan almost certainly reflects another aspect of Alfred's careful planning!

88

Kingston Lisle: The Blowing Stone, Oxfordshire

This curious stone, called the 'Blowing Stone', used to stand upon the Great Ridgeway above the village on Blowing Stone Hill. The hill commands extensive views of the fertile Vale of the White Horse, which was the northern granary of the kingdom of Wessex.

When someone used to playing large brass instruments such as the tuba blows into the hole at the top of the stone, a loud echoing note is produced from a hole in the side. Traditionally this stone was used to alert the Saxon farmers in the Vale of impending Viking attack. When the Blowing Stone sounded, the thanes gathered their 'fyrd' or militia about them and proceeded to mustering places in order to resist the invader.

The truth of this legend is inevitably beyond direct proof, but the Stone does emit a loud booming note, and it all seems just a little too circumstantial to be lightly dismissed.

The Blowing Stone. It is blown through the small hole near the centre of the top of the stone; this connects with a small aperture low down on the left-hand side.

The Blowing Stone blown! This particular West Saxon is David Dawson, Keeper of Archaeology at Bristol City Museum.

Map Reference: SU 324870 (metric map 174. 1-inch map 158)
Nearest Town: Wantage
Location: Kingston Lisle is on the edge of the Lambourn Downs between Swindon and Wantage, 5 miles (8 km) west of Wantage on the B4507. At the junction of the minor road to Kingston Lisle north of Lambourn, turn south and pull up by the row of cottages close to this junction. The stone is to be found in a fenced enclosure in front of the cottages.

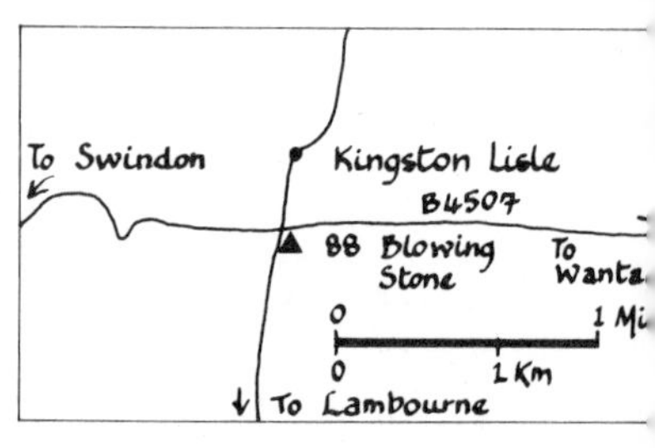

89

Ramsbury Crosses and Sculpture, Wiltshire

The increasing importance of Wessex during the early 10th century encouraged an extension of the church. In 909 three new bishoprics were created, one of which was sited at Ramsbury. The new see lasted until 1058, when it was reunited with Sherborne. Nothing is left of the cathedral church at Ramsbury, although some foundations were observed during 19th-century restoration work. Recent excavations have failed to reveal evidence of Anglo-Saxon occupation, but it seems likely that there was a substantial settlement here. Indeed, it is also probable that Ramsbury existed as a settlement before the see was established.

The most spectacular of the Ramsbury carvings is the great cross-shaft, which is decorated with spirited serpents set against a background of complicated interlacing tendrils. Apart from the serpents on the main faces, the sides of the cross bear interesting knotwork and wheel patterns. The whole belongs to the first half of the 11th century when, with a Danish king on the throne of England, Scandinavian influences penetrated to the heart of Wessex. The serpents show strong links with the Ringerike style which was particularly popular in southern England at the time.

Apart from the fragments of cross-shaft, there are also two fine coped tombstones with interlace decoration. These are quite late in character, since the foliate ornament on the stones has been reduced to barbed points. They presumably date to the late 10th century when the see of Ramsbury was still in operation. The form of these coped stones, and there are several at Ramsbury, perhaps owes something to the Anglo-Danish 'hog-back' stones of Northumbria, but such matters would doubtless have meant little to the prominent Wessex citizens who were buried beneath them.

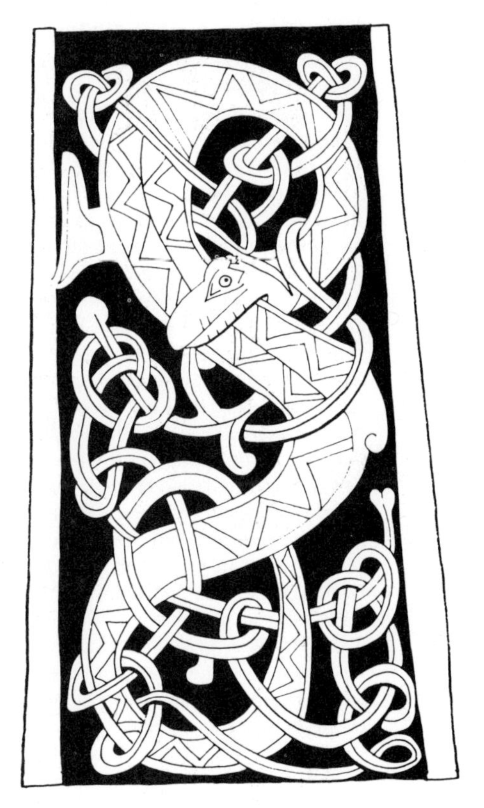

One face of the 11th-century cross-shaft. The serpent shows strong Danish Ringerike influence and, although carved in low relief, has great vitality.

Map Reference: AU 273716 (metric map 174 1-inch map 157)
Nearest Town: Hungerford
Location: Ramsbury is on the River Kennett, just off the A419 Hungerford to Swindon road, about 4½ miles (7 km) north-west of Hungerford.

One of the 10th-century coped tombstones. The foliate decoration has been reduced to regular scrolls and barbed points, rather than sinuous stems and leaves.

90

Wansdyke: A Wessex Frontier, Wiltshire and Avon

As with the Cambridgeshire Dykes, much speculation has been engendered by the great earthwork called Wansdyke which stretches intermittently for some 45 miles (72 km) between Dundry Hill south-east of Bristol in the west and Great Bedwyn or thereabouts on the Berkshire/Wiltshire border to the east. The work appears to be divided into two sections, one on the crest of the hills south of the valley of the Bristol Avon between Bristol and Bath, and the other beginning at Morgan's Hill near Devizes and continuing over the southern edge of the Marlborough Downs to a point west of Savernake Forest. The central section is occupied by the line of the Roman road from Silchester to Bath which was once thought to have formed part of the dyke itself. The easterly section across the downland to Savernake is the more impressive, and it is rewarding to walk this length.

The origins of Wansdyke are something of a mystery. The name means 'Dyke of the God Woden'. Woden was chief amongst the Anglo-Saxon gods, and it appears that this area of southern England was something of a centre of his cult. This is indicated by other place names such as 'Woden's Valley' near West Overton and a place formerly called Wodnes Beorgh or 'Woden's Barrow', now called Adam's Grave, near Alton Priors. Since the dyke has an Anglo-Saxon name, it might be tempting to adduce this as evidence for its origin, but we know that the Anglo-Saxons often referred to Roman works as the 'works of giants', so they might just as easily have decided that this great dyke was created by a God.

Various theories for the dyke's origins have been advanced, including an attempt by Ambrosius, leader of the Britons, to stem the Anglo-Saxon advance southwards before the Battle of Mount Badon in the late 5th century. Perhaps the most likely explanation sees the dyke as having been constructed in two stages: the eastern section as a check by Wessex to the Middle Anglian expansion after the Battle of Fethanleag in 584, and the western as a counter to Mercian aggression under Penda around 628. Whatever its original purpose, the earthwork is a splendid sight, and it is well worth following its bank and ditch across the Marlborough Downs on a fine summer's day!

Map Reference: SU 127652 (metric map 173. 1-inch map 167)

Nearest Towns: Bristol, Bath, Marlborough

Locations: As can be seen from the map, Wansdyke stretches from Bristol in the west to Marlborough in the east. The most complete section stretches for over 10 miles (16 km) from Grid Reference SU 030670 to 195665. Further sections can be seen south of Bristol and Bath at ST 601655 to ST 624651, ST 660641 to 672639 (metric map 172.) The Wansdyke can be walked along its whole length, but for the motorist the best viewing point is on the minor road between Fyfield and Alton Priors, a south turning off the A4 one mile (1.6 km) west of Marlborough. About 3 miles (5 km) from Fyfield the dyke, which is tree-grown, cuts across the shallow valley.

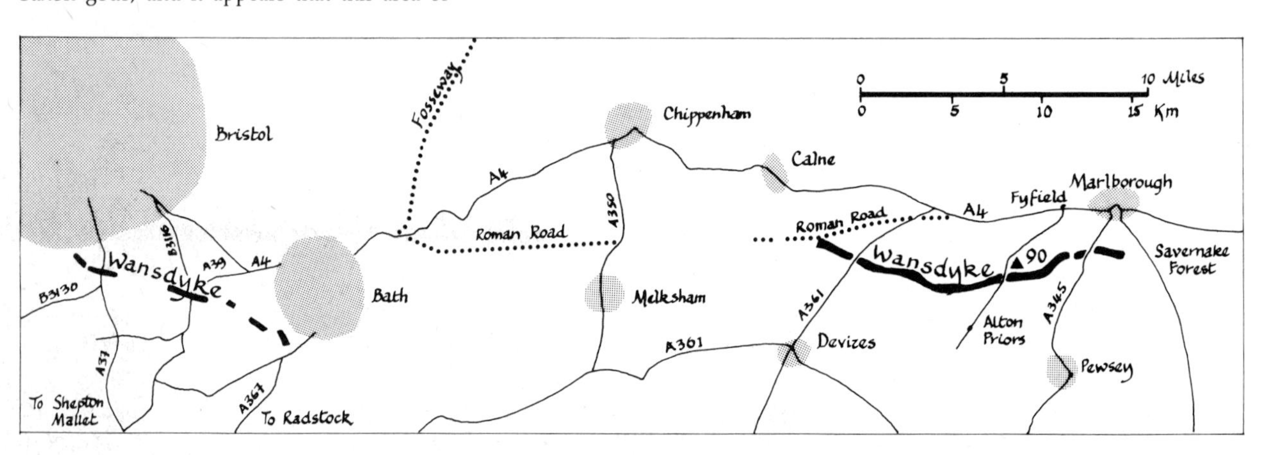

The dyke where it crosses the minor road between Fyfield and Alton Priors.

91
Whitchurch Sculpture, Hampshire

Although nothing of the fabric of All Hallows church is known to be of pre-Conquest date, it houses an interesting piece of Anglo-Saxon sculpture. This stone was discovered embedded in the north wall of the nave during restoration work in 1868. The form of the piece is unique in England, and is closer to Roman funerary monuments than to other known Anglo-Saxon gravestones. That this was a gravestone is evident from the inscription cut into the top of the stone:

+HIC CORPUS FRIDBURGAE REQUIESCIT IN PACEM SEPULTUM

'Here the body of Frithburga lies buried in peace'

The figure on the front has generally been identified as a bust of Christ, but the composition bears a striking resemblance to a wall panel bust of the Virgin Mary at Breedon-on-the-Hill in Leicestershire. Although the

Map Reference: SU 460480 (metric map 185. 1-inch map 168)
Nearest Town: Andover
Location: Whitchurch is just to the east of the A34 dual carriageway, between Newbury and Winchester, about 12 miles (19 km) north of that city. The church of All Hallows is on the south side of this pleasant little town.

The front and back of the Whitchurch stone. The form of the monument appears to be unique in Anglo-Saxon England, and may derive from Roman funerary sculpture.

Breedon piece is rather earlier, being 8th century rather than late 9th or 10th as here, the pose of the figure, the form of the blessing administered by the right hand, and the appearance of a book in the left hand are closely similar. Sadly the weathering on the Whitchurch stone makes it difficult to be sure. The reverse has graceful incised scrollwork upon its upper part which is in contrast to the rather crude representation on the front. The identity of Frithburga is uncertain though it has been plausibly suggested that she may have been abbess of the nearby monastery at Wherwell.

92

Romsey Roods, Hampshire

Map Reference: SU 350212 (metric map 185. 1-inch map 168)
Location: Romsey stands on the east bank of the River Test 5 miles (8 km) north of the Southampton Water, on the A3057 road from Southampton to Andover.

The early history of Romsey abbey is obscure, but traditionally Edward the Elder, son of Alfred, founded a small nunnery here in 907. Merewenna, later canonized as a saint, became

The Great Rood, an image of Christ Triumphant; note the hand of God appearing from the rather woolly cloud above Christ's head.

abbess in 967, and the house flourished under her rule. Princesses were numbered among the inmates, and one of her disciples, called Ethelfleda, supposedly a daughter of Ethelwold of Essex, was also canonized. Ethelfleda is reputed to have indulged in nude nocturnal bathing for ascetical reasons, and died at an advanced age. Both these remarkable Anglo-Saxon ladies were buried in the abbey church.

No trace now survives above ground of that church, but excavations during the 19th century revealed traces of an apsidal structure of imposing proportions. In 1975, further excavations revealed the foundations of a large northern porticus which incorporated substantial re-used Roman stones in its footings.

The dearth of structural evidence is more than compensated for by the two Romsey roods, which are among the major achievements of Anglo-Saxon art. The first is a small gilded stone panel set in a later wooden frame which now stands on the altar in the south aisle. The figure of Christ is rigid and formalized, whilst the Cherubim on the arms of the cross and the acanthus scrolls which curl from behind are both characteristic of Byzantine models. The Virgin Mary and St John are here joined by the Roman soldier Longinus who plunges his spear into Our Lord's side, and Stephaton, who offers a sponge mounted on a reed.

The second Romsey rood is life size, and is built into the outside of the west wall of the south transept. This carving is almost certainly a relic of the original monastic church, where it would have occupied a prominent position, perhaps in the east wall of the nave. Carved from huge blocks of stone, the Crucifixion has no hint of sadness about it. Rather, it is a scene of Christ crucified yet triumphant, eyes open and head erect, he surveys the world which he rules.

Arguments have been raised about the date of this sculpture, and it has been claimed as post-Conquest work; but it must surely belong to the great tradition of later Saxon figure sculpture in southern England of which Langford in Oxfordshire and the mutilated example at Breamore elsewhere in the same county are important representatives.

93

Corhampton: Church and Sundial, Hampshire

Map Reference: SU 610203 (metric map 185. 1-inch map 168)
Nearest Town: Fareham
Location: Corhampton is on the A32 Reading to Fareham road about 8 miles (13 km) north of Fareham. The church stands on the west side of the main road, in a raised churchyard.

Set in a raised churchyard beside a prodigious yew tree, this little church is a fine survival of a pre-Conquest structure. Corhampton has not come through entirely unscathed; the east end of the chancel was rebuilt after a collapse in 1855, and various other patchings of the fabric have been carried out, but it is sufficiently intact to provide a very clear impression of its original appearance.

The walls are built of flints, with freestone being reserved for the long and short quoins and the pilaster strips which form such a

The Anglo-Saxon sundial in the south wall with its unusual foliate and 'capstan' tide-marks.

The church from the south. Traces of the stripwork scheme can be seen above and to the east of the porch.

notable exterior feature. At the west end, a horizontal string-course can be seen about a third of the way up the wall. This line was probably carried right round the building originally at or slightly below eaves level; it is therefore likely that the walls have been lowered by about three feet (90 cm). The vertical strips are set on a low plinth around the bottom of the walls, and their bases are unusually decorated with a design of three small leaves, the one to the west of the south door being the best preserved. The window above the string-course in the south wall was used as a bell-cote and the marks made by the bells on the jambs are still clearly visible; it is possible that this was the Anglo-Saxon arrangement.

Before entering the church, note the Anglo-Saxon sundial east of the south porch. Carved in reddish brown stone, it is divided into eight sections or 'tides'. Divisions on the dial are marked either by strange bulbous shapes, or by trefoil leaves. The hole for the gnomon is still visible at the centre.

Inside, the chancel arch dominates the scene. It is a fine piece of masonry, and shows careful composition in the balance of its voussoirs and in the unusual device of advancing the keystone at the head of the hood mould. These features, together with its simplicity of form, serve to emphasize the stature of the arch. Attention is thus focused towards the east end of the nave, and the rather limited space is skilfully extended.

94

Bosham: Holy Trinity Church, West Sussex

Map Reference: SU 804039 (metric map 197. 1-inch map 181)
Nearest Town: Chichester
Location: A popular sailing spot, Bosham is about 4 miles (6.5 km) west of Chichester, a south turning off the A27. The church stands dramatically, close to the harbour, in a well-kept churchyard.

It is curious that for a church so well documented as that at Bosham we have no knowledge of the dedication before the 14th century, since which time it has been known as Holy Trinity. This apart, the first reference

Perhaps these two gentlemen were late! This picture from the Bayeux Tapestry purports to show Bosham church. It is, of course, a stylized representation of 'a church'; we know that the western tower would have been standing and acting as a landmark to seamen when King Harold made his ill-starred voyage.

to Bosham occurs in the Venerable Bede's *History of the English Church and People*, which records that when St Wilfrid of Ripon came to preach the gospel to the South Saxons in 681 there was already 'among them a certain monk of the Scottish nation called Dicul who had a very small monastery at a place called Bosenham, encompassed with sea and woods, and in it five or six brothers who served the Lord in peace and humility.' Bede also tells us that Dicul's mission was not very successful: the natives were not interested. We are assured that Wilfrid made some progress before returning to Northumbria in 686, for he enjoyed the support of the South Saxon King Ethelwalch who had previously been baptized in Mercia.

Bosham was a busy port in Anglo-Saxon times, and it was from here that King Harold made his ill-starred trip to Normandy. The feasting hall of the manor house at Bosham is shown in the Bayeux Tapestry, as is a highly stylized representation of Bosham church. The manor of Bosham was held by Edward the Confessor, and there is reason to believe that it

The tower from the west. The quoins, double belfry light and some of the windows remain from the 11th-century church.

was held by Canute before him. A centuries-old tradition relates that a small grave near the chancel steps is that of a younger daughter of Canute. When the grave was opened in 1865, the skeleton of a young girl was found lying in a stone coffin. Although there is no certain evidence that this was Canute's daughter, the tradition is very strong, and a modern tablet near the spot bears the Black Raven of Denmark, Canute's emblem. Legend also relates that during a 10th-century Viking raid the tenor bell of Bosham church was stolen. When the raiders put to sea, the church bells rang the 'all clear' and the tenor bell in the Viking boat tried to join in. The boat capsized, drowning the miscreants, and the bell fell into deep water at a place still called 'Bell Hole'.

Fable aside, Bosham church retains interesting Anglo-Saxon features, since the western tower, nave and chancel arch are all of the 11th century. The tower is of three stages divided by simple string-courses. All the openings save one double belfry light, a blocked window in the south side and another on the north are post-Saxon, though the second-floor window on the north side retains its Anglo-Saxon frame. The western nave quoins can be seen to either side of the tower.

Inside, the tower arch is fine but cannot match the superb chancel arch. A gabled doorway above the tower arch may have led onto a timber gallery like the one at Wing in Buckinghamshire. The other openings near the doorway are probably to provide ingress to the roof-space above the nave. The nave retains three circular windows high up in the north wall. The western third of the chancel is of Saxon date, the rest being Norman and later; note the perverse angle at which the chancel joins the nave. One blocked window survives in the north wall, though it was partially cut away when a 12th-century window was inserted.

The chancel arch itself is prodigious and decidedly elegant, one of the best in the country. The matching capitals and bases are of very advanced design, and bespeak the influence of the holy King Edward, whose penchant for elaborate Continentally-inspired designs is also indicated at Great Paxton in Cambridgeshire. It is interesting to note in this connection that both the chancel arch here at Bosham and the nave arcade at Paxton have markedly horseshoe-shaped arch heads. It has been suggested that the mighty plinths upon which the Bosham arch rests are re-used Roman work, but there is no evidence for this. Rather we must view this remarkable composition as a monument to the religious zeal of King Edward, who was aptly nicknamed 'the Confessor'.

Right: *The southern capital of the chancel arch – a remarkable composition!*

95

Selham: St James's Church, West Sussex

Map Reference: SU 933206 (metric map 197. 1-inch map 181)
Nearest Town: Chichester
Location: Only 3 miles (5 km) west of Petworth House, Selham is a delightful village in the South Downs. It can be reached by a minor road, a south turning off the A272, about halfway between Petworth and Midhurst.

Although no church is mentioned in the entry for 'Seleham' in Domesday Book, the simple parish church of St James the Apostle was almost certainly constructed in Anglo-Saxon times. The west wall of the nave has been rebuilt, a small aisle has been added to the south, and the north porch is later, but the presence of herringbone work in the remaining walls reassures us as to its likely pre-Conquest origins. The overall simplicity of the structure belies the interior. The chancel arch is a rustic late Saxon composition, with beasties, acanthus leaves and interlace work in riotous profusion.

Upon entering the church by its original north door, note the tall narrow proportions and simple imposts which proclaim its Anglo-Saxon character. The chancel arch immediately claims the attention, not least for the notable dissimilarity between the decoration on its two capitals. The arch itself is a straightforward enough feature, with a simple round head enriched with roll-mouldings on its western face. Similarly the jambs and bases are of sober form, but uniting the head and jambs are two capitals bearing highly imaginative decoration.

The southern capital has a rather cheeky serpent upon the west face of the impost, with linked palmettes below. The whole is supported on the head of a monster whose interlacing body fills the remaining space. The

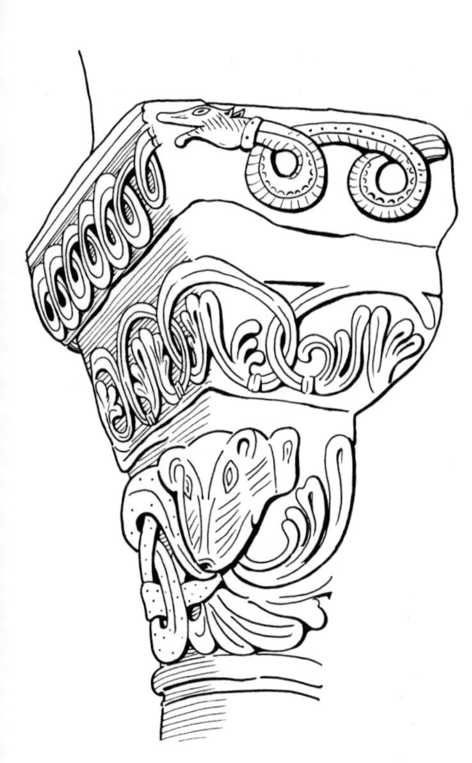

northern capital is more restrained. The impost may be a re-used piece of Roman string-course or similar, since it bears severe classical mouldings on the soffit face. The outer face has been enlivened by the Saxon mason by the addition of palmettes similar in design to those on the southern capital. Below is a competent zone of two-strand interlace work. The whole rests on well-formed volutes at the angles, the stems of which turn upwards to form palmettes which match the rest.

Why the two sides of the arch should differ so markedly is a matter for conjecture. The variety of the decoration suggests that some pupil-mason was displaying his art. Perhaps this was a trial piece, designed to display technical skill rather than good design!

96

Sompting: Saxon Tower and Sculpture, West Sussex

The helmet-shaped roof of St Mary's church tower must be one of the best-known sights of Anglo-Saxon England. This is the only such roof which survives intact, but there is evidence for at least one other, at St Bene't's church in Cambridge. The openings in the tower, which are both round- and triangular-headed, are largely original, though there are later lights above the west door. Externally, the tower is divided into two storeys separated by a string-course which bears unusual 'fluted' ornament not precisely paralleled elsewhere. Single vertical strips appear in the centre of each face of the tower. These terminate in corbels at the top, whilst the bases rest on the string-course on all save the eastern side. Traces of an elaborate stripwork scheme on the bottom stage are particularly noticeable on the south side. There is a persistent tradition that the tower was 'lowered' during the 18th century, but in view of the close parallels to the 'helm' form in the Rhineland, we may safely assume that the present form of the roof follows the original arrangement.

Inside, the capitals of the tower arch are decorated with scrolls, exaggerated volutes, and what are perhaps intended as bunches of grapes. Some of the work appears to be executed in plaster, and may be a later restoration. The principal entry into the church was through the tower. An altar was apparently placed against the west wall of the tower, and this would have faced worshippers as they entered. This can be deduced from the fact that the western tower arch is displaced towards the south, suggesting the presence of an altar to the north.

Apart from the tower, nothing of the Anglo-Saxon fabric survives except some interesting sculpture. This consists of sections of friezes,

Map Reference: TQ 161056 (metric map 198. 1-inch map 182)
Nearest Town: Worthing
Location: Situated at the foot of the Downs facing the Channel, Sompting is between Worthing and Brighton. The village is about a mile (1.6 km) north-west of Worthing but the church of St Mary's, which is signposted off the A27, stands apart from the village to the west.

The notable tower from the south-west. The quoins, stripwork and belfry lights are very fine, whilst the string-course round the lower part of the tower has unique ornament upon it.

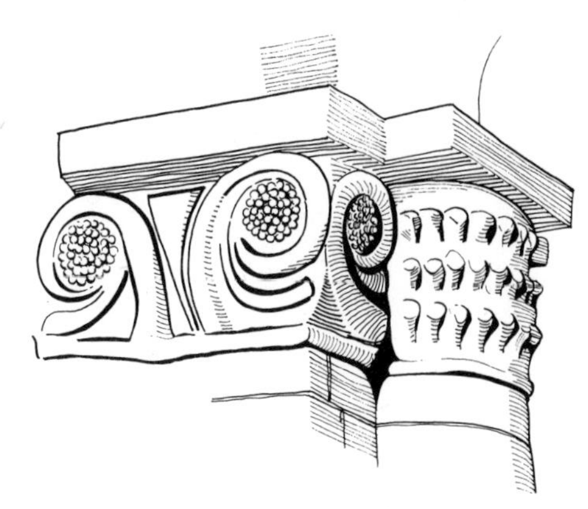

One of the capitals of the tower arch.

wall arcades and a fragment of scroll ornament. These fragments are built into the heads of recesses in the chancel, in the east wall of the south transept, opposite the organ, and on the north side of the nave. One of the stones in the south transept has a carving of an abbot upon it, with his crozier to the left and a desk to the right. The fragment in the nave is of particular interest since it seems to have formed part of a stone screen or 'chancellum', which must have divided the sanctuary from the nave. The back of this stone bears a later, probably Norman, carving of Christ in Majesty surrounded by the four symbols of the Evangelists.

97

Worth: St Nicholas's Church, West Sussex

Despite the creeping onset of Crawley new town, the little village of Worth is today a somewhat isolated settlement, and it must have been the more so in Anglo-Saxon times. Domesday Book records that the village was small and impoverished, and only one other village called Ifelt – modern Ifield – is recorded nearby. The reason for this low settlement density is not hard to find: the parish still includes the forests of Worth and Tilgate, more than 13,000 acres in extent, and Anglo-Saxon Worth must have been little more than a clearing in the great forest called Andredswald.

What is more difficult is to account for the presence of a large and fine 11th-century church in such a place. Plainly it was far too large for the requirements of the local inhabitants, and the explanation for its existence must lie elsewhere. Since Worth formed part of a royal estate, it may be that this little village in the forest was a favoured retreat for the royal house. The great forest doubtless provided good hunting, to which every high-born Saxon was devoted, and we may imagine that the aristocracy retired to St Nicholas's church of a Sunday to thank God for the pleasures of the chase.

The church, which was apparently built from new in the 11th century, had a cruciform plan with a relatively broad nave and eastern apse. Despite a thoroughgoing restoration in 1871, which included the insertion of divers openings as well as the addition of a northern tower in dubious taste, the main elements of the pre-Conquest church are clearly discernible. Externally, the decorative scheme of broad pilaster strips is particularly evident on the south side of the church and on the apse which was actually rebuilt during the restoration. The strips are rebated to take plaster, and we may therefore be certain that the roughly coursed rubble walls would have been hidden. The south-east nave quoin is particularly fine and displays the same quality of entasis which is to be found at Odda's Chapel, Deerhurst.

There are three sets of double windows in the side walls of the nave, two on the north side and one on the south. Originally there was a further set in the south wall, but it was replaced during the 15th century by a three-light opening. Before entering, stand to the

Map Reference: TQ 302362 (metric map 187. 1-inch map 182)
Nearest Town: Crawley
Location: Despite the proximity of Crawley to the north-west, and the close proximity of the M23 to the east, Worth church is picturesquely situated in a lovely quiet churchyard. It is signposted off the B2036.

One of the double windows in the north wall of the nave.

south-east of the apse and look back towards the church. If you are in the right position a convenient tree masks the Victorian tower, and you are confronted with one of the most perfect views of an Anglo-Saxon church in England. The sturdy simplicity of the strip-work, the pleasant curvature of the chancel roof and the stubby projection of the south transept are redolent of all that is best in Anglo-Saxon architecture.

The three original arches opening into the chancel and transepts dominate the east end of the nave. The chancel arch is particularly fine,

The apse was rebuilt during the 19th-century restoration, but it is likely that it closely reflects the original appearance.

with stout rounded jambs, simple cushion capitals and an arch with one plain square order. The south transept arch has been heavily restored, but the north transept arch is very largely in its original condition. The eastern walls of the transepts have arched recesses cut into them; both are post-Saxon, but they might reflect the earlier arrangements.

Further west in the nave, the Anglo-Saxon north and south doors may be seen. Both preserve their elegant tall and narrow Anglo-Saxon proportions which, although extreme, do not rival the southern nave opening at Ledsham in West Yorkshire. Traces of outlining stripwork may be seen on the exterior of the north doorway, though it has been hacked back flush with the wall surface.

We must thank the isolated position of Worth for the survival of this splendid church which, despite the zealous attentions of Victorian church restorers, retains much of its original character.

98
Orpington Sundial, Greater London

There is some dispute as to whether or not the nave of All Saints is of Anglo-Saxon origin. Long and short quoins are claimed to have existed at the south-west angle of the nave before drastic restoration in 1874, but more recent opinion holds that no part of the structure is earlier than the 12th century. Be that as it may, it is clear that a late Saxon church must have stood here since a particularly fine sundial was re-used as a common building stone in the south wall of the nave. This treasure was discovered in 1957, and is one of the best sundials to survive from Anglo-Saxon England.

The fact that the stone itself is so unworn suggests that it was taken down from its original setting shortly after it was placed

The Orpington sundial.

there. The sundial must have been out of doors in order to function properly, and any prolonged exposure to the elements would have resulted in erosion of the surface. This suggests that the dial belongs to the very end of the Anglo-Saxon period, just before the Conquest.

The dial has lines which divided the Anglo-Saxon day into eight 'tides'. Each tide was three hours long, and ran from 7.30 a.m. to 10.30 a.m. and so on. The main tides are divided into two halves on the dial by crossed lines. Round the outer part of the dial, just inside the handsome cable-moulded rim, is a long inscription in seriffed Roman capitals. This text, which is incomplete, has been interpreted as meaning 'to count [or to tell] and to hold, to [or for] him who knows how to seek out how', and perhaps 'it increases' or part of a longer word. This fragmentary translation might suggest that the inscription described the dial's function of marking and keeping hours, which was of benefit to those who understood its marks.

Around the inner part of the dial are other Roman and runic characters; the OR on the left and IUM on the right are probably the beginning and end of the Latin word orlogium, whilst the runes are apparently meaningless, or at least their meaning cannot now be ascertained.

Map Reference: TQ 466666 (metric map 177. 1-inch map 171)
Location: Orpington is a busy commuter suburb rather than a separate town. All Saints church, which was considerably enlarged in the 1950s, is between the High Street and the main Sevenoaks road (A224).

99

Canterbury: Shrine of English Christendom, Kent

The city of Canterbury was the capital of the early Saxon kingdom of Kent, and its Anglo-Saxon name *Cantwaraburg* meant 'fort of the dwellers of Kent'. The story of the Canterbury Anglo-Saxon monuments begins not here but in Rome. The famous tale of how Pope Gregory saw the 'angelic Angles' in the slave market is well known. This event probably happened in about 586, and it determined Gregory to attempt the conversion of the heathen Anglo-Saxons. For this great task he chose Augustine, who was prior of his own monastery at Rome. There is evidence that Augustine was reluctant to embark upon this arduous task; he accepted only because Gregory was, as Pope, the 'Vicar of Christ' whose word could not be gainsaid. Augustine set out for the barbaric northern lands, but on his way through France he was so appalled by tales of English savagery that he decided to return to Rome. Gregory would brook no excuses, and Augustine set out once more for the island which lay on the edge of the world.

Things weren't nearly as bad as Augustine had expected. When he landed he was met not by howling barbarians but by a strong and relatively civilized kingdom ruled by King Ethelbert. Though a pagan himself, he was married to Bertha, daughter of Caribert, who was the Christian king of the region about Paris. The Venerable Bede tells us in his *History* that Ethelbert allowed Bertha to practise her religion, and that she had with her her personal chaplain Bishop Liudhard. Bede also tells us that: 'There was on the east side of the city a church dedicated to St Martin which had been used by the Roman Christians in Britain. To this church the Queen, accompanied by Bishop Liudhard, came to worship.'

This small medallion, which bears the legend 'LEVDARDVS EPS' – EPS being short for Episcopi, the Latin for bishop – was found in St Martin's churchyard, and is a remarkable confirmation of Bede's account of Queen Bertha and her chaplain Liudhard's use of the church.

The little church of St Martin still stands, but although Roman finds have come from the site, few would date any part of the structure earlier than the beginning of the 7th century. The chancel of the present church is of very great antiquity, however, and it is generally accepted that it was the nave of the original church in which Queen Bertha worshipped. It is of course very likely that St Martin's stands on the site of the Roman church mentioned by Bede.

After Augustine and his monks landed, King Ethelbert went to talk to them. Being a somewhat cautious pagan, he declined to meet them indoors, since he feared their 'magic', so an open-air conference was held instead. Augustine was afterwards given leave 'to preach his religion provided he used no compulsion or force in making converts' – a nice example of early English fairness!

Having been thus accepted, Augustine set

Map References: **St Augustine's Abbey** TR 155577 (metric map 179. 1-inch map 173)

St Martin's Church TR 158577

Locations: St Augustine's Abbey, which is a popular site, is in the care of the Department of the Environment and is open standard hours. The site is on the south side of the city about 100 yards (90 metres) from the city walls in Broad Street. The entrance is at the junction of Monastery Street and Lady Wootton's Green. An admission fee is charged. There is a car park beside the city walls in Broad Street.

St Martin's church is about a quarter of a mile (0.4 km) further east from St Augustine's Abbey, in the direction of Sandwich and Deal. It can be reached by turning left at the east end of Langport Street at the bottom of St Martin's Hill.

The south wall of the chancel of St Martin's church. The door on the left behind the gravestones opened into a porticus, the foundations of which were excavated during the 19th century. The round-headed doorway to the right is a later Saxon insertion, perhaps of the same date as the nave. This chancel, with its many re-used Roman tiles, was almost certainly the nave of the first church in which Bertha and Liudhard worshipped, and in which King Ethelbert was baptized.

about his work of conversion. He made great strides, and Ethelbert himself was baptized soon afterwards, probably in St Martin's church. On Christmas Day 597, Augustine is said to have baptized over 10,000 converts in and around Canterbury. Ethelbert gave Augustine a site within the walled city for his church, which lay on the site of the great cathedral. All trace of this early structure was destroyed when Archbishop Lanfranc rebuilt the cathedral after a disastrous fire in 1067.

Apart from the cathedral, Augustine also built a monastery east of the city walls. Bede tells us that King Ethelbert 'erected from the foundations and endowed the church of the blessed Apostles Peter and Paul in which the bodies of Augustine and all the bishops of Canterbury and kings of Kent might be laid.' This was the monastic church, the foundations of which can still be seen. It was unfinished at the time of Augustine's death, so his body was first buried outside the church and later in the north porticus. Many of the succeeding Anglo-Saxon bishops of Canterbury were buried here, and the building underwent a complex series of alterations.

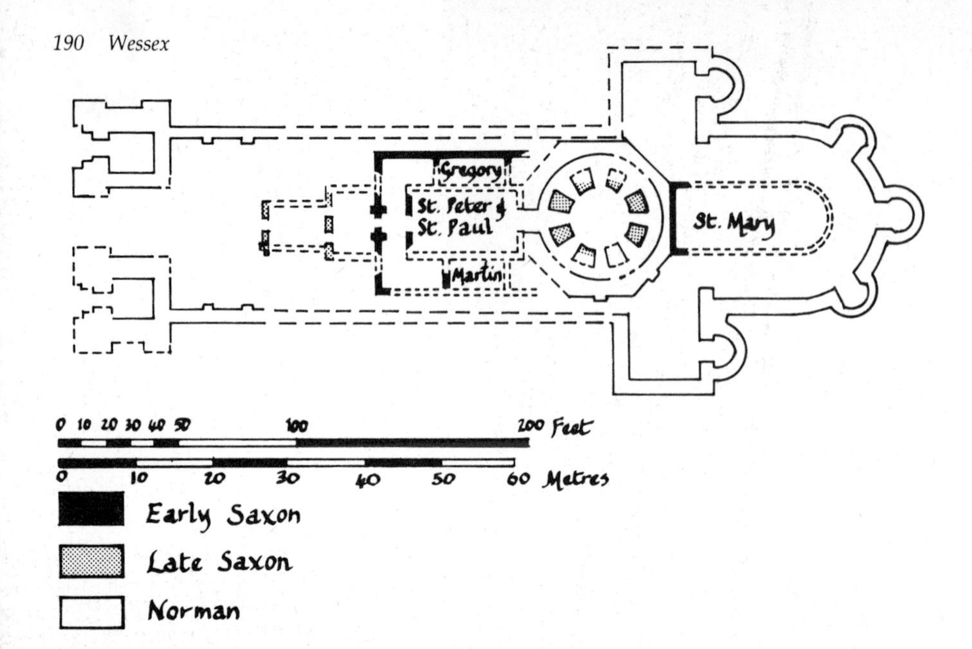

Plan showing the remains of the church built by Ethelbert, with his son Edbald's chapel of St Mary to the east. Bishop Wulfric's octagon is shown in a lighter tone, whilst Abbot Scotland's great cruciform church is shown in outline.

The ruined church of St Pancras, which is supposed to have begun life as a 'heathen temple' before Ethelbert was converted to Christianity.

The great crypt beneath Bishop Wulfric's octagonal rotunda, now one of the imposing features of the site.

The first monastic church was rectangular, with a broad nave and flanking chapels. The chancel was probably apsidal, and there was a porch or 'narthex' at the west end. The porticus on the north side of the nave was the burial place of the early bishops, and eight of them, including Augustine, were laid either inside or against the north wall of the nave. King Edbald, who was Ethelbert's son, built a small chapel dedicated to St Mary immediately to the east of St Augustine's monastic church in about the year 620.

During the middle of the 11th century, Abbot Wulfric conceived a grandiose scheme to link up the two buildings, and to this end he built a great octagonal rotunda with a crypt beneath. This structure is one of the most striking features of the abbey remains, and its great crypt lies over the site of the chancel of the monastic church. An 11th-century monk called Gocelin relates that when Wulfric died in 1059, it was widely believed that his death had been due to the displeasure of the Virgin Mary which he had incurred when he destroyed the west wall of her chapel! After the Conquest, the Norman Abbot Scotland demolished all the earlier buildings and replaced them with a great cruciform church which covered the entire site, but the foundations of the Saxon churches have all been recovered by excavation, and are clearly marked out on the site.

Further east of this main complex was yet another church, dedicated to St Pancras. The lower parts of the early walls survive, and are thought to date from the early 7th century. Traditionally this was the site of a heathen temple used by King Ethelbert before his conversion.

Canterbury must qualify as the foremost shrine of English Christendom; not only is it the see of the Archbishop of Canterbury, Primate of all England, but it was also the site of the earliest churches associated with the 7th-century Latin conversion. As if on some great ley line, the three early churches follow a common east-west axis, and the remains of these structures, which are rich in historical associations, are a remarkable sight.

100

Reculver: Bassa's Monastery, Kent

Map Reference: TR 228694 (metric map 179. 1-inch map 173)
Nearest Town: Herne Bay
Location: Reculver perches on the north coast of Kent between Margate and Herne Bay. The twin towers can be seen silhouetted against the sky from the main A299 road, from where the minor road to Reculver is signposted. The site is in the care of the Department of the Environment, and is open standard hours. There is a small admission charge; postcards and guidebooks can be purchased on the site.

For the year 669, the Anglo-Saxon Chronicle has the following laconic entry: 'In this year King Egbert gave Reculver to Bassa the priest to build a church there.'

This grant marks the starting point of the Anglo-Saxon history of Reculver, but the site had a long history of occupation before this. Bassa, like St Cedd at Bradwell-on-Sea in Essex, had been granted not an empty site but a ruined Roman Saxon shore fort. These forts, which formed a chain stretching along the south and east coasts of England, were com-

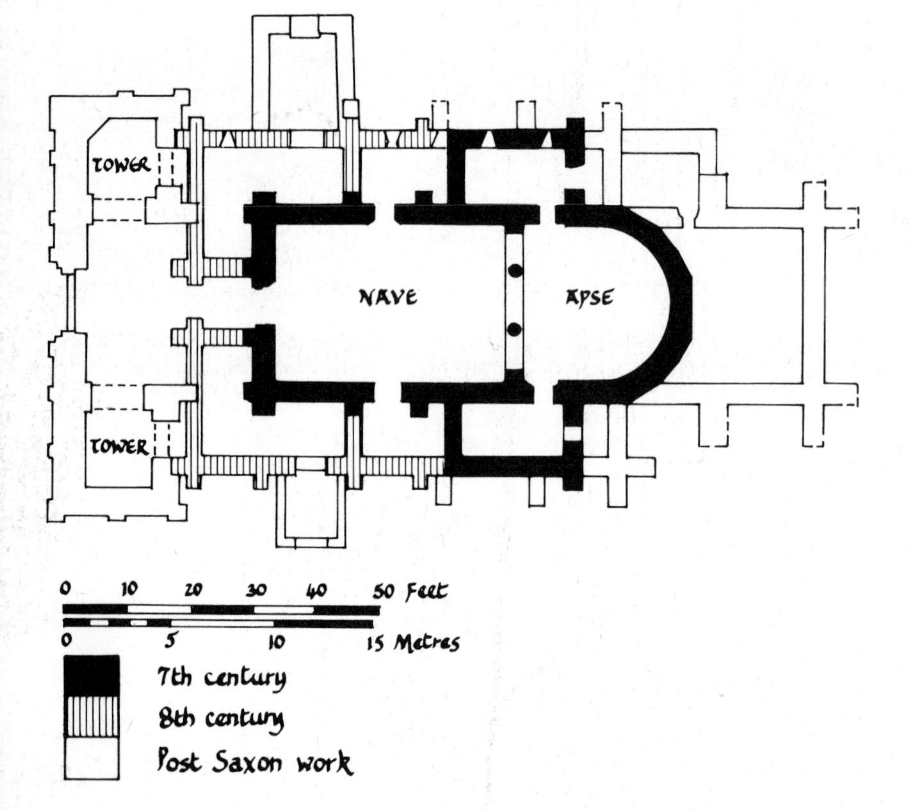

Ground plan of the church. Bassa's church is shown in black.

manded during the 4th century by the *Comes Litoris Saxonici* – the Count of the Saxon Shore. They were used as bases for the Roman fleet which was charged with the defence of the coast against the piratical attacks of the early Anglo-Saxons, hence the Count's title.

Bassa and Cedd were probably given the old forts because their defences, although ruined, still acted as a barrier between the outside world and the land within. Both men led small communities of monks, and the forts made ideal sanctuaries in which they could carry on

The church from the air. The foundation walls of Bassa's church show up clearly where they are marked out in white. The towers at the west end are 12th century, and were all that remained after the vandal-vicar had finished! Bassa built his church near the centre of the roman fort; the seaward half of it has been eroded away. (Courtesy Aerofilms Ltd)

their religious life. This idea of a 'closed community' physically separated from the world of men was an essential element of many early monastic traditions; the defences of the shore forts provided ready-made precinct walls.

A further advantage of the shore forts was that their ruined buildings afforded a handy source of building materials. We know from the remains of Bassa's church that he plundered the ruins of Regulbium – as the fort had been called by the Romans – for bricks and tiles as well as for stone. The plan of his church, which is marked out on the site, was excavated in 1927. It resembled that of St Augustine's abbey at Canterbury, having a broad nave with flanking porticus and a rounded apse. This basic plan was extended during the 8th century by the addition of a western porch or 'narthex'.

Between the nave and chancel was an elegant arcade of three arches made from Roman bricks and supported on two tall stone columns. A low seat running round the inside of the apse was for the use of the abbot and his monks. The abbot sat in the centre, directly behind the altar, with his monks ranged around the sides. The doorways into the porticus from the chancel are thought to have been lined with stone. Slots for this purpose may be seen in the stone threshold of the north door close to the jambs. The linings may have resembled the somewhat later work at Britford in Wiltshire. In the north porticus the sills of the original windows may be seen, whilst in the north wall of the later western narthex the seating for a wooden window frame is preserved under glass.

The little church at Reculver, with its commanding seaside site, must have attracted the attention of Viking pirate bands at an early date. We do not know when the church was sacked, nor for how long its congregation braved the menace before withdrawing inland, but monastic life had ceased here by the early 10th century. Later it served as a parish church, and was considerably extended during the Middle Ages.

The church resisted wind and tide until 1805 when the young clergyman of the parish, urged on by his Philistine mother, rashly besought his parishioners to demolish this shrine of early Christendom. This they duly did and all save the western towers, which still act as a landmark for shipping, was razed to the ground. The sad history of Reculver was not yet done. Shortly after World War II a caravan site was established below the church which has since grown so large that much imagination is now required to conjure up the majesty of its former setting.

101

Battle: Turning Point of History, East Sussex

This famous site of Senlac – the name refers to a 'sand stream' near the English position – is a melancholy place for lovers of Anglo-Saxon England. As we follow the neat Department of the Environment signs and gaze upon the grassy slope of the hill where the Normans attacked, we should not forget that the last king of Anglo-Saxon England died here, and with him the hopes of a nation.

As with most old battlefields, all traces of the conflict have long since vanished and only memorials remain. The ruins of the great abbey, whose high altar stood on the very spot where Harold was slain, still dominate the summit of the hill, a physical memorial of the Conqueror's thanks to God upon the occasion of his great victory.

The story of Harold's forced march south from Stamford Bridge where he had defeated the Norwegian host of Harold Hardrada, to whom he had freely granted 'six feet of English ground' is well known. Harold must have realized that his enemies had been in collusion

Map Reference: TQ 746163 (metric map 199. 1-inch map 184)
Nearest Town: Hastings
Location: The site of the Battle of Hastings was recently purchased for the nation, and is now in the care of the Department of the Environment. The site is entered through the great gatehouse of Battle Abbey, and is open standard hours. An entrance fee is payable. Perhaps surprisingly, the town of Battle is 6 miles (9.5 km) north-west of Hastings itself, and is reached by the A2100. The abbey, which was built on the site of the Saxon position, is in the centre of the town and is now a private school. When visiting the site, look out for the monument erected in 1903 to mark the spot where King Harold fell.

This peaceful hillside where sheep graze and daffodils bloom was where the Normans stormed up to the Anglo-Saxon shield wall; this is a Saxon's eye view of the field.

when word reached him of William's landing in the south. Nothing daunted, he set off at a brisk pace and covered the 250 miles from York in under twelve days.

On the evening of 13 October his army camped for the night at the place which is now called Battle, hoping to take William by surprise in Hastings the following morning. But William's intelligence was good, and he moved out early on the morning of the 14th. Harold decided to retain the advantage of his elevated camp, and his troops 'dug in'. The two armies were approximately the same size – around 7,000 men each, but William had more archers than Harold, as well as the only cavalry on the field. The Saxon front line was held by the 'huscarles' – the king's bodyguard, who were known as 'the King's Hounds'. They formed the famous shield wall which stood until the end of the battle like the 'Thin Red Line' of the Crimea.

After close reconnaissance, William drew up his army below the hill, about 150 yards away from Harold's front line. The fight began at about 9.30 a.m. on the morning of 14 October with heavy fire from William's archers, but the Saxons stood fast. William then ordered a full-scale infantry attack, which was nearly disastrous since his left flank was routed, the Norman infantry being pursued down the hill against Harold's orders. William annihilated the pursuers with his cavalry. After the archers and the infantry, a cavalry attack was mounted, but still the shield wall held.

The armies had by now been fighting for eight hours, and it was growing dark. William was becoming desperate and decided on a combined operation, with the archers providing saturation fire, under which the infantry advanced with the cavalry close behind. The entire Norman host rushed the hill-top, and Harold's faithful huscarles finally broke under sheer weight of numbers. Harold and his two brothers were killed, and the English army virtually annihilated.

The qualities of bravery and loyalty which kept Harold's men about him, even though they must have know the fight was hopeless, are enduring memories of Anglo-Saxon England. Loyalty between a Lord and his retainer was the foundation of Anglo-Saxon society; at Senlac we see its tragic passing.

Seventy years before, at the Battle of Maldon, Bryhtwold, Earl of Essex, and his retinue had also faced certain death; their heroic last stand gave birth to the finest battle poem in the English language. Harold's huscarles must have known the Maldon poem, and we can imagine them repeating these lines to themselves in the moments before the Norman attack struck home:

Thought shall be the harder, heart the keener,
Courage the greater, as our strength faileth.
Here lies our leader, in the dust of his greatness.
Who leaves him now, be damned for ever.
We who are old now shall not leave this battle,
But lie at his feet, in the dust with our leader.
(Trans. Henry Treece)

After Hastings, nothing was ever quite the same again. William the Bastard (as the Anglo-Saxon Chronicle calls him!) rode about England establishing his lieutenants in place of the old Saxon aristocracy, and there was hardly an estate left in English hands by the time of Domesday Book in 1086. But he didn't have it all his own way, and revolts broke out in the north and south-west which caused much bloodshed before they were put down. William controlled the country, but the chronic Norman shortage of manpower must always have meant that some 'give and take' was necessary. In the words of the dying Norman lord to his son in Kipling's 'Norman and Saxon':

The Saxon is not like us Normans. His manners are not so polite.
But he never means anything serious till he talks about justice and right.

When he stands like an ox in the furrow with his
sullen set eyes on your own,
And grumbles, 'This isn't fair dealing,' my son,
leave the Saxon alone.

You can horsewhip your Gascony archers, or torture
your Picardy spears;
But don't try that game on the Saxon; you'll have
the whole brood round your ears.
From the richest old Thane in the county to the
poorest chained serf in the field,
They'll be at you and on you like hornets, and, if you
are wise, you will yield.

The Norman cavalry crashes into the shield wall. Note the great Danish two-handed axe wielded by the leading huscarle in front of the gonfanon *or pennon. (From the Bayeux Tapestry)*

Glossary

AISLE Division of a church normally running parallel to the nave, and divided from it by an arcade.
AMBULATORY An aisle enclosing an apse or straight-ended sanctuary, often used for processional purposes.
ANGLO-SAXON CHRONICLE The historical traditions of the Anglo-Saxons, in the form of annals – i.e. events recounted year by year – set down in Alfred's time for the benefit of Wessex readers, and afterwards continued in various monasteries, at some of them well into the Norman period.
APSE A semi-circular termination of a chapel or chancel.
ARCADE Row of arches on pillars or columns.
ASHLAR Masonry constructed of square hewn stones.
BALDRIC Belt for a sword hung from shoulder to opposite hip.
BALUSTER A short pillar often found at the centre of a two-light window.
BARROW A burial mound made of earth heaped over the cremated or inhumed bodies of the dead.
BASILICA Originally a Roman word which described a building divided into a nave and two or more aisles, the nave being higher and wider than the aisles to each side. This basic form was used for early Christian churches in the Mediterranean, and can be seen in England at Hexham, Canterbury and elsewhere.
BATTER The inclined face of a wall, normally at the base.
BEOWULF Anglo-Saxon epic poem of the early 8th century or earlier.
BURGH A fortified place, a town.
BYZANTINE A civilization which can be dated from 330 when Constantine I transferred the capital of the Roman Empire to Byzantium (renamed Constantinople). Byzantine architects mastered the dome, and borrowed both from Roman and Persian building traditions to develop a distinctive style. Byzantine art is formal and deeply spiritual; it exerted a strong influence on Western Europe and Asia.
CABLE DECORATION Carving imitating thick twisted rope.
CAPITAL The head of a column, often enriched with moulded decoration.
CAROLINGIAN A dynasty of the Franks named after Charlemagne (742–814). It lasted until the death of Louis V in 987. During this period there was a Classical revival, and Carolingian art and architecture reflect Roman models.
CELTIC A general term for the peoples and cultures of Cornwall, Wales, north-western England and the rest of the British Isles outside Anglo-Saxon England.
CHAMFER Surface produced by cutting away the sharp edge of a stone block, normally at an angle of 45 degrees to the other planes.
CHANCEL The east end of a church where the main altar is placed; reserved for clergy and choir.
CHEQUER A squared pattern producing a chessboard effect.
CLERESTORY The upper stage of the main walls of a church above the aisle roofs, pierced by windows.
COUNT OF THE SAXON SHORE *(Comes Litoris Saxonici)* Commandant of the British coastal defences, mentioned in 367 in the *Notitia Dignitatum*, and apparently in charge of the great stone fortresses arranged round the east and south-east coasts of England, and intended to prevent seaborne invasion.
CRYPT Underground room beneath a church, often used for burials and the display of relics.
DANEGELD Tax on land levied in England in 991 and later in order to buy off the Danish Vikings.
DANELAW East Midlands and north of England: a name given (contemptuously) to the area which had been conquered and settled by the Danish Vikings, and which was subject to Danish rather than English customary law. The Danelaw was officially recognized by a treaty between Alfred and the Danish leader Guthrum in 886.
DOMESDAY BOOK A description of England compiled in 1086 at the order of William the Conqueror giving, under counties, and then under landowners, answers to questions about the former and present owner, taxable value, present population and so on.
ENTASIS Slight convex curve used on columns and quoins to correct the optical illusion of concavity which would result if the sides were straight.
FOLIATE Leaf-like.
FRANKS Germanic confederacy of small tribes which conquered France during the 6th century.
FREESTONE Any stone that cuts well in all directions, especially fine-grained limestone or sandstone.
FRIEZE A decorative band of carving set into the surface of a wall.
FRISIANS Inhabitants of the Dutch coastal plain (Frisia).
FYRD The national militia of Anglo-Saxon England in which all able-bodied freemen were expected to serve.
GENEALOGY An account of descent from an ancestor by means of listing the intermediate persons.

GNOMON Rod or pin at the centre of a sundial which shows the time by its shadow falling on a marked surface.

GREEK KEY DECORATION A geometrical ornament of vertical and horizontal straight lines repeated to form a band.

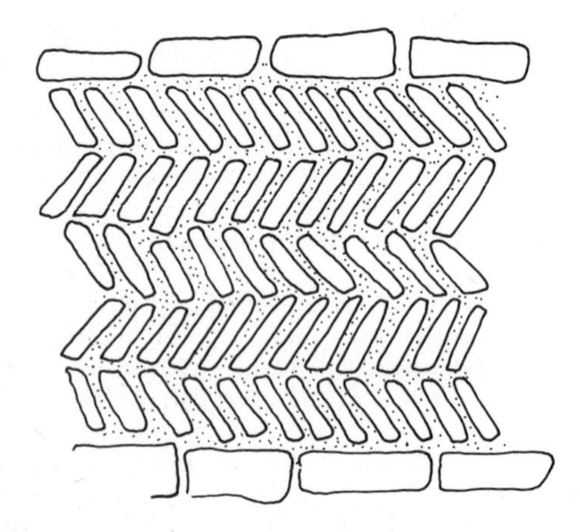

HERRINGBONE WORK Type of walling in which the stones are laid diagonally rather than horizontally. Alternate courses lie in opposite directions, forming a zigzag or herringbone pattern on the wall face.

HIDE The English unit of land, the amount required to support one family; varying in size between forty and a 120 acres.

HOG-BACK Tombstone in the form of a stylized house; the roof ridge of which has a 'hog-back' shape, being higher at the centre than the ends.

HOST The Anglo-Saxon army in the field, led by the king and his retinue, followed by the peasantry.

ICONOGRAPHY The use of drawings and symbols to illustrate a theme or subject.

IMPOST Bracket set into a wall upon which the end of an arch rests.

INHUMATION Name given to the burial custom by which the body was laid unburned in the grave (in contrast to cremation).

INTERLACE A pattern created by intertwining one or more ribbons.

JAMB The straight side of an archway, door or window.

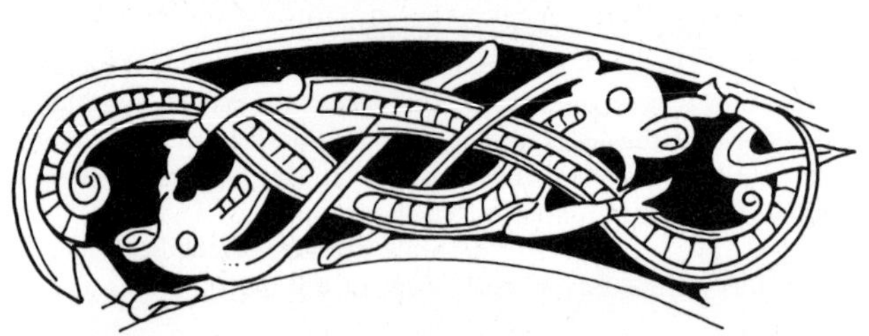

JELLINGE STYLE Named after the Danish royal site at Jelling, Jutland. Scandinavian settlers introduced the style into Britain late in the 9th century, and it remained popular through much of the 10th century. The basic motifs are ribbon-like animals with double outlines. The head appears in profile with open jaws, and there is often a fold or tendril-like extension of the upper lip.

LINTEL Horizontal stone over a door or window opening.

MINSTER The mother church (not necessarily a cathedral or monastery) serving an area eventually divided up into parishes.

MONOLITH A single stone.

NARTHEX A porch or vestibule at the entrance of a church.

NAVE The western arm of a church, which normally forms the main body of the structure.

NIMBUS Bright cloud or halo around or over the head of a saint.

ORATORY A small chapel used for private worship.

ORDER On a doorway or a window, a series of concentric steps receding towards the opening.

PALMETTE A fan-shaped ornament composed of narrow divisions like a palm leaf.
PECTORAL CROSS A decorative cross worn on the chest.
PELLET Circular decorative boss.

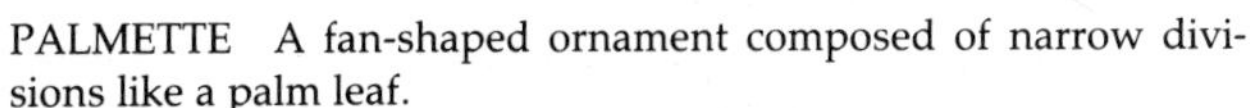

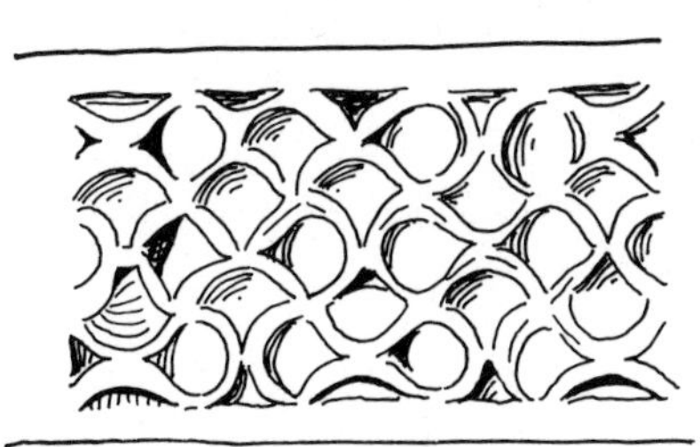

PELTA DECORATION Originally a small light shield carried by the ancient Greeks. Pelta decoration is so-called because it is similarly shaped.
PILASTER Shallow rectangular column projecting only slightly from a wall.
PLINTH The projecting base of a wall or column pedestal; generally chamfered or moulded on the top.
POMMEL Knob at the end of a sword hilt.
PORTICUS (Singular and plural) These were side chapels built against the main walls of a church. Many were used for burials, since the burial of the dead was originally forbidden in the main body of a church.
PRECINCT A reserved space round a monastic settlement, normally divided off from the outside world by a wall or ditch.

QUATREFOIL Symmetrical four-lobed shape.
QUOINS The squared stones at the corner of a building; side alternate and long and short are the two most distinctive Anglo-Saxon techniques.

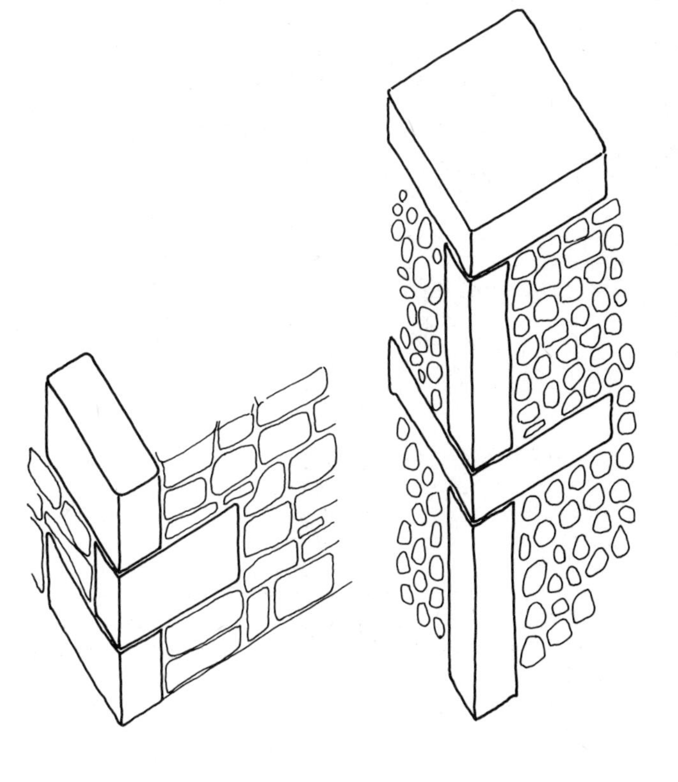

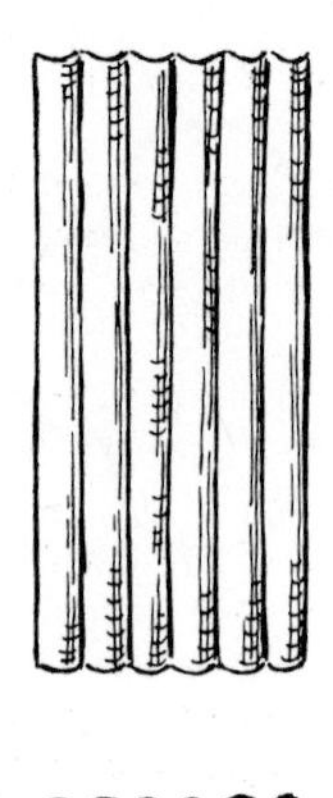

REEDING Decoration consisting of parallel convex mouldings touching one another.
RELIC A revered object associated with a saint. This could either be a piece of clothing or some similar item, or else a fragment of the saint's body. Such relics were often displayed to pilgrims at shrines, and were kept in RELIQUARIES, which were suitably shaped caskets, often bearing rich decoration.
REPOUSSÉ Ornamental metalwork hammered into relief from the reverse side.
REREDOS A wall or screen set behind an altar which is normally decorated.
RING-CHAIN PATTERN A complex running motif much used in north-west England by Anglo-Scandinavian sculptors; there are several variations on the basic type illustrated here.

RINGERIKE STYLE The latest Viking style in England, named after a district near Oslo where several finds in this style have been made. The style began during the late 10th century, and continued into the 11th. It developed from the earlier Jellinge style, but the animal panels are enriched by the addition of long curling tendrils.
ROOD This simply means a crucifix, but also refers to the elaborate stone carvings of the Crucifixion which depict figures of the Virgin Mary and others.
ROTUNDA Building of circular ground plan, often with a dome.
RUBBLEWORK Rough unhewn building stones or flints, generally not laid in regular courses.
RUNE A letter of the Germanic alphabet which was developed by modifying Greek and Roman characters to suit carving in wood and stone. There are several versions of the *futhorc* or alphabet, so-called after its first few letters.
SARCOPHAGUS Stone coffin, usually decorated with sculpture.
SOFFIT The underside of an arch.
SPANDREL The triangular space between the side of an arch and its frame.
SPLAY A sloping, chamfered surface cut into a wall. The term

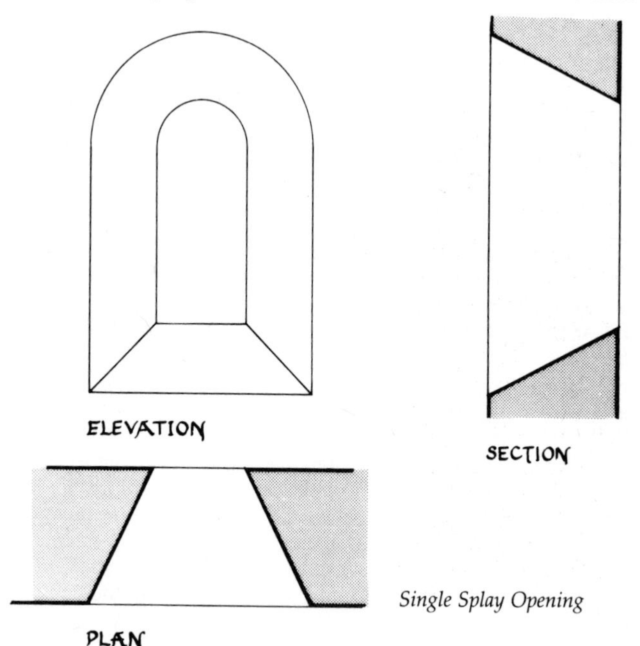

Single Splay Opening

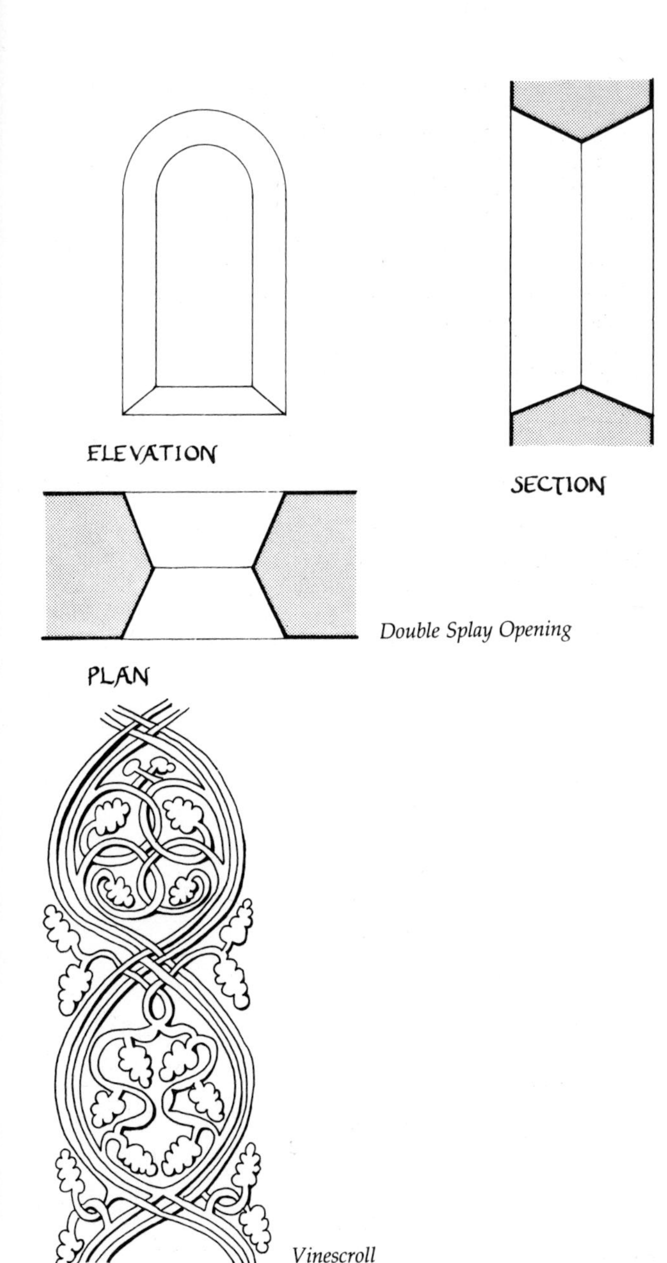

Double Splay Opening

Vinescroll

refers to the widening of doorways and windows by slanting the sides.

STRING-COURSE   A continuous projecting horizontal band set into the surface of a wall, sometimes decorated.

STRIPWORK   Narrow lines of decorative stonework, often used to outline windows and doors.

SYNOD   An ecclesiastical council or meeting.

TRANSEPT   The transverse arms of a cross-shaped church, normally between nave and chancel.

TRANSOM   Horizontal bar of wood or stone across a window.

TYMPANUM   Space between the lintel of a door and the arch above it; often decorated.

VINESCROLL   The vine was a very popular motif, and is often depicted with bunches of grapes. It is probable that its popularity derived from biblical allusions such as that in John, 15: 5, 'I am the vine, ye are the branches. He that abideth in me and I in him, the same bringeth forth much fruit: for without me ye can do nothing.'

INHABITED VINESCROLL was a type of ornament popular in Northumbria in which animals and birds 'inhabit' the stylized vinescrolls, and are often shown plucking or eating the grapes.

VOLUTE   A spiral scroll.

VOUSSOIR   A wedge-shaped stone used in the head of an arch.

WHEEL-HEAD CROSS   Cross-head in which the ends of the arms are joined together by a ring or 'wheel'.

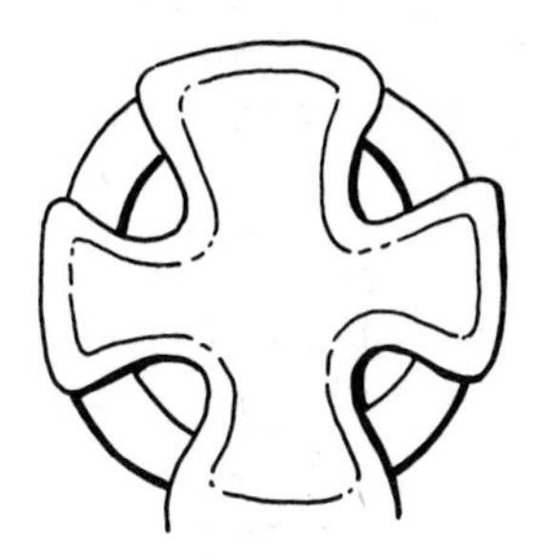

Museums with Important Anglo-Saxon Collections

Abingdon Borough Museum, Berkshire
Birmingham City Museum and Art Gallery
Bury St Edmunds, Moyse's Hall Museum
Cambridge University Museum of Archaeology and Ethnology
Canterbury Royal Museum
Colchester Castle Museum
Durham Cathedral Library, Dormitory Museum
Huddersfield, Tolson Memorial Museum
Hull, Transport and Archaeological Museum, Mortimer Collection
Jarrow Hall (Site Museum)
Leicester, Jewry Wall Museum
Lincoln City and County Museum
Lindisfarne Priory (Site Museum)
Liverpool City Museum
London, British Museum
London, Museum of London
London, Victoria and Albert Museum
Maidstone Museum (Kent Archaeological Society Collection)
Newark Museum
Newcastle University Museum of Antiquities
Norwich Castle Museum
Nottingham Castle Museum
Oakham Museum
Oxford, Ashmolean Museum
Salisbury Museum
Sheffield City Museum
Winchester Museum
York, The Yorkshire Museum

General Reading

Hunter Blair, P., *An Introduction to Anglo-Saxon England*, Cambridge University Press, 2nd edition, 1977, paperback.
Loyn, H. R., *Anglo-Saxon England and the Norman Conquest*, Longmans, 2nd edition, 1968, paperback.
Page, R. I., *Life in Anglo-Saxon England*, Batsford, 1970.
Whitelock, D., *The Beginnings of English Society*, Pelican History of England, 1974.
Wilson, D. M., *The Anglo-Saxons*, Penguin, 1972.
Wilson D. M. (ed.), *The Archaeology of Anglo-Saxon England*, Methuen, 1976.

All these books contain good bibliographies which can be used for more detailed reading as desired.

Index